I0214755

The Poetry of Cao Zhi

Library of Chinese Humanities

The Poetry of Cao Zhi

Translated by Robert Joe Cutter

Volume edited by Paul W. Kroll

De Gruyter

This book was prepared with the support of the Andrew W. Mellon Foundation.

ISBN 978-1-5015-1563-7
e-ISBN (PDF) 978-1-5015-0703-8
e-ISBN (EPUB) 978-1-5015-0697-0
ISSN 2199-966X
DOI https://doi.org/10.1515/9781501507038

Library of Congress Control Number: 2020948090

Bibliografische Information published by the Deutsche Nationalbibliothek
The Deutsche Nationalbibliothek lists this publication in the Deutsche Nationalbibliografie; detailed bibliographic data are available on the Internet at http://dnb.dnb.de.

Typesetting: Meta Systems Publishing & Printservices GmbH, Wustermark
Printing and binding: CPI books GmbH, Leck

www.degruyter.com

Table of Contents

Shi

For David R. Knechtges

Acknowledgments

Readers of this volume will be able to tell from the Introduction and notes throughout the book how great a debt I owe to many distinguished scholars past and present. Without them, this work would have been impossible. Here I want to express my gratitude to a number of people who have influenced this project more directly. The book is dedicated to David R. Knechtges, whose kindness and inspirational mentorship changed everything. He is the founder of this repast. Long ago, the late C. H. Wang was one of the first to suggest that I study Cao Zhi. He will be greatly missed by all who knew him as mentor and friend. I have also benefitted from the work and cordiality of Xu Gongchi of the Chinese Academy of Social Sciences, who was for twenty years the editor of *Literary Heritage*. Dr. Liu Qian of Arizona State University's Hayden Library aided me on a question involving editions and provided references. Colleagues and students alike can attest to Liu Qian's expertise and generosity. To Paul W. Kroll, editor of this volume, any expression of thanks will be inadequate, so I can only trust that Paul knows how much I appreciate his work. Xiaofei Tian has been extraordinarily kind – and patient – during the time this book was being born. We overlap in various areas, and I have profited a great deal from her research. To the many graduate students at the University of Wisconsin-Madison and Arizona State University with whom I have had the pleasure of reading and discussing Jian'an literature over the years, I am incredibly grateful. Finally, to Carolyn Marie Warner for her love and support, my fondest thanks. She proves that social scientists and humanists *can* communicate.

https://doi.org/10.1515/9781501507038-203

Introduction

Background

Cao Zhi 曹植 (192–232), one of China's most famous poets, lived during a tumultuous age, when the dissolution of the four-centuries-old Han dynasty (206 BCE–220 CE) was well underway. Within a decade or so of his birth, his father Cao Cao 曹操 (155–220) emerged as the most powerful single leader in a ravaged and divided empire, and in 220, Cao Zhi's elder brother Cao Pi 曹丕 (187–226) accepted the abdication of the last Han emperor and established himself as the founding emperor of the Wei Dynasty (220–265); he is posthumously known as Emperor Wen of Wei 魏文帝 (r. 220–226). Near the end of his too short life, Cao Zhi famously wrote that he "was born into disorder, grew up among armies."

This was a time of intrepid and astucious figures and of bold and violent acts that captured the Chinese imagination across the centuries. Commonly known as the Three Kingdoms, in all it lasted fewer than a hundred years, but its impact on Chinese history and culture remains far out of proportion to its length. History and popular tradition eventually came together in a famous fourteenth-century novel, which in turn "has since generated numerous fictional, dramatic, and visual representations, from opera plays and storytelling performances, to films, television shows, manga, video games, and card games" whose popularity has spread beyond China to other parts East Asia and the world beyond.[1]

The Caos were from Qiao 譙 (modern Bo 亳 county, Anhui) in the princedom of Pei 沛國. Within four generations, almost precisely a hundred years, the family rose from humble beginnings to place a ruler on the throne of its own dynasty. Although the Wei was short-lived and occupied only a fraction of the territory the Han had controlled, the Caos left an indelible mark on Chinese history and culture. Their origins are, however, lost in time. What remain are various traditions,

1 Xiaofei Tian, *The Halberd at Red Cliff: Jian'an and the Three Kingdoms* (Cambridge, Mass.: Harvard Univ. Asia Center, 2018), 3. See also J. Michael Farmer, *The Talent of Shu: Qiao Zhou and the Intellectual World of Early Medieval Sichuan* (Albany: State Univ. of New York Press, 2007), 1–2.

https://doi.org/10.1515/9781501507038-204

almost hopelessly confused and largely fictitious, regarding their early ancestors.

According to *Records of the Three States*, Cao Cao was a descendant of Cao Shen 曹參 (d. 190 BCE), a famous minister under Liu Bang 劉邦 (256–195), the founder of the Han Dynasty.[2] One account traces Cao Shen's ancestry and the surname itself back to legendary antiquity to An 安, one of the sons of Luzhong 陸終.[3] Legend has it that Luzhong was descended from Zhuanxu 顓頊, who was a descendant of the Yellow Emperor and an ancestor of Yu 禹, founder of the Xia dynasty.[4] Later, when Zhou conquered Shang, the Cao family was enfeoffed in Zhu 邾, where they remained until scattered by the destruction of Zhu by the state of Chu 楚 in the Warring States Period.[5]

The epitaph of Cao Cao's adoptive grandfather Cao Teng 曹騰 also says that the Caos were from Zhu.[6] But Cao Cao himself gives a different genealogy. He reports that he was descended from Caoshu Zhenduo 曹叔振鐸; that is, from a maternal uncle of King Wu of Zhou 周武王 who had been enfeoffed in Cao.[7] Cao Zhi apparently subscribed to his

2 *Sgz* 1.1. The family connection with Cao Shen is surely spurious; see Xu 3.

3 *Sgz* 1.1, n. 1, Pei Songzhi's 裴松之 (372–451) commentary quoting Wang Chen's 王沈 (d. 266) *Wei shu* 魏書. An's birth was miraculous. His father is said to have married a Guifang 鬼方 woman. She was pregnant for three years without delivering, so they opened her ribs on the right and left and took out three individuals from each side; see Wang Liqi 王利器, ed., *Fengsu tongyi jiaozhu* 風俗通義校注 (Beijing: Zhonghua shuju, 1981), 1.28 Yuan Ke 袁珂, comp., *Zhongguo shenhua chuanshuo cidian* 中國神話傳說祠典 (Shanghai: Shanghai cishu chubanshe, I980), 218.

4 Wang, *Fengsu tongyi jiaozhu*, 1.28; Yuan, *Zhongguo shenhua chuanshuo cidian*, 218; K. C. Chang, "Sandai Archaeology and the Formation of States in Ancient China: Processual Aspects of the Origins of Chinese Civilization," in *The Origins of Chinese Civilization*, ed. David N. Keightley, 497 (Berkeley: Univ. of California Press, 1983).

5 *Sgz* 1.1, n. 1; Zhu's capital was southeast of modern Qufu 曲阜, Shandong.

6 *Sgz* 14.455, n. 2. Pei's quote from the epitaph comes from Jiang Ji's 蔣濟 (d. 249) "Li jiao yi" 立郊議. On Jiang's "opinion," see Howard Goodman, *Ts'ao P'i Transcendent: The Political Culture of Dynasty-Founding at the End of the Han* (Seattle: Scripta Serica, 1998), 184. Cao Teng served in the Han court as a palace official for over thirty years. See *HHs* 78.2519.

7 *Sgz* 14.455, n. 2 (Pei's commentary quoting Cao Cao's "Jia zhuan" 家傳); Carl Leban, "Ts'ao Ts'ao and the Rise of Wei: The Early Years" (Ph.D. diss., Columbia Univ., 1971), 45.

father's opinion on the origins of the family, for in the dirge he wrote for him, "Dirge for Emperor Wu" 武帝誄, he writes: "How august our King! / Descended from [Lord] Millet, succeeding Zhou."[8] Cao Pi's son and successor Cao Rui 曹叡 (206–239) had yet another understanding of the family's lineage. He accepted the assertion of Gaotang Long 高堂隆 that the Caos were descendants of the legendary sage ruler Shun.[9]

There was nothing abnormal in the Caos' various attempts to provide themselves with heroic ancestors from the ancient past. This was a normal endeavor on the part of the Chinese upper and ruling classes and served a legitimating function. Especially in times of conflict, attacks on rivals could include aspersions about someone's relatives. In Jian'an 5 (200), Chen Lin 陳琳 (d. 217), then in the employ of Cao Cao's rival Yuan Shao 袁紹 (154–202), famously wrote a scathing criticism of Cao entitled "Wei Yuan Shao xi Yuzhou" 為袁紹檄豫州. In it, he not only vilifies Cao Cao but also refers insultingly to his father and grandfather.[10]

Reliable information on the Caos' background really goes back only as far as Cao Cao's grandfather Cao Teng 曹騰. Cao Teng's own father may have been a farmer.[11] Cao Teng was castrated while still a child so that he might become a palace eunuch.[12] The strategy worked. Throughout the Later Han, the number and the power of the eunuchs was on

---

8 Cutter, "Saying Goodbye: The Transformation of the Dirge in Early Medieval China," *EMC* 10–11.1 (2004): 98; Zhao 198.

9 *Sgz* 14.455–56, n. 2. See also Leban, "Ts'ao Ts'ao and the Rise of Wei," 46. Gaotang Long's assertion was disputed by Jiang Ji. Pei's commentary also mentions "Shan Jin wen" 禪晉文, which says Youyu 有虞, a reference to Shun 舜, was the ancestor of the Caos; *Sgz* 14.456, n. 2.

10 See *Sgz* 6.197, n. 1 (quoting Sun Sheng's 孫盛 [fl. ca. 350] *Wei shi chunqiu* 魏氏春秋); *HHs* 64A.2393; and *Wx* 44.1968. See also Leban, "Ts'ao Ts'ao and the Rise of Wei," 50–51, and Rafe de Crespigny, *Imperial Warlord: A Biography of Cao Cao 155–220 AD* (Leiden: Brill, 2010), 129, 240.

11 See *Sgz* 1.1, n. 2 (quoting Sima Biao's 司馬彪 [243–306] *Xu Han shu* 續漢書). See also Leban, "Ts'ao Ts'ao and the Rise of Wei," 46, n. 10, and de Crespigny, *Imperial Warlord*, 17.

12 *Sgz* 1.1, n. 2 (quoting *Xu Han shu*); Leban, "Ts'ao Ts'ao and the Rise of Wei," 47; and de Crespigny, *Imperial Warlord*, 17. See also Paul W. Kroll, "Portraits of Ts'ao Ts'ao: Literary Studies on the Man and the Myth" (Ph.D. diss., Univ. of Michigan, 1976), 2.

the rise.[13] While serving in a minor eunuch office, Cao Teng was selected to be a companion to the heir-designate. From then on, he advanced in office, serving four emperors during a period of over thirty years.[14]

Cao Teng's adopted son was Cao Song 曹嵩. There were good reasons for a eunuch like Cao Teng to adopt a son. For one thing, the son could carry out sacrifices to the family ancestors and to the father after his death. For another, he could beget his own sons to ensure that these sacrifices continued. After 135, the adopted son of a eunuch was allowed to inherit from his father, thereby allowing for the preservation of the family position.[15]

Cao Song's origins were already something of an enigma at the time of the compiling of *Records of the Three States*.[16] Two works often quoted in its commentary – the anonymous *Cao Man zhuan* 曹瞞傳 and Guo Ban's 郭頒 *Wei Jin shi yu* 魏晉世語 – maintain that Cao Song was a member of the Xiahou 夏侯 clan of Qiao.[17] If that were true, then Cao Cao later broke a taboo by marrying women from his family into the Xiahou clan. Some scholars argued in the past that it is extremely unlikely that Cao Song was originally a Xiahou.[18] Chen Shou writes, "No one has been able to discover from what stock Song was born,"[19] and *Records of the Three States* nowhere says outright that Cao Song was a Xiahou. But in fascicle 9, where Chen Shou deals with the leading generals of the Cao clan, he lists Xiahou generals, too, which can be interpreted as an endorsement of the *Cao Man zhuan* and *Wei Jin shi yu* information. Furthermore, the discovery of Xiahou names on tomb

13 Hans Bielenstein, "Wang Mang, the Restoration of the Han Dynasty, and Later Han," in *The Cambridge History of China*, vol. 1, *The Ch'in and Han Empires, 221 B.C.–A.D. 220*, ed. Denis Twitchett and Michael Loewe, 287–88 (Cambridge: Cambridge Univ. Press, 1986).

14 *Sgz* 1.1, n. 2 (quoting *Xu Han shu*); Leban, "Ts'ao Ts'ao and the Rise of Wei," 47. See also Kroll, "Portraits of Ts'ao Ts'ao," 2–3; de Crespigny, *Imperial Warlord*, 17–8.

15 Leban, "Ts'ao Ts'ao and the Rise of Wei," 48; Bielenstein, "Wang Mang, the Restoration of the Han Dynasty, and Later Han," 287–88.

16 *Sgz* 1.1.

17 *Sgz* 1.2, n. 3; Leban, "Ts'ao Ts'ao and the Rise of Wei," 48; Kroll, "Portraits of Ts'ao Ts'ao," 3. Both *Cao Man zhuan* and *Wei Jin shi yu* have an anti-Cao bias.

18 See Leban, "Ts'ao Ts'ao and the Rise of Wei," 48–52.

19 *Sgz* 1.1.

bricks that have been excavated at the Cao clan cemetery at Bozhou since 1974 can also be seen as proof of the Xiahou origins of Cao Song. Fang Beichen 方北辰 says that Chen's statement about the obscurity of Cao Song's origins was a distortion.[20] Since Cao Teng was so successful in office, when he died Cao Song was naturally left in favorable circumstances, and he held high posts in the central government during the reign of Emperor Ling 靈帝 (r. 168–189). The *Later Han History* states that he obtained office through bribes and purchase, common practice at the time.[21]

Emperor Ling died in the summer of 189, and the Han dynasty essentially died with him, though it survived in an attenuated form for another three decades.[22] During that time, there was almost constant warfare. A key moment came in 196, for that was the year that Emperor Xian 獻帝 (r. 189–220), the last Han emperor, and his court came under Cao Cao's protection and control. With that event, Cao Cao became preeminent in the Han and was able both politically and militarily to operate from a position of imperial legitimacy against opponents and enemies. At the same time, he was able to advance his own interests to the benefit of his family. The year 196 is significant for another reason, as well, for to mark the change in the emperor's circumstances, a new reign period was inaugurated – Jian'an 建安 (196–220). This name also came to be applied to a literary period, and as such, it is inseparable from Cao Zhi. Chronologically speaking, the literary period has a somewhat broader scope than the reign period.[23] At the risk of getting ahead of the story, let us just note that when used as a period name in literature, Jian'an can be understood to begin earlier and end later than the reign period. Whatever specific dates may be assigned to it, it essentially includes the productive years of both Cao Cao and Cao

20 On the Xiahou issue, see Fang Beichen, trans., *San guo zhi zhu yi* 三國志注譯 (Xi'an: Shaanxi renmin chubanshe, 1995), 1.2, n. 8; de Crespigny, *Imperial Warlord*, 20–25; Xu 5, 104.

21 *HHs* 78.2519; Leban, "Ts'ao Ts'ao and the Rise of Wei," 53. See also B. J. Mansvelt Beck, "The Fall of the Han," in *The Cambridge History of China*, 1: 323, 329, 331–33.

22 On the events of 189 and their immediate aftermath, see de Crespigny, *Imperial Warlord*, 41–55; Mansvelt Beck, "The Fall of the Han," 340–50.

23 See Tian, *The Halberd at Red Cliff*, 2–3; Cutter, "To Make Her Mine: Women and the Rhetoric of Property in Early and Early Medieval *Fu*," *EMC* 19 (2013): 39–40.

Zhi. A useful approach is to understand that "Jian'an literature" refers to the works of a particular group of writers who were active around the end of the second century and the beginning of the third, including but not limited to Cao Cao, Cao Pi, Cao Zhi, and the writers that later came to be called the Jian'an qi zi 建安七子, the Seven Masters of the Jian'an Period: Kong Rong 孔融 (153–208), Chen Lin 陳琳 (d. 217), Wang Can 王粲 (177–217), Xu Gan 徐幹 (171–218), Ruan Yu 阮瑀 (ca. 165–212), Ying Yang 應瑒 (d. 217), and Liu Zhen 劉楨 (d. 217).[24]

Life

Cao Zhi was born sometime in 192, most likely in Dongwuyang 東武陽, the seat of Dong commandery 東郡 in Yan province 兗州.[25] Cao Cao had become grand administrator of Dong commandery, with his base in Dongwuyang, in mid-191, and in 192, the rest of Yan province came under his power.[26] In addition to Cao Zhi himself, three of his brothers were also born to his mother, known posthumously as Empress Bian 卞后: Cao Pi, Cao Zhang and Cao Xiong 曹熊. Cao Zhi ultimately had twenty-five or twenty-six brothers and half-brothers and an unknown number of sisters, with only a few of the latter mentioned in our sources. He seems to have been closest to Cao Zhang and to Cao Biao 曹彪, a half-brother. His relationship with Cao Pi was fraught from the beginning and grew extremely tense once Cao Pi became emperor.

Up to 196, Cao Zhi had lived in parts of Yan province, but once Cao Cao settled the emperor and court at Xu 許 (later renamed Xuchang 許昌), the family probably moved there.[27] Then, in 200, Cao Cao defeated his rival Yuan Shao 袁紹 (d. 202) for control of northern China at the Battle of Guandu 官渡. Yuan's seat of power, the city of Ye 鄴, remained for a time in the hands of his son Yuan Shang 袁尚 (d. 207), but in 204, Cao Cao captured it.[28] Ye was an old city, its

---

24 For a study of the discovery, reception, and influences of the Jian'an period, see Tian, *The Halberd at Red Cliff.*

25 Xu 7.

26 *Sgz* 1.9. See also de Crespigny, *Imperial Warlord*, 61–68.

27 Xu 32.

28 *Sgz* 1.25. Ye was in modern Linzhang 臨漳, Hebei.

region “the homeland of former kings, / Where the traces of the sages may be found,” according to a *fu* written some decades later by Zuo Si 左思 (ca. 250–ca. 305).[29] Strategically situated, it became a monument to Cao Cao’s success, and he embarked upon an ambitious building program there as he rose in power and status.[30] Some of Cao Zhi’s poems make reference to features of Ye, notably Bronze Bird Terrace 銅雀臺 and its nearby park or garden, as well as Wenchang Palace 文昌殿.

Cao Cao was skilled in war and politics, but he was also a person of culture who had a gift for writing.[31] Even during the almost constant battles and social upheaval at the end of Han, he saw to it that his sons received both a classical education and military training. In a famous passage from his *Dian lun* 典論, Cao Pi writes, “At that time I was five *sui*, and because the world was in chaos, His Highness [Cao Cao] had me learn archery. When I was six, I knew how to shoot. He also had me ride horses. When I was eight, I knew how to shoot while riding. Because the age had many unforeseen developments, whenever he went on a campaign, I always accompanied him” 余時年五歲，上以世方擾亂，教余學射，六歲而知射，又教余騎馬，八歲而能騎射矣。以時之多故，每征，余常從.[32] Cao Zhi must have had a similar experience, for in his “Memorial Seeking to Prove Myself” 求自試表, he writes, “In the past I went with my father the late August Emperor Wu south as far as Red Bank, in the east we approached the glaucous sea, in the west we gazed on Jade Gate, in the north we went out to the Great Wall. I saw the conditions under which he marched his army and used arms; it can be called ingenious” 臣昔從先武皇帝南極赤岸，東臨滄海，西望玉門，北出玄塞，伏見所以行軍用兵之勢，可謂神妙矣![33]

---

29 David R. Knechtges, trans., *Wen xuan, or Selections of Refined Literature*, vol. 1, *Rhapsodies on Metropolises and Capitals* (Princeton: Princeton Univ. Press, 1982), 435. See *Wx* 6.266.

30 See Joanne Tsao, *The City of Ye in the Chinese Literary Landscape* (Leiden: Brill, 2020).

31 Jean-Pierre Diény, *Les poèmes de Cao Cao (155–220)* (Paris: Institut des Hautes Études Chinoises, Collège de France, 2000), 7.

32 *Sgz* 2.89.

33 *Sgz* 19.567. The references to the sea and to the Dark Fortress 玄塞 (Great Wall) indicate that he is probably referring to Cao Cao’s expedition against the Wuhuan 烏桓 (or Wuwan 烏丸) in Jian’an 12 (207); Xu 85. On this expedition,

The humanistic side of Cao Zhi's education is evident early. At the very outset of his biography in *Records of the Three States* we read, "When he was something over ten *sui*, he could recite poetry, treatises, and *fu* totaling several hundred thousand words, and he was skilled at writing" 年十餘歲，誦讀詩、論及辭賦數十萬言，善屬文.[34] The biography goes on to say that he was by nature easygoing and unaffected and that he did not care about showy carriages or clothes. Clearly some of the language used in this section of Cao Zhi's biography is conventional; Cao Pi is depicted as similarly precocious in one text.[35] That does not necessarily mean, however, that the information should be dismissed out of hand.

One of the earliest *fu* by Cao Zhi that is still extant dates from Jian'an 17 (212). This is "*Fu* on Ascending the Terrace" (**2.6**).[36] Cao's biography states, "When Bronze Bird Terrace in Ye was newly completed, Cao Cao ascended it with all of his sons and ordered them each to compose a *fu*. Cao Zhi took up his brush and was done in an instant. It was marvelous and Cao Cao thought him highly exceptional" 時鄴銅爵臺新成，太祖悉將諸子登臺，使各為賦。植援筆立成，可觀，太祖甚異之.[37] There is obviously a performative component captured by this narrative. Performance and, less often remarked, entertainment, were important in Jian'an times. Hsiang-Lin Shih has studied Jian'an period poetry by looking at the compositions as poetic dialogues and performances. For example, she imagines Ying Yang reciting his banquet poem "Poem in Attendance at the Jianzhang Terrace Gathering of

---

see de Crespigny, *Imperial Warlord*, 230–39. Mention of the Red Bank may point to Cao Zhi's presence as a teenager at the famous Battle of the Red Cliff, site of a major defeat for Cao Cao's armies; Xu 93.

34 *Sgz* 19.557.

35 *Sgz* 2.57, Pei Songzhi quoting Wang Chen's *Wei shu*. On such conventions, see Hans H. Frankel, "T'ang Literati: A Composite Biography," in *Confucian Personalities*, ed. Arthur F. Wright and Denis Twitchett, 72–73, 80–81 (Stanford: Stanford Univ. Press, 1962).

36 Bold numbers are the numbers of the poems in this book.

37 *Sgz* 19.557. On Bronze Bird Terrace, see Niu Runzhen 牛潤珍, *Gudu Yecheng yanjiu: Zhongshiji Dongya ducheng zhidu tanyuan* 古都鄴城研究：中世紀東亞都城制度探源 (Beijing: Zhonghua shuju, 2015), 49–53; Shih, "Jian'an Literature Revisited," 98–100; Tian, *The Halberd at Red Cliff*, passim; Tsao, *The City of Ye in the Chinese Literary Landscape*, 45–56.

the General of the Gentlemen of the Household for All Purposes" 侍五官中郎將建章臺集詩 and perhaps pacing back and forth with his arms folded behind him as he spoke in the voice of a goose.[38] In this highly conjectural reconstruction of the moment, the poet-courtier becomes part entertainer, but then goes on to deliver a serious message about the precariousness of life.

The idea of entertaining in order to instruct was already an old one. We tend to approach the poems and *fu* of Cao Zhi and his cohort with a uniform sobriety that works like "*Fu* on the Bat" (**3.8**) and "*Fu* on the Sparrow Hawk and Sparrow" (**3.7**) belie. There is ample evidence that the Caos were interested in performance arts. We know that music was important to Cao Cao, Cao Pi, and others of the time. There is an interesting anecdote about Cao Zhi's behavior on meeting the noted classical scholar Handan Chun 邯鄲淳 (ca. 130–ca. 225) that may deserve more attention than it usually gets. It is from the *Wei lüe* 魏略, as quoted in Pei Songzhi's commentary to *Sgz*:

> Cao Zhi was delighted when he first received Handan Chun. He invited him in to take a seat, but did not at first talk to him. At the time, the weather was blazing hot, so Cao Zhi called for an attendant to fetch water. After he had bathed himself, he put on powder. Then, hatless and slapping his bared shoulder, he did the foreign dance "Five Hammer Forge," juggled balls and fenced, and having recited several thousand words of comedic small talk, asked Chun, "What does Master Handan make of that?" Thereupon, he changed his clothes and headwrap, assumed a proper countenance, and together with Chun critically discussed facets of the primal chaos and creation, and the significance of the differences of the multitude of things. After this they discussed the differences in the strengths and weaknesses of worthy sages, famous officials, and intrepid men from august Fu Xi on down. Next they paid tribute to ancient and contemporary literary texts, rhapsodies, and dirges, and got to what the priorities in government affairs of officials

38 Hsiang-Lin Shih, "Jian'an Literature Revisited: Poetic Dialogues in the Last Three Decades of the Han Dynasty" (Ph.D. diss., Univ. of Washington, 2013), 53.

> should be. They also deliberated on fluctuating conditions in the use of arms and deploying troops. Then Cao Zhi gave orders to the kitchen steward, and wine and roasted meat came out together. Seated silently on the mat, there was no one who could compare with him. At nightfall, Chun returned home and extolled Cao Zhi's talent to those he knew, calling him a genius.
>
> 植初得淳甚喜，延入坐，不先與談。時天暑熱，植因呼常從取水自澡訖，傅粉。遂科頭拍袒，胡舞五椎鍛，跳丸擊劍，誦俳優小說數千言訖，謂淳曰：「邯鄲生何如邪？」於是乃更著衣幘，整儀容，與淳評說混元造化之端，品物區別之意，然後論羲皇以來賢聖名臣烈士優劣之差，次頌古今文章賦誄及當官政事宜所先後，又論用武行兵倚伏之勢。乃命廚宰，酒炙交至，坐席默然，無與伉者。及暮，淳歸，對其所知歎植之材，謂之「天人」.[39]

As Timothy Davis observes, "this passage is valuable for the insight it provides into the variety of social and cultural activities enjoyed by the elite of the early medieval period."[40] Even dirges perform a social function as a topic of entertaining conversation. Cao Zhi "wowed" Handan Chun, as was no doubt his aim.

The Handan Chun anecdote provides a template. It is a simple idea to view some of Cao's literary pieces as performances in which an early medieval Chinese poet plays two roles at once, on the one hand seeking, to "impress, persuade, entertain, or even challenge" his audience,[41] while on the other perhaps addressing a serious topic through a veiled allegorical message. The question of allegory will be addressed later.

In Jian'an 16 (211), Cao Zhi received his first title of nobility – he was made Marquis of Pingyuan 平原侯, which was located in the modern county by the same name in Shandong province.[42] The Cao sons, however, did not go to their fiefs before Cao Pi became emperor, so Cao Zhi was able to remain in Ye, the center of cultural activity. In Jian'an 19 (214), he was switched to be Marquis of Linzi 臨淄侯.[43] A

39 *Sgz* 21.603.

40 Timothy M. Davis, "Potent Stone: Entombed Epigraphy and Memorial Culture in Early Medieval China" (Ph.D. diss., Columbia Univ., 2008), 245.

41 Shih, "Jian'an Literature Revisited," 10.

42 *Sgz* 19.557.

43 Linzi was to the south of modern Guangrao 廣饒, Shandong.

few years later, in Jian'an 22 (217), five thousand households were added to Cao Zhi's income base, bringing the total to ten thousand.[44] But this was the year that Cao Pi was named Cao Cao's heir-designate, and Cao Zhi's fortunes were soon to change.

For a time, Cao Zhi had been Cao Cao's favorite son and potential successor. When Cao Cao launched in 204 a military expedition against his rival Sun Quan 孫權 (182–252), he had Cao Zhi, then just twenty-three *sui*, stay behind in charge of Ye (see **1.1**). But ultimately, due to Cao Zhi's undisciplined behavior or the machinations of Cao Pi or both, his attitude toward Cao Zhi changed. One event behind the change was a serious violation of law: Cao Zhi drove his carriage down the speedway that was reserved for the emperor's use and exited through the major's gate, opened it, and went out. His biography says, "Cao Cao was incensed, and the Prefect of [the Majors in Charge of] Official Carriages was condemned to death. Thenceforth, he increased the prohibitions regarding the sundry lords, and his favoritism toward Cao Zhi declined daily" 太祖大怒，公車[司馬]令坐死。由是重諸侯科禁，而植寵日衰.[45]

In 220, after Cao Cao's death, Cao Zhi's elder brother Cao Pi accepted the carefully engineered abdication of the last Han emperor and established himself as the founding emperor of the Wei dynasty.[46] Cao Zhi's behavior had shown on more than one occasion that he lacked self-control and discipline, so Cao Pi was made heir. Both brothers had their backers, and the rivalry between the two sides was intense. Once Cao Pi became ruler, all of his brothers were sent separately to their fiefs, and his treatment of them, especially Cao Zhi, was harsh. Cao Zhi seems to have come close to being executed, and one story, perhaps

44 *Sgz* 19.557.

45 *Sgz* 19.558. See also Cutter, "The Incident at the Gate: Cao Zhi, the Succession, and Literary Fame," *TP* 71 (1985): 229.

46 On Cao Pi's acceptance of Emperor Xian's abdication and the founding of the Wei, see Knechtges, "The Rhetoric of Imperial Abdication and Accession in a Third-Century Chinese Court," 3–35 and Howard L. Goodman, *Ts'ao P'i Transcendent: The Political Culture of Dynasty-Founding in China at the End of the Han* (Seattle: Scripta Serica, 1998). See also Andrew Chittick, "Dynastic Legitimacy during the Eastern Chin: Hsi Tso-ch'ih and the Problem of Huan Wen," *AM*, 3rd ser., 11.1 (1998): 25–26.

apocryphal, says that Cao Pi murdered his brother Cao Zhang.[47] Some of Cao Zhi's supporters, including the brothers Ding Yí 丁儀 and Ding Yì 丁翼, along with their sons, were, in fact, killed.

The second year of Cao Pi's reign as emperor, Huangchu 2 (221), was a precarious time for Cao Zhi, a year in which he was nearly put to death. His biography says, "In Huangchu 2, Guan Jun, Superintendent of the Vassal State, catering to the emperor's wishes, memorialized that 'While drunk, Cao Zhi was defiant and arrogant and threatened and menaced Your envoy.' Those in charge all asked that the offense be punished, but because of the empress dowager, he only demoted Cao Zhi to be Marquis of Anxiang" 黃初二年，監國謁者灌均希指，奏「植醉酒悖慢，劫脅使者。」有司請治罪，帝以太后故，貶爵安鄉侯.[48] This was a real demotion. Marquis of Anxiang was a district marquis, not a commandery marquis as had been the case with Linzi. It was a distinctly lower rank, and as a result his position was lower than that of the least of his brothers. His title and rank were now actually the same as those of a man who was not even a member of the royal family. Furthermore, his income was greatly reduced. Before his demotion, it was set at 10,000 households. Afterwards, even following two subsequent promotions, his income was only up to 2,500 households. After his demotion was announced, Cao Zhi did not go to a place called Anxiang. It is likely that this was a titular rank with no connection in terms of revenue or residence to a place. It is this near-death experience that is behind the first half of **4.27** (lines 1–56).

After a few months, Cao Zhi was made Marquis of Juancheng 鄄城侯. But Huangchu 3 and 4 (222–223) were to be another critical period for Cao Zhi. He had only been designated Prince of Juancheng 鄄城王, with a fief of 2,500 households, the previous year, and soon he was transferred to be Prince of Yongqiu 雍丘王.[49] He was thirty-two *sui* at the time. A piece he later wrote, known as "Order of Huangchu 6"

---

47 See Cutter, "*Shishuo xinyu* and the Death of Cao Zhang," *JAOS* 129 (2009): 403–11.

48 *Sgz* 19.561. On this incident, see Cutter, "Personal Crisis and Communication in the Life of Cao Zhi," in *Rhetoric and the Discourses of Power in Court Culture, China, Europe, and Japan*, ed. David R. Knechtges and Eugene Vance (Seattle: Univ. of Washington Press, 2004), 151–54. See also Xu 276–84.

49 *Sgz* 2.80, 19.562.

黃初六年令, states that he was once more under investigation by Wang Ji 王機 and others.[50] Although he avoided punishment, he was extraordinarily apprehensive at this time, a fact that is evident in **4.15**, **4.27**, and the memorial submitting them. He initially received an edict cutting him and unspecified other lords off from court, but that was rescinded and he and the other marquises and princes did go to Luoyang in the fifth month.[51] There he lodged in a "west mansion." According to one account, he was so concerned that he left his retinue east of Xuanyuan Pass 軒轅關 and went ahead incognito with two or three others to see the Senior Princess of Qinghe 清河長公主 and ask her to offer apologies to the emperor on his behalf. But officers at the pass found out about this and notified the emperor, who sent people to keep Cao Zhi from seeing the princess. The account goes on to describe a tearful scene involving the emperor, Empress Dowager Bian, and Cao Zhi, the reliability of which is open to question.[52] But in any case, Cao Zhi's biography reports that Cao Pi's reaction to Cao Zhi's memorial and poems was that he "appreciated the sincerity of his words and graciously issued an edict in response to encourage him" 嘉其辭義，優詔答勉之.[53]

In Huangchu 6 (225), Cao Pi led a large expedition to the east. On his return, he visited Cao Zhi in Yongqiu and added 500 households to his income.[54] Cao Pi died of illness in Huangchu 7 (226) and was succeeded by his son Cao Rui, known posthumously as Emperor Ming 明帝. In the first year of the Taihe 太和 reign period (227), Cao Zhi's fief was changed to Junyi 浚儀, but it reverted back to Yongqiu the following year. And in Taihe 3 (229), Cao Zhi's fief was changed again to Dong'e 東阿.[55]

Cao Zhi was an excellent writer of memorials (or expressions) 表. A recurrent theme in these and certain other writings is his desire to be of use to the state, but he never got the chance. This is perhaps the

50 Ding 128–29; Xu 295–301, 310–11.
51 *Sgz* 19.562. See also **4.20**.
52 *Sgz* 19.564, Pei's commentary quoting *Wei lüe*. See also Xu 8, 311–12.
53 *Sgz* 19.564.
54 *Sgz* 19.565.
55 Sgz 19.565, 569.

great tragedy of his life – that his desire to accomplish great deeds was never achieved. Near the end of Cao Zhi's biography, we read,

> In the winter of that year, the emperor ordered all the princes to come to court in the first month of Taihe 6 [232]. In the second month he gave Cao Zhi four counties of Chen and made him Prince of Chen, with a fief of 3,500 households. Cao Zhi always wanted to get a separate audience to talk alone and discuss current governmental issues. He hoped to be employed on a trial basis but in the end was not able to get his wish. Once he returned to his fief, he was despondent and disappointed. Since the regulations of that time were very harsh toward the princedoms, his subordinates were hucksters and second-raters, and the soldiers given him were either crippled or old. At most there were fewer than 200 men. Furthermore, because of Cao Zhi's prior transgressions, his income had also been reduced by half, and in the course of eleven years the seat of his fief was moved three times. Often anxious and unhappy, he subsequently fell ill and died. He was forty-one at the time. He left orders to bury him simply.
>
> 其年冬，詔王朝六年正月。其二月，以陳四縣封植為陳王，邑三千五百戶。植每欲求別見獨談，論及時政，幸冀試用，終不能得。既還，悵然絕望。時法制，待藩國既自峻迫，寮屬皆賈豎小才，兵人給其殘老，大數不過二百人。又植以前過，事事復減半，十一年中而三徙都，常汲汲無歡，遂發疾薨，時年四十一。遺令薄葬。[56]

Cao Zhi was buried at Yushan 魚山 in Dong'e. His tomb was excavated in 1951, and twenty-eight bones were recovered, but these have since been lost. "Unfortunately we have no idea of the whereabouts of Cao Zhi's bones," reported Liu Yuxin, director of the Cultural Relics Administration of Dong'e county, during the controversy surrounding the discovery of a tomb thought to be Cao Cao's.

Poetry

Nothing like a complete and totally reliable edition of Cao Zhi's collected works exists. We will discuss editions later, but for now let us note

56 Sgz 19.576. An error in the 1995 reprint of the second edition has 韶 for 詔.

that some of his works have been lost, some exist as incomplete fragments, and many are hard or impossible to date. There are also occasional issues of attribution and authenticity. This is not unusual for an early medieval poet. As I have written elsewhere, "The more we learn about early medieval Chinese literature, the more conscious we are of how much is missing and how bereft we are of a store of materials adequate to lend real clarity to our assertions. Fluctuations in taste and the ravages of time have depleted what was once a more varied and robust corpus, and what remains, of course, presents with all of the philological symptoms and infirmities of authenticity that come with great age."[57] But something is not nothing, and a substantial amount of Cao Zhi's writing has survived.

Cao Zhi wrote in a variety of genres of prose and poetry, and has important works in several genres not represented here. The excellence of his memorials was mentioned above. Among the most personal and expressive are "Memorial Presenting the Poems 'Blaming Myself' and 'Responding to an Edict'" 上責躬應詔詩表 (see **4.27**), "Memorial Seeking to Prove Myself" 求自試表, "Memorial Seeking to Convey Familial Affection" 求通親親表, and "Memorial Explaining Judicious Appointments" 陳審舉表.[58] These memorials all date from the reigns of Cao Pi and Cao Rui.

This book deals with his more narrowly poetic works: the translation contains works in the *fu* 賦 genre, as well as both *shi* 詩 and *yuefu* 樂府 poems. It contains forty-four in the former category, and eighty-four in the latter.[59] These include numerous pieces that have not survived fully intact.

57 Cutter, "Letters and Memorials in the Early Third Century," in *Handbook of Chinese Letter Writing*, ed. Antje Richter (Leiden: Brill, 2015), 307. See also Xiaofei Tian, "The Twilight of the Masters: Masters Literature (*zishu*) in Early Medieval China," *JAOS* 126 (2006): 471–72.

58 See *Wx* 20.927–35, 37.1675–90; *Sgz* 19.562–64, 565–68, 569–74; Zhao 2.268–78, 3.368–79, 3.436–43, 3.444–52; Cutter, "Letters and Memorials," 322–26.

59 This translation follows the text and arrangement of Ding Yan's 丁晏 (1794–1875) edition, on which more below. Ding sometimes includes isolated lines, both titled and untitled, as at the end of his *juan* 5; these are usually not translated here.

The genre name *fu* has been translated in several ways, most notably as "rhapsody" and "poetic exposition," but in the case of so important a genre, it may make sense to at least try to accustom general readers to the homegrown name. Some of the characteristics of *fu* include mixture of rhymed and unrhymed parts, extensive description and enumerative cataloguing of things or attributes, and hyperbole. Cao Zhi's *fu* include a number that are *fu* on objects 詠物賦, not infrequently on the same topics as fellow Jian'an writers. As in the case of other poets of the time, some of his *fu* tend to be shorter and more lyrical than early works in the genre. *Yuefu* means "Music Bureau." Without going into the origins of the term or scholarship on the category, suffice to say that it typically designates musical poetry. But individual poems could drift into or out of the category, depending on vagaries of transmission and editorial choices.[60] For example, poems like **5.4** and **5.47** are in some sources classified as *yuefu* and in others not.

The Jian'an period was a time when many of the elements associated with classical Chinese poetry were first formed or ratified through use. One of the main features of the poetry is the use of the pentasyllabic line by known poets like Cao Zhi. However, the older tetrasyllabic line did not disappear. It remained important throughout the early medieval period.[61] In this book there are numerous poems that are either completely or partly composed in tetrasyllabic lines. Nonetheless, the use of the pentayllabic line by Cao Zhi and other poets was a significant development in the history of Chinese literature. Cao Zhi's most famous and often anthologized poems are mainly in this form.

Another notable facet of Jian'an poetic life and praxis was group composition, in the sense of poets writing on a common theme.[62] Sometimes these were occasional poems written for the outings, banquets, and drinking parties in Ye that characterize and were used by later writers and scholars – notably Xie Lingyun 謝靈運 (385–433), Liu Xie 劉勰 (ca. 465–ca. 532), and Xiao Tong 蕭統 (501–531) – to define

60 See Stephen Owen, *The Making of Early Chinese Classical Poetry* (Cambridge, Mass.: Harvard Univ. Asia Center, 2006), 31–33.

61 See David Zebulon Raft, "Four-syllable Verse in Medieval China" (Ph.D. diss., Harvard Univ., 2007).

62 On Jian'an group composition, or poetic "dialogues," see Shih, "Jian'an Literature Revisited," 4–11.

the period.[63] Although Cao Cao took Ye in 204, it was really only after the death of Liu Biao 劉表 in 208, and his son's subsequent surrender to Cao Cao, that the Ye gatherings begin, for it was then that Wang Can – who in a sense is the first Jian'an poet – and others sought protection and refuge with Cao Cao's regime. Cao Zhi, of course, was an active participant in these moments of bonding, in which poetry was deployed for aesthetic and sociopolitical purposes. This is evident in a number of the works translated herein. In a sense, these were command performances – the writers present were expected to express their gratitude for the event and to praise the host. Sometimes, as in the case of certain *fu* and works in the related Sevens 七 genre, they had a topic set for them by the host, generally one of the Caos. *Fu* on a shared topic composed by Cao Zhi and others include: **2.2** (Wang Can); **2.3** (Wang Can, Ying Yang, Chen Lin); **2.9** (Cao Pi, Wang Can, Ying Yang, Xu Gan); **2.10** (Cao Pi, Wang Can, Ying Yang, Chen Lin); **3.2** (Wang Can); **3.4** (Wang Can, Ying Yang, Chen Lin, Ruan Yu, Mi Heng 禰衡 [173–198]); **3.5** (Wang Can).[64]

It is a commonplace that to read Cao Zhi's poetic writings is to face repeatedly the question of allegory, since so many of his works have traditionally been read as metaphorical depictions of his own fraught relationship with his imperial brother. Frustration with this hermeneutical tradition, coupled with the then "New Criticism," led to Hans H. Frankel's 1964 article "Fifteen Poems by Ts'ao Chih: An Attempt at a New Approach," which was rightly intended as a corrective to this habit of reading.[65] But carried too far this approach can fail to take into account the fact that many of Cao Zhi's poems *are* informed by his life, even when not strictly autobiographical. Some influential and valuable

63 See Tian, *The Halberd at Red Cliff*, 30–62. See also Tian Xiaofei 田曉菲, "Yanyin yu huiyi: chongxin sikao Jian'an" 宴飲與回憶:重新思考建安, *Zhongguo wenxue xuebao* 中國文學學報 (Dec. 2010): 21–34; Cutter, "Gastropoetics in the Jian'an Period: Food and Memory in Early Medieval China," *EMC* 24 (2018); idem, "Cao Zhi's (192–232) Symposium Poems," *CLEAR* 6.1/2 (1984): 1–32; Huang Yazhuo 黃亞卓, *Han Wei Liuchao gongyan shi yanjiu* 漢魏六朝公宴詩研究 (Shanghai: Huadong shifan daxue chubanshe, 2006).

64 The works listed under **2.3** are titled "*Fu* on the Goddess" 神女賦.

65 Hans H. Frankel, "Fifteen Poems by Ts'ao Chih: An Attempt at a New Approach," *JAOS* 84.1 (1964):1–14.

contemporary scholarship focuses so much on palimpsestic relationships and shared compositional techniques that poets almost disappear. This problem of allegorical readings is never going to go away, and it is difficult to know where to stand. For example, in a marginal note to the "*Fu* on the Bat" (**3.8**) in his critical edition of Cao's works, Ding Yan indicates this is an attack on malevolence.[66] A long time ago I questioned the notion that it was possible on the basis of so few remaining lines – all of which can be understood as describing attributes of bats – to say with certainty this *fu* has a hidden meaning and was written to attack the likes of Guan Jun or even Cao Pi, as is sometimes said. Cao Haidong (see *List of Abbreviations*) agreed that it is difficult to ascertain who is the target of the *fu*, but then went on to state unequivocally that there is no doubt that the *fu* lashes out at a type of real person who was as freakish and perverse as bats.[67] Ma Jigao 馬積高, an important historian of the *fu*, has written, "This type of short satirical *fu* was entirely Cao Zhi's invention and from Tang times on it gradually developed into the subgenre of *fu* richest in immediate significance" 這種諷刺小賦，完全是曹植的首創，到唐以後，逐漸發展成為賦體作品中最富於現實意義的一種.[68] Liao Guodong also sees this *fu* as a sharp rebuke to Cao Zhi's enemies. Furthermore, Liao understands from Cao Zhi's use of *yang* and *yin* in "*Fu* on the Parrot" (**3.4**) and "*Fu* on the Cicada" (**3.3**) that they are intended as symbols of enlightened and benighted times, respectively. Thus, the "Bat" line "They hide by day and move at night" takes on special meaning beyond the behavior of bats.[69] "*Fu* on the Cicada" uses first-person pronouns, which facilitates the kind of allegorical/autobiographical reading many prefer. If this feels like a game of hide-and-seek, a scavenger hunt for poetic clues to the events of Cao Zhi's life, it often times is – but it is an old and mostly honorable one played by centuries of scholars steeped in the praxis of Chinese poetics, so one should be chary of willy-nilly casting it aside, just as one should be judicious about engaging in it.

66 Ding 31.

67 Cao Haidong 106.

68 Ma Jigao, *Fu shi* 賦史 (Shanghai: Shanghai guji chubanshe, 1987), 154.

69 Liao Guodong 廖國棟, *Wei Jin yongwu fu yanjiu* 魏晉詠物賦研究 (Taipei: Wenshizhe chubanshe, 1990), 247.

Cao Zhi's most famous *fu* is "*Fu* on the Goddess of the Luo River" (**2.3**), but he seems to have written others that are almost unimaginably different from that iconic piece. Among Cao Zhi's surviving *fu*, two are especially unusual stylistically. This is perhaps a reminder of how incomplete is our knowledge of what poets actually did, as opposed to what later editors and critics thought they should have done. The two *fu* are "*Fu* on the Sparrow Hawk and Sparrow" (**3.7**) and "*Fu* on a Bat." "*Fu* on the Sparrow Hawk and Sparrow" is a *su fu* 俗賦, a popular vernacular narrative *fu* in a style similar to the "*Fu* on the Swallow" 燕子賦 that was found in two manuscript versions at Dunhuang 敦煌.[70] It can also be seen as part of the tradition represented by the much earlier "*Fu* on the Divine Crow" 神烏賦 discovered in 1993 in a Han tomb and dated to 10 BCE.[71] "*Fu* on the Sparrow Hawk and Sparrow" is quite colloquial. Ma Jigao has noted, for example, that early on *Yanshi jiaxun* 顏氏家訓 already identified the term *ke suan* 果(=顆)蒜 (**3.7**, line 20) as an "everyday usage among the common people" 俗閭常語.[72] In short, "*Fu* on the Sparrow Hawk and Sparrow" is very different from the rest of Cao Zhi's surviving corpus. Commenting on this *fu*'s place in the tradition, Qian Zhongshu 錢鍾書 (1910–1998) very remarkably states:

> This is a playful work and, though not ornate, it fully expresses the author's state of mind. … After the sparrow gets released, the

---

70 Fu Junlian 伏俊璉, "Dunhuang su fu zhi yanjiu fanchou ji su fu zai wenxueshi shang de yiyi" 敦煌俗賦之研究範疇及俗賦在文學史上的意義, *Zhengda Zhongwen xuebao* 政大中文學報 18 (Dec. 2012): 37.

71 See Cao Daoheng 曹道衡 (1928–2005), *Han Wei Liuchao cifu* 漢魏六朝辭賦 (Shanghai: Shanghai guji chubanshe, 1989), 113; Wilt Idema, "Dunhuang Narratives," in *The Cambridge History of Chinese Literature*, vol. 1, *To 1375*, ed. Kang-I Sun Chang and Stephen Owen (Cambridge: Cambridge Univ. Press, 2010), 378; David R. Knechtges and Taiping Chang, eds., *Ancient and Early Medieval Chinese Literature: A Reference Guide, Part One* (Leiden: Brill, 2010), 325; and Hans van Ess, "An Interpretation of the *Shenwu Fu* of Tomb No. 6, Yinwan," *MS* 51 (2003): 605–28. "*Fu* on the Divine Crow," "*Fu* on the Sparrow Hawk and Sparrow," and other such popular *fu* are discussed in Fu Junlian, *Su fu yanjiu* 俗賦研究 (Beijing: Zhonghua shuju, 2008), 158–65.

72 Ma Jigao 馬積高, *Fu shi* 賦史 (Shanghai: Shanghai guji chubanshe, 1987), 155. See Zhou Fagao 周法高, *Yanshi jiaxun hui zhu* 顏氏家訓彙注 (Taipei: Tailian guofeng chubanshe, 1975 rpt.), 106.

> male and female converse, and he brags, "I counted on the speed of my moves, and I've always been glib and ingratiating," and so on. Very like the story in the "Li Lou" section of *Mengzi* about the man of Qi's behavior on coming home and being arrogant before his wife and concubine, it opens the way for the satirical mode in later fiction. Of Cao Zhi's *fu*, "*Fu* on the Goddess of the Luo" [**2.3**] is the most famous, but although it has eloquence, it's still just dust trailing Song Yu's carriage; it's no match for the novelty and groundbreaking qualities of this piece.[73]
>
> 游戲之作，不為華縟，而盡致達情，筆意已似《敦煌掇瑣》之四《燕子賦》矣。雀獲釋後，公嫗相語，自誇："賴我翻捷，體素便附"云云，大類《孟子．離婁》》中齊人外來驕其妻妾行逕，啟後世小說中調侃法門。植之詞賦，《洛神》最著，雖有善言，尚是追逐宋玉車後塵，未若此篇之開生面而破餘地也。

Perhaps only someone as iconoclastic and learned as Qian Zhongshu could dare make such a statement. It certainly moved the discourse on "*Fu* on the Sparrow Hawk and Sparrow."[74]

The final lines of "*Fu* on the Sparrow Hawk and Sparrow" make it clear that we are dealing with allegory, placing the work rather clearly in the tradition of other pieces, like Zhao Yi's 趙壹 (ca. 130–ca. 185) "*Fu* on the Cornered Bird" 窮鳥賦, that use birds for allegorical purposes. It is almost too easy to read "*Fu* on the Sparrow Hawk and Sparrow" as being about the strained relationship between Cao Zhi and his emperor brother, and if we do so, we are in some old company. It happens that "*Fu* on the Sparrow Hawk and Sparrow" is so far the earliest *fu* for which there is a stone inscription.[75] That inscription, which dates from the Sui 隋 dynasty (589–618), is listed in Zhang Zhongxin's 張仲炘 (*jinshi* 1877) *Hubei shi jin zhi* 湖北石金志, which says:

73 Qian Zhongshu 錢鍾書 *Guanzhui bian* 管錐編 (Hong Kong: Zhonghua shuju, 1980), 1059–60. The preface to "*Fu* on the Goddess of the Luo" will explain the reference to Song Yu here.

74 For example, Qian's evaluation is mentioned in Fu, *Su fu yanjiu*, 164, and Zhao Chenglin 趙成林, *Tang fu fenti xulun* 唐賦分體敘論 (Changsha: Hunan daxue chubanshe, 2009), 151–52.

75 Cf. Mao Yuanming 毛遠明, *Beike wenxian xue tonglun* 碑刻文獻學通論 (Beijing: Zhonghua shuju, 2009), 230–31.

> In Zhijiang district, at the residence of Palace Writer Yang; in cursive script. At the front is a preface by the Daye Emperor of the Sui [隋煬帝] saying, "Prince Si of Chen [曹植] was a son of the Wei royal house." The inscription at the end says, "Written in the second month of the second year of the Huangchu reign period [221]."
>
> 在枝江縣楊內翰宅，係草書。前有隋大業皇帝序云：陳思王，魏宗室子也。后題云：黃初二年二月記。[76]

As we know from the account of his life above, the second year of Huangchu was a perilous time for Cao Zhi, a year in which he was nearly put to death. The question is, did scholars (and the emperor) in the Sui period have access to information about the date of the composition of "*Fu* on the Sparrow Hawk and Sparrow" that we no longer have, or was this just a surmise based on what they knew of Cao Zhi's life? As Cheng Zhangcan has noted, "If '*Fu* on the Sparrow Hawk and Sparrow' really was composed in Huangchu 2, then the fight between the sparrow hawk and sparrow isn't just a fable concocted by a rhapsodist, but may be the reflection of a genuine brutal political struggle" 如果《鷂雀賦》確實作於黃初二年，那麼，賦中所寫的鷂雀相爭就不僅僅是賦家的假設寓言，而也可能是現實中殘酷的政治鬥爭的映現.[77]

"*Fu* on the Goddess of the Luo" is very commonly read as an allegory of Cao Zhi's failed attempts to gain a position to serve the regime. That is possible, but not overtly evident in the piece, which can just as well be seen as a performance in competition with other writers on this topic. It is important, too, to debunk the common notion that this *fu* has something to do with an infatuation for Empress Zhen 甄后, Cao Pi's wife.[78]

Cao Zhi's *shi* and *yuefu* poems tend toward certain topics and themes. There are parting poems, some of which have content that is

76 Cheng Zhangcan 程章燦, "Shixue yu fuxue: yi Tang Song Yuan shike zhong de fu wei li" 石學與賦學：以唐宋元石刻中的賦為例, in *Cifu wenxue lun ji* 辭賦文學論集, ed. Nanjing daxue Zhongwen xi (Nanjing: Jiangsu jiaoyu chubanshe, 1999), 622, 629.

77 Cheng, "Shixue yu fuxue," 629. Xu 290 dates it to that year.

78 See Cutter, "The Death of Empress Zhen: Fiction and Historiography in Early Medieval China," *JAOS* 112 (1992): 577–78.

not so evidently about parting (see **4.4**). Many poems are occasioned by or descriptive of feasts and outings. The popularity of this topic is significant, for it reflects the lifestyle of the period, especially in Ye, and encapsulates a number of issues: the nearness of death and brevity of life in a time of frequent war and recurrent disease; issues of rank and social status in a shifting court environment; obligations between superior and inferior; the nature of friendship; literary display and competition. A notable feature of Jian'an verse in general and Cao Zhi's writing in particular is the prevalence of poems about women. Among his writings not included here are dirges 誄 and laments 哀辭 for deceased women and girls, but in this book we see poems dealing with abandoned or rejected women, sometimes wholly or partly in the voice of the woman. Although these may reflect a genuine concern for the situation of a specific woman or for an unhappy social phenomenon, such poems were also associated with group composition, complicating our ability to discern their import.

Hand-in-hand with group composition was the subgenre of poetry called *zengda shi* 贈答詩. These are poems of "presentation and reply," in a sense, epistolary poems. They are perhaps the most overt form of poetic dialogue. Cao Zhi has several poems written to friends and associates in this category.

A final group of Cao Zhi's poems that should be mentioned are the poems on roaming into transcendence 遊仙詩. These are pieces about seeking immortality (or high longevity) and sometimes include encounters with such ethereal beings. Cao Zhi was not the only one to write such poems in Jian'an times. It is not clear where the impetus for this poetry came from. Certainly there was an earlier tradition of works of a different sort that involved celestial and terrestrial journeys in quest of immortals. Perhaps the surrender of Zhang Lu 張魯, leader of the Daoist denomination Way of the Celestial Masters 天師道, to Cao Cao in 215 had an effect, for Cao Cao had Zhang and his family and followers move from the theocratic realm he had established in the Hanzhong 漢中 region to the cities of Luoyang and Ye.[79] Daoist beliefs apparently did gain some currency during the Wei.[80] Interestingly, Cao

79 *Sgz* 1.45, 8.265, 23.666.

80 Timothy Wai Keung Chan, *Considering the End: Mortality in Early Medieval Chinese Poetic Representation* (Leiden: Brill, 2012), 88.

Zhi also has a prose work entitled "Disputing Dao" 辨道論 in which he criticizes the quest for immortality. (Another piece, entitled "Dispelling Doubts" 釋疑論, reverses opinions expressed in "Disputing Dao," but the attribution to Cao Zhi is not reliable.)

It is hoped that the non-specialist and specialist alike will find this book interesting and helpful. Cao Zhi's broad range of styles, topics, subgenres, and voices is impressive. The formal and vernacular, the humorous and deadly serious, the autobiographical voice and the poet speaking as a woman, all of these are present. Reading closely, sometimes it is possible to think, "Oh, I see, he was reading (or remembering or consulting) *x* when he wrote this." I am referring not just to allusions but to sustained echoes in a given piece from an earlier particular work or tradition. A bit of this comes out in the footnotes and the *Additional Notes*. In this regard, one question that has long been posed is which version of the *Classic of Poetry* 詩經 did Cao Zhi use. Given when he lived, he may have known more than one, but commentators often seem to think he relied on the Han 韓 school text and interpretation.[81] Others might challenge this view, but any opinions should consider the full range of Cao's works, not just his poetry.

Editions

Cao Zhi has the most remaining works attributed to him – over two hundred pieces of poetry and prose – of any of the writers of his day. Not surprisingly, no contemporary manuscript of his collected works exists. The earliest extant versions are from the Song 宋 dynasty (960–1127), hundreds of years after his death. But collections of Cao Zhi's writings already existed in his own time. He himself compiled a manuscript of seventy-eight of his works in the *fu* genre, calling it the *Qian lu* 前錄. It was lost very early. In the "Preface" to that work, he noted: "I have liked *fu* since I was young. As for what I value in them, I am fond of impassioned spirit, and those I have composed are numerous. Even though they were based on earlier examples, still many were turgid, so, by deleting and revising, I have separately compiled this *First*

81 See, for example, the *Additional Notes* to the preface of **2.3**.

Manuscript of seventy-eight pieces" 余少而好賦、其所尚也、雅好慷慨、所著繁多。雖觸類而作、然蕪穢者眾、故刪定、別撰為前錄七十八篇。[82]

A posthumous rehabilitation of Cao Zhi began with his nephew Emperor Ming, who ordered the compilation of Cao Zhi's writings:

> In the Jingchu period [237–239] the emperor issued an edict which said, "Although in times past King Si of Chen committed errors, he overcame himself and became circumspect in his behavior and thereby made up for his former faults. Moreover, from the time he was a young boy until he died, books were never out of his hands, something that is not easy. As to all the indictments against Cao Zhi during the Huangchu period, the highest officials have already given their decision to the Masters of Writing, the Archivists, and the Palace Writers, as well as to the Grand Herald, to expunge them. Compile and copy the over one hundred rhapsodies, eulogies, poems, inscriptions, and miscellaneous prose written at various times by Cao Zhi and deposit them both inside and outside the palace.
>
> 景初中詔曰：「陳思王昔雖有過失，既克己慎行，以補前闕，且自少至終，篇籍不離於手，誠難能也。其收黃初中諸奏植罪狀，公卿已下議尚書、祕書、中書三府、大鴻臚者皆削除之。撰錄植前後所著賦頌詩銘雜論凡百餘篇，副藏內外。」[83]

The number of works mentioned, "altogether over one hundred pieces," is not specific and was surely not intended to be, so this passage cannot be used to determine the number of pieces written by Cao Zhi.[84]

---

82 Ding 143.

83 *Sgz* 19.576.

84 David Zebulon Raft, "Poetry in the Communication Model: Cao Zhi," unpublished paper, 18–19, criticizes Hans Frankel for understanding the phrase in question as indicating over, but not much over, one hundred pieces and using that as an indication of the approximate size of Cao Zhi's corpus. Chao Gongwu 晁公武 (d. 1171) seems to have made an assumption not dissimilar to Frankel's in his *Junzhai dushu zhi* 郡齋讀書志; Chao Gongwu, comp., *Junzhai dushu zhi*, in *Zhongguo lidai shumu congkan* 中國歷代書目叢刊, comp. Xu Yimin 許逸民 and Chang Zhenguo 常振國, 17.6b (Beijing: Xiandai chubanshe, 1987).

The bibliographical treatise of the *Sui shu* 隋書 (*History of the Sui Dynasty*; presented to the throne in 636) lists a *Chen Si wang Cao Zhi ji* 陳思王曹植集 (Collected Works of Cao Zhi, Prince Si of Chen), in thirty fascicles.[85] *Jiu Tang shu* 舊唐書 (Old Tang History) and *Xin Tang shu* 新唐書 (New Tang History) list *Chen Si wang ji* in both twenty- and thirty-fascicle formats.[86] The versions that existed in Sui and Tang times have long been lost. The oldest extant text of Cao Zhi's collected works is a ten-fascicle large character Song dynasty woodblock edition entitled *Cao Zijian ji* 曹子建集 (the table of contents uses the title *Cao Zijian wenji* 曹子建文集). It is perhaps most likely to date from the reign of the Southern Song emperor Xiaozong 孝宗 (r. 1162–1189). In Qing times, the sole surviving copy of this book entered the famous Tiejin tongjian lou 鐵琴銅劍樓 library of Qu Yong 瞿鏞 (1794–1875) and is now held in the Shanghai Library.[87] It may be smaller (i.e., contain fewer pieces) than the Song imperial library text that was used earlier in compiling *Taiping yulan* in Northern Song times.[88] What is more interesting is the possibility that the extant Southern Song edition falls in a textual lineage going back to the Tang. It appears to be based on the Northern Song edition that Chao Gongwu catalogued, which in turn has indications of a connection with a Tang version.[89]

In 1922, this Song edition was reproduced as part of *Xu Gu yi congshu* 續古逸叢書. It was also reproduced, with some small changes to the

85 *Sui shu* (Beijing: Zhonghua shuju, 1973), 35.1059.

86 *Tang shu "Jing ji" "Yi wen" he zhi* 唐書經籍藝文合志 (Taipei: Shijie shuju, 1976 rpt.), 289. See also Ji Yun 紀昀 (1724–1805) et al., comps., *Qinding Siku quanshu zongmu* 欽定四庫全書總目 (Beijing: Zhonghua shuju, 1997), 2: 1982.

87 On the date of this edition, see Park Hyun-kyu 朴現圭, "Cao Zhi ji de bianzuan yu sizhong Song ben zhi fenxi" 曹植集的編纂與四種宋本之分析, *Wenxian* 文獻, 1995.2: 44–46; idem, "Cao Zhi ji bianzuan guocheng yu sizhong Song ban zhi fenxi" 曹植集編纂過程與四種宋版之分析, *Wenxue yichan* 文學遺產, 1994.4: 30–31 (the contents of Park's two titles appear to be the same); Xie Jin 謝津, "*Cao Zhi ji* banben yanjiu ji bianzuan zhuangkuang kao" 曹植集版本研究及編纂狀況考, *Qingchun suiyue* 青春歲月, 2012.7: 41. Cf. *Shanghai tushuguan cang Song ben tulu* 上海圖書館藏宋本圖錄 (Shanghai: Shanghai guji chubanshe, 2010), 172–73; Liu Ming 劉明, "Cao Zhi ji yanjiu san ti" 曹植集研究三題, *Xuchang xueyuan xuebao* 許昌學院學報 36.4 (2017): 49–50.

88 Liu, "Cao Zhi ji yanjiu san ti," 50.

89 Ibid., 51.

front matter, in the series *Miyun lou ying Song ben qizhong* 密韻樓景宋本七種, also known as *Miyun lou congshu* 密韻樓叢書 (1923–24).[90] Zhu Zuzeng 朱緒曾 (1805–1860) and Ding Yan, the Qing dynasty editors of important critical editions of Cao's collected works, employed a number of editions and other sources in producing their respective works, but neither was aware of this Song edition.[91]

Although neither is entirely satisfactory, the two most useful editions of Cao Zhi's works today are Ding Yan's *Cao ji quanping* 曹集銓評 and Zhao Youwen's 趙幼文 (d. 1993) *Cao Zhi ji jiaozhu* 曹植集校注. Ding based his critical edition on a Ming edition from the Wanli 萬曆 period (1573–1620) by a Mr. Cheng 程 of Xiuyang 修陽. This he collates with *Chen Si wang quan ji* 陳思王全集 from Zhang Pu's 張溥 (1602–1641) *Han Wei Liuchao baisan mingjia ji* 漢魏六朝百三名家集 and twenty-one other works.[92] One advantage of Ding's edition – and a testament to its value – is that it is the edition chosen to be used for Jean-Pierre Diény's *Concordance des oeuvres completes de Cao Zhi*, although that advantage has been vitiated by digital searches. Diény notes:

> Le recueil de Ding Yan n'est pas sans défauts. Il inclut des œuvres d'authenticité improbable; il omet quelques pieces fragmenatires; sa punctuation est parfois critiquable; il comporte des leçons erronées et des coquilles; la réédition de 1957, qui corrige certaines erreurs de éditions précédentes, en commet aussi de nouvelles. Bien que cette version des œuvres completes de Cao Zhi ne puisse donc etre considérée comme vraiment satisfaisante, nous l'avons choisie comme texte de base, en lui apportant quelques corrections indispensables.
>
> [Ding Yan's collection is not without flaws. It includes some works of unlikely authenticity; it omits some fragmentary pieces; its punctuation is sometimes open to criticism; it has some erroneous readings and typos; the new edition of 1957, which corrects certain mistakes in preceding editions, introduces some new ones. Even

90 There is a reprint from 2014 by Fenghuang chubanshe in Nanjing.

91 See also Park, "Cao Zhi ji de bianzuan yu sizhong Song ben zhi fenxi," 47, and "Cao Zhi ji bianzuan guocheng yu sizhong Song ban zhi fenxi," 31.

92 Frankel, "The Problem of Authenticity in the Works of Ts'ao Chih," 184–86.

> though this version of the complete works of Cao Zhi cannot therefore be considered truly satisfactory, we have chosen it as our base text and have added some essential corrections.][93]

Zhao Youwen's *Cao Zhi ji jiaozhu* takes Ding Yan's edition as its base text, but while Ding adopted the traditional arrangement of the works by genre, Zhao, based on his notion of when they must have been composed, rearranged them chronologically by period. The value of Zhao's book lies in the fact that it was the first annotated edition of a recension of Cao Zhi's complete works. In addition, Zhao made use of the Southern Song edition and other works to emend in places the readings found in Ding. Among the problems with Zhao Youwen's edition are its inconvenient and moot chronological arrangement and occasionally debatable readings and notes.[94] It also omits, apparently through oversight rather than intent, at least two poems. Even so, it remains an essential tool for reading Cao Zhi's works. There is likely a link between the Southern Song edition and those available in Sui and Tang times, and the most important editions available today, such as those of Ding Yan, Zhu Xuzeng, and Zhao Youwen, draw extensively upon Tang and Song commonplace books and compendia both for collation purposes and as sources for texts.

The present book uses Ding as its base text. The poems herein are numbered according to their sequence in his *Cao ji quanping*. The first number is the fascicle (*juan* 巻), and the second number is the sequential position of the piece in that fascicle. Ding provides the variants he is aware of, and Zhao Youwen often refers to these and provides others. Where I have accepted a variant mentioned by one or both, or have used a variant from a source they do not mention, that fact is indicated in the *Additional Notes* to the poem in question. The Chinese texts accompanying the translations incorporate the variants. It should be

93 *Concordance*, iv. The advent of text databases and searchable PDF files has greatly reduced, though not eliminated, the usefulness of Diény's *Concordance*. His corrections and additional textual notes may still be consulted.

94 Reviews include Jiang Yin 江般, "*Cao Zhi ji jiao zhu* deshi ping" 曹植集校注得失評, *Wenxue yichan*, 1987, no. 4: 118–23; Xiong Qingyuan 熊清元, "*Cao Zhi ji jiao zhu* shangdui" 曹植集校注商兑, *Guji zhengli yanjiu xuekan* 古籍整理研究學刊, 1997, no. 1: 36–9.

noted that stanza breaks in the original texts and the English translations are added by me and reflect changes of rhyme in the Chinese.

Because Cao Zhi is such a famous and accomplished poet, some of the pieces translated here have been translated before, the most popular ones multiple times. I have not provided references to those earlier translations unless there is a specific reason to do so. There are at least two vernacular Chinese translations of Cao's collected works. These are in the *List of Abbreviations* as 1) Cao Haidong and 2) Fu Yashu. I have occasionally found these useful and mentioned them in the *Additional Notes*.

Some of Cao Zhi's poems can be dated, and the compulsion to relate nearly every work to events in Cao's life means that there have been attempts to date virtually all his writings. The difficulty of doing so can be seen in the different dates suggested for the same poem by different scholars. Consider, for example, the sixth of the six "Unclassified Poems" 雜詩. Due to the influence of *Wen xuan*, these poems are often grouped together. Li Shan's *Wen xuan* commentary says that they were written after Cao Zhi had left the capital and was in Juancheng homesick.[95] Cao Zhi was made marquis of Juancheng in Huangchu 2 (221). Huang Jie argues that the sixth "Miscellaneous Poem" dates from Jian'an 19 (214), whereas Cao Haidong dates that poem to Huangchu 4 (223).[96] The arcana of this cottage industy of Cao Zhi studies will not be of particular interest to most people for most purposes, but it sometimes has real relevance to understanding the poems, and it will often be of interest to the specialist. This book cites a number of opinions on the dating of particular pieces, but it most frequently mentions those of Xu Gongchi 徐公持. Xu has produced a very useful chronological biography 年譜 of Cao that takes into account the arguments of virtually all of the previous scholars who have done such work. It is cited by the abbreviation "Xu" (see *List of Abbreviations*). Although this is the best work of its kind on Cao Zhi, and although the evidence and arguments it brings to bear are exhaustive, Xu cannot provide an answer in every case, which sometimes leads to complicated inferences and unavailing speculation.

95 *Wx* 29.1363.

96 Huang Jie 1.15; Cao Haidong 137–38.

Translations

1.1 東征賦

建安十九年，王師東征吳寇，余典禁兵、衛宮省。然神武一舉、東夷必克、想見振旅之盛、故作賦一篇。

登城隅之飛觀兮
望六師之所營
幡旗轉而心異兮
4 舟楫動而傷情
顧身微而任顯兮
愧責重而命輕
嗟我愁其何為兮
8 心遙思而懸旌

師旅憑皇穹之靈佑兮
亮元勳之必舉
揮朱旗以東指兮
12 橫大江而莫御

https://doi.org/10.1515/9781501507038-001

Fu

1.1 *Fu* on the Eastern Campaign (fragment)

In the nineteenth year of the Jian'an reign period [214 CE], the royal army is launching an eastern campaign against the Wu brigands. I am in charge of the imperial guard and defending the palace precinct. Ipso facto, as soon as the divine warrior strikes, the eastern barbarians will perforce be vanquished.[1] Envisioning the magnificence of the triumphant returning troops, therefore I compose a *fu*.

I ascend a soaring lookout at a corner of the city-wall,
Gaze upon the operations of the imperial army:
When the pennons and banners turn, my heart feels left out;
When the boat oars move, I am broken-hearted.[2]
I am mindful that I am insignificant while my post is illustrious,
I am abashed at how weighty my duty and modest my lot.
O, why am I so sorrowful?
Thinking of one far away, my heart is like a fluttering flag.[3]

The army relies on august heaven's divine assistance,
Trusts that great merit will surely be attained.
Waving vermilion flags, they head eastward,[4]
Cross the Great River with no resistance:[5]

1 The divine warrior is Cao Cao.
2 Cao Zhi is wishing he could be part of the military expedition. The expedition had a naval component. From the evidence, it appears that the boats gathered on the Xuanwu Reservoir and then entered the Zhang River, which gave access to the Yellow River and ultimately the Huai River.
3 "The one far away" is his father Cao Cao, who is leading the campaign.
4 The flags are vermilion because the color red corresponds to fire, the one of the cosmological five phases (or five agents) under which the Han dynasty ruled.
5 "Great River" means the Yangzi.

循戈櫓於清流兮
氾雲梯而容與
禽元帥於中舟兮
16 振靈威於東野

1.2 遊觀賦

靜閑居而無事
將遊目以自娛
登北觀而啟路
4 涉雲際之飛除
從羆熊之武士
荷長戟而先驅
罷若雲歸
8 會如霧聚
車不及回
塵不獲舉
奮袂成風
12 揮汗如雨

They let their halberd ships follow the clear current;[1]
Spread scaling ladders all about with effortless ease.
They take the enemy commander prisoner in a boat,
6 Ply their divine might in the fields of the east.

1.2 *Fu* on Visiting a Lookout (fragment)

Living quietly and idly, I had nothing to do
And would take in the sights to amuse myself.
Ascending the northern lookout, we clear the way,
4 March up soaring steps as high as the clouds.
The accompanying brown- and black-bear-like warriors
Shouldering long halberds lead the way.
When they stop, it is like clouds receding;
8 When they assemble, it is like fog amassing:
The carriages have no way to turn around,
Dust cannot even fly up.
Their waving sleeves create a wind,
2 Their spattering sweat is like rain.

1 Various explanations of the term "halberd ships" (or "dagger-axe ships") have been offered by commentators, including ships carrying soldiers armed with dagger-axes, ships armored for ramming, and ships outfitted with dagger-axes on the hulls to prevent attack or boarding.

1.3 懷親賦

濟陽南澤有先帝故營，遂停駕住駕造斯賦焉。

獵平原而南鶩
覩先帝之舊營
步壁壘之常制
4 識旌旗之所停
存官曹之典列
心髣髴於平生
回驥首而永游
8 赴脩途以尋遠
情眷戀而顧懷
魂須臾而九反

1.3 *Fu* on Longing for a Loved One (fragment)

Nanze of Jiyang has an old encampment of the late emperor, so I reined in the horses, halted my rig, and made this *fu*.[1]

Hunting on the plains, I gallop south
And behold the late emperor's old encampment.
I stroll the customary arrangement of the ramparts,
Recognize where the standards and flags were placed.
Thinking back to when he held a standard rank in office,
My mind almost seems to be in old times.
I turn my steed's head and endlessly roam,
Pursue a long trail coursing afar.
But with feelings of fond affection and nostalgic longing,
My soul is repeatedly brought back in an instant.

1 "Late emperor" refers to Cao Zhi's father Cao Cao. Cao Cao was never an emperor, but when Cao Pi became emperor of Wei, Cao Cao was posthumously given the title Emperor Wu. Jiyang was a county in Chenliu 陳留 commandery. Nanze was a place east of modern Lankao 蘭考, He'nan.

1.4 玄暢賦

夫富者非財也，貴者非寶也。或有輕爵祿而重榮聲者，或有反性命而徇功名者。是以孔老異旨，楊墨殊義。聊作斯賦，名曰《玄暢》。庶以司馬相如為上林，控引天地古今，陶神知機，摛理表微……

夫
何希世之大人
磬天壤而作皇
該仁聖之上義
據神位以統方
補五帝之漏目
綴三代之維綱
□□□□□□
[緪日際而來王]
僥餘生之倖祿
遘九二之嘉祥

---

1 Yang and Mo are the Warring States period philosophers Yang Zhu 楊朱 and Mo Di 墨翟. Yang was a kind of egoist, whereas Mo promoted a concept of universal love wherein all were treated equally.

2 Sima Xiangru (179–117 BCE) was one of the greatest *fu* writers of all time, and his long "*Fu* on the Imperial Park" is a masterpiece of the genre.

1.4 *Fu* on Communicating with the Mysterious (fragment)

Now, wealth is not property, and what is valuable is not treasure. There are some who disdain rank and emolument but prize glory and fame; there are others who go against their natures and die for merit and reputation. Therefore, Confucius and Laozi differed in viewpoint; Yang and Mo diverged in opinion.[1] I have tentatively written this *fu*, calling it "Communicating with the Mysterious." I hope, along the model of the "*Fu* on the Imperial Park" composed by Sima Xiangru, to draw in heaven and earth and the ancient and modern, to cultivate spirit and know the signs of things to come, to set forth the principles of things and make known the imperceptible.[2]

That Great Man, so rare in the world,
To the ends of Heaven and Earth is become emperor.[3]
He possesses the superior righteousness of benevolence and sagacity,
Occupies the sacred seat to govern the four quarters of the world,
Remedies the omissions of the five emperors,
Mends the braces and stays of the Three Dynasties[4]
. . . .
[From the farthest places lit by the sun, they come to audience at court.][5]
Serendipitous, the happy good fortune of my life:
Encountering the auspicious sign of "nine in the second."[6]

---

3 It seems he is referring to Cao Pi.

4 The Five Emperors are Huang di 黄帝 (the Yellow Emperor), Zhuan Xu 顓頊, Yao, Shun, and Yu 禹, although the list is sometimes given as the Yellow Emperor, Zhuan Xu, Di Ku 帝嚳, Yao, and Shun. The Three Dynasties are Xia, Shang, and Zhou.

5 On lines 7–8, see the Additional Notes to this *fu*.

6 This is an allusion to the *Classic of Changes* 易經, which says of the hexagram *qian* 乾, that a *yang* (i.e., solid, indicated by the number nine) line in the second position of the hexagram is a sign of the appearance of a great man, who is "one who has the virtue of a true sovereign." Again, the great man is Cao Pi.

上同契於稷卨
降合穎於伊望

思薦寶以繼佩
怨和璞之始鐫
思黃鐘以協律
怨伶夔之不存

嗟所圖之莫合
悵蘊結而延佇
希鵬舉以傅天
蹶青雲而奮羽

舍余駟而改駕
任中才之展御
望前軌而致策
顧後乘而安驅
匪逞邁之短修
取全貞而保素

弘道德以為宇
築無怨以作藩

Above, I will match tallies with Ji and Xie;
Below, I will be equally clever as Yi and Wang.[1]

I want to present a precious stone to add to his pendants,
But regret that He's matrix has already been carved.[2]
I want a yellow bell to harmonize the pitches,
But regret that Ling and Kui no longer exist.[3]

Alas, my plans did not come together at all;
Despondent, knotted with frustration, I stand craning my neck.
I wish to rise like a *peng* to reach the sky,[4]
Beat my wings and tread the clouds in the blue.

Casting off my team of four, I change rigs;
I employ the orderly driving of a man of middling talent:
Watch the tracks ahead to apply the whip;
Look back at vehicles behind and proceed slowly.
I repudiate the defect of bounding impulsively forward,
And will ever preserve integrity to remain unsullied.

I exalt the Way and its virtue, taking them as my abode;
I erect "no rancor" to make a fence;

---

1 Ji is the culture hero Hou Ji 后稷 (Lord Millet), who reputedly served as agricultural minister to the legendary ruler Shun and who was considered an ancestor of the founders of the Zhou dynasty. Xie, better known as Qi 契, was also a minister to Shun. Legend makes him an ancestor of the Shang dynasty. Yi is Yi Yin 伊尹, a celebrated officer who aided in the founding of the Shang. Wang is Lü Shang 呂尚 – also known as Lü Wang 呂望, Jiang Taigong 姜太公, and Taigong Wang 太公望, among other names – who was discovered fishing on the banks of the Wei River by King Wen of Zhou 周文王 and who aided King Wu of Zhou in the conquest of the Shang.

2 For the story of Bian He and his jade, see **4.16**, n. 4.

3 "Yellow bell" is one of the twelve pitch pipes. There was a connection between control of the yellow bell and the inception of a new dynasty. Ling is Ling Lun 伶倫, reputed music official of the legendary Yellow Emperor, who was sent north of the Kunlun Mountains to harvest bamboo to make the twelve pitch pipes. Kui is said to have been a music official under Shun.

4 The *peng* is a huge mythical bird mentioned, for instance, in *Zhuangzi*. Its vast wings are like clouds spread across the sky.

播慈惠以為圃
畊柔順以為田

不愧景而慚魄
32 信樂天之何欲
逸千載而流聲
超遺黎而度俗

1.5 幽思賦

倚高臺之曲隅
處幽僻之閒深
望翔雲之悠悠
4 羌朗霽而夕陰
顧秋華而零落
感歲莫而傷心
觀躍魚於南沼
8 聆鳴鶴於北林
搦素筆而慷慨
揚大雅之哀吟
仰清風以嘆息
12 寄餘思於悲弦
信有心而在遠
重登高以臨川

I sow compassion and kindness, taking them to be my garden;
I till softness and compliance, taking them to be my fields.

I am neither abashed before my reflection nor ashamed in my soul;
32 Truly what is there to desire when one delights in the will of Heaven?
Spanning a thousand years, one leaves a good name;
Outlasting remnant peoples of lost states, one passes beyond the
mundane world.

1.5 *Fu* on Hidden Thoughts

I take advantage of an out-of-the-way corner of a tall terrace,
Come to rest in unoccupied depths of hidden seclusion.
I gaze afar at an endless sweep of soaring clouds,
4 Clear of a morn, then eve overcast.
Watching the autumn blossoms, they fall and wither;
Touched by the close of the year, I feel broken-hearted.
I observe the leaping fishes in the southern pond,
8 Hear a calling crane in the northern wood.
I pick up a plain cither, forlornly impassioned;
Lift the mournful tones of the *Greater Odes*.
Looking up into a fresh breeze, I heave a sigh;
12 Consign my thoughts to these sad strings.
In truth my mind is set on one far away,
Again I climb high to look out over the river.

何餘心之煩錯
16 寧翰墨之能傳

1.6 節遊賦

覽宮宇之顯麗
實大人之攸居
建三臺於前處
4 飄飛陛以凌虛
連雲閣以遠徑
營觀榭於城隅
亢高軒以回眺
8 緣雲霓而結疏
仰西嶽之崧岑
臨漳滏之清渠
觀靡靡而無終
12 何渺渺而難殊
亮靈后之所處
非吾人之所廬

於是
仲春之月
16 百卉叢生
萋萋藹藹

So troubled and bewildered is my mind!
How could it be conveyed by brush and ink?

1.6 *Fu* on Curtailing Excursions

I scan the manifest beauty of the palace,
It is truly a place for a great man to dwell.
He erected the Three Terraces in front of it,
Floated flying steps to surmount the void.
He joined cloud-high passages to lengthen walkways,
Built towers and kiosks at corners of the city-wall.
Raised high galleries for gazing afar,
Traced clouds and rainbows to form fretwork windows.
Looking up, the peaks and ridges of the western mount;
Looking down, the clear channels of the Zhang and the Fu.
The view is exquisite and endless.
How far, far distant and hard to surpass!
Clearly where a sacred sovereign abides,
Not where we mere mortals reside.

Thereupon,
In the second month of spring,
The hundred plants grow in clusters.
Lush and luxuriant, rampant and riotous

翠葉朱莖
竹林青蔥
珍果含榮
凱風發而時鳥歡
微波動而水蟲鳴
感氣運之和順
樂時澤之有成

遂乃
浮素蓋
御驊騮
命友生
攜同儔
誦風人之所嘆
遂駕言而出遊
步北園而馳鶩
庶翱翔以解憂
望淇池之滉瀁
遂降集乎輕舟
沈浮蟻於金罍
行觴爵於好仇
絲竹發而響厲
悲風激於中流

The blue-green leaves, the vermilion stalks.
The bamboo grove is dark green,
Precious fruit trees are about to blossom.
Balmy breezes blow and seasonal birds twitter happily,
Small ripples move and aquatic insects chirr.
I feel the pleasant and gentle weather of the seasonal rotation,
Delight in the good harvests of timely precipitation.

And then,
Gliding my carriage canopy,
Driving Dappled Roan,[1]
Bidding friends,
Leading companions,
Chanting that which the poets declaimed,
Thereupon we harness up and go on an excursion.[2]
We go at a walk to the Northern Garden, then gallop fast,
Hoping to soar to relieve our cares.
Having gazed at the massive and measureless grand reservoir,
We then alight and gather in skiffs.
We drown floating ants in bronze ewers,[3]
Serve chalices and cups to boon companions.
Strings and woodwinds play, the sound strident;
A sad wind springs up midstream.

---

1 Dappled Roan was one of the eight horses of King Mu (r. 956–918 BCE) mentioned in the cosmographic romance *Traditions about Son of Heaven Mu* 穆天子傳.

2 Lines 29–30 allude to the last two lines of a poem in the *Classic of Poetry* (*Mao shi* 59): "I will harness up and go on an excursion, / In order to dispel my cares" 駕言出遊，以寫我憂.

3 "Floating ants" is a term for the lees or foam that formed on the surface of wine during fermentation. It also comes to be used for the wine itself.

且容與以盡觀
聊永日而忘愁

嗟羲和之奮迅
怨曜靈之無光
念人生之不永
若春日之微霜
諒遺名之可紀
信天命之無常
愈志蕩以淫游
非經國之大綱
罷曲宴而旋服
遂言歸乎舊房

1.7 感節賦

攜友生而遊觀
盡賓主之所求
登高墉以永望
冀消日以忘憂
欣陽春之潛潤
樂時澤之惠休
望候雁之翔集
想玄鳥之來游

For the moment at leisure, we exhaust the view;
Temporarily we while away the day and forget our sorrows.

O, the way Xihe plies the whip:
We rue the Sparkling Numen's lack of light.[1]
Pondering the impermanence of human life,
It is like a slight frost on a spring day.
I assume that the reputation one leaves will likely be recorded,
And I believe in the mutability of the destiny ordained by Heaven.
To be ever more intemperate and excessively make pleasure excursions
Contradicts the great principles for regulating the state.
We end the private feast and go back,
And so return to our familiar abodes.

1.7 *Fu* on Responding to the Season

Leading friends, I roam to the lookout,
To satisfy the desires of guests and host.
We climb the high wall to gaze afar,
Hoping to while away the day to forget our cares.
We rejoice in the muted moistening of sunny spring,
Delight in the gentle blessing of timely rains.
We gaze at a soaring flock of migratory wildgeese,
Envisage the coming visit of the black birds.[2]

1 Xihe is the charioteer of the sun, and Sparkling Numen is the sun itself.
2 I.e., swallows.

嗟征夫之長勤
雖外逸而懷愁
懼天河之一回
12 沒我身乎長流
豈吾鄉之足顧
戀祖宗之靈丘

唯人生之忽過
16 若鑿石之末耀
慕牛山之哀泣
懼平仲之我笑
折若華之翳日
20 庶朱光之常照
願寄軀於飛蓬
乘陽風而遠飄

亮吾志之不從
24 乃拊心以嘆息
青雲鬱其西翔
飛鳥翩而上匿
欲縱體而從之
28 哀余身之無翼

O, the long labors of the soldiers on campaign;
Though I live secure, I am beset with sorrow.
I fear a change in the Sky River's course[1]
Will drown my body in its long stream.
How could my native place be worth caring about?
But I hold dear the numinous tumuli of my forebears.

Indeed, human life swiftly passes,
Like the sparks from chiseling stone.
I admire the mourning tears shed at Ox Mountain,
But I fear Pingzhong's laughing at me.[2]
I would break off a Ruo blossom to hinder the sun,[3]
Hoping its vermilion rays will constantly shine.
I wish to consign myself to a flying tumbleweed,
Ride an easterly wind and be tossed afar.

Truly my ambitions have not come to pass,
So I strike my breast and sigh.
Clouds in the blue grow dense and soar westward;
Flying birds glide to a halt and hide.
I wish to spring upwards and join them,
Lament that I have no wings.

1 Sky River is one of the names of the Milky Way.

2 A parable repeated in a number of texts tells of Duke Jing of Qi 齊景公 (r. 547–490 BCE) ascending Ox Mountain, looking down on his state, and shedding tears over the fact that he would die someday, leaving it behind. Others with him also cried – only Pingzhong laughed. When asked why, he pointed out that if the duke's predecessors had not died, he would not have been able to rule Qi. Pingzhong was the style of Yan Ying 晏嬰, or Yanzi 晏子.

3 The Ruo tree was a mythical tree in the far west where the sun came to rest after crossing the sky.

大風隱其四起
揚黃塵之冥冥
鳥獸驚以求群
32 草木紛其揚英
見游魚之涔灂
感流波之悲聲
內紆曲而潛結
36 心怛惕以中驚
匪榮德之累身
恐年命之早零
慕歸全之明義
40 庶不忝其所生

1.8 離思賦

建安十六年，大軍西討馬超，太子留監國，植時從焉。意有憶戀，遂作離思之賦云

在肇秋之嘉月
將曜師而西旗
余抱疾以賓從
4 扶衡軫而不怡
慮征期之方至
傷無階以告辭

Strong winds abound and rise on every side,
They raise a gloom of yellowish dust.
Birds and beasts are alarmed and seek their kind,
Plants and trees though tangled flaunt their blossoms.
I see the splish-splash of swimming fish,
Am moved by the sad sound of the rolling waves.
My insides are twisted and stifled,
My heart is anxious and apprehensive:
It is not over glory and favor accruing to my person,
I just am afraid that my life span will wither away early.
I aspire to the lucid rectitude of dying with reputation intact,
And hope not to dishonor my parents.

1.8 *Fu* on Thoughts at Parting (fragment)

In Jian'an 16 [211], a great army went west to suppress Ma Chao [176–222]. The heir-designate [Cao Pi] stayed behind to keep guard over the capital. I, Zhi, at that time followed along with them. My mind held reminiscences and a reluctance to part from him, so I wrote "*Fu* on Thoughts at Parting."

In a fine month at the beginning of autumn,
[My father] took a vaunted force and led the banners westward.
I went along in the retinue although I was ill,
And holding on to the carriage for support, I was not of good cheer.
Pondering on when the term of the expedition will be complete,
I grieve that I have no cause to bid farewell to it.

念慈君之光惠
庶沒命而不疑
欲畢力於旌麾
將何心而遠之
願我君之自愛
為皇朝而寶己
水重深而魚悅
林脩茂而鳥喜

1.9 釋思賦

家弟出養族父郎中，伊餘以兄弟之愛，心有戀然，作此賦以贈之。

彼朋友之離別
猶求思乎白駒
況同生之義絕
重背親而為疏
樂鴛鴦之同池
羨比翼之共林
亮根異其何戚
痛別幹之傷心

But mindful of our loving father's splendid benevolence,
8 I hope to give up my life without any qualms.
I want to use all my strength midst standards and ensigns –
With what sort of mind would I keep them far away?
I wish my lord to take care of himself,[1]
2 For the sake of the imperial court to value himself.
When the water is doubly deep, the fish are pleased;
When the woods are tall and dense, the birds are glad.

1.9 *Fu* on Relieving Troubled Thoughts (fragment)

My youngest brother was adopted out to my uncle, the Gentleman-of-the-Palace. O, I, because of brotherly love, have a fond feeling for him in my heart and wrote this *fu* to present to him.[2]

On the parting of friends,
One still turns to "White Colt."[3]
How much more so when sibling bonds are broken,
4 And even more so when leaving parents and becoming estranged?
One delights in mandarin ducks sharing a pond,
Envies linked-wing birds together in a wood.[4]
Truly, how distressing it is when a root is divided;
8 Painful the heartbreak of forking off from the trunk.

---

1 It is not clear whether he means Cao Pi or Cao Cao here.

2 The brother was Cao Zheng 曹整 (d. 218). He and Cao Zhi had different mothers. The "uncle" is Cao Cao's cousin Cao Shao 曹紹. Cao Zheng was moved to Cao Shao's family to maintain his lineage.

3 "White Colt" is a *Classic of Poetry* poem (*Mao shi* 186). That poem speaks of trying to prevent estrangement from, in the Mao tradition, a worthy person one is trying to recruit to office.

4 This refers to mythological linked-wing birds (*biyiniao* 比翼鳥) that, each having only one wing and one eye, flew in mated pairs.

1.10 臨觀賦

登高墉兮望四澤
臨長流兮送遠客
春風暢兮氣通靈
草含乾兮木交莖
丘陵崛兮松柏青
南園薆兮果載榮

樂時物之逸豫
悲余志之長違
嘆東山之愬勤
歌式微以詠歸
進無路以效公
退無隱以營私
俯無鱗以遊遁
仰無翼以飜飛

1.10 *Fu* on Looking Out from a Lookout

Ascending the high city-wall, I gaze out at the surrounding wetlands;
Looking out over the long current, I see off a guest from afar.
Spring breezes are pleasant, the weather agreeable and fair;
Plants are full of shoots, tree stems intertwine.
The barrows jut upwards, pines and cypresses are verdant;
The South Garden is rank, fruit trees laden with blossoms.

I rejoice at the peace and happiness of the things of the season;
But I am saddened that my ambitions have long been unfulfilled.
I recite "Eastern Mountains" to tell of toil,
Sing "No Use" to chant of going home.[1]
Advancing, I have no route to do my utmost in public service;
Withdrawing, I have no refuge for making personal plans.
Looking down, I have no scales with which to swim and get away;
Looking up, I have no wings with which to flap and fly off.

1 These are allusions to two *Classic of Poetry* poems. "Eastern Mountain" (*Mao shi* 156) is spoken by a soldier going home after three years away. The poem is attributed to the Duke of Zhou, who relates the feelings of returning soldiers and sympathizes with their toil. "No Use" (*Mao shi* 36) is spoken by a person who is away from home in the service of his lord and wishes to return.

1.11 潛志賦

潛大道以遊志
希往昔之遐烈
矯貞亮以作矢
當苑囿之呈藝
驅仁義以為禽
必忠信而後發

退隱身以滅跡
進出世而取容
且摧剛而和謀
接虔肅以靜恭
亮知榮而守辱
匪天路以焉通

1.12 閒居賦

何吾人之介特
去朋匹而無儔
出靡時以娛志
入無樂以銷憂

何歲月之若驚
復民生之無常

1.11 潛志賦 *Fu* on Focusing the Will

Steeped in the great Way, let your mind roam;
Set aside your high ambitions of former days.
Shape "upright" and "steadfast" to make an arrow,
And in the hunting park display your skill.
Drive benevolence and righteousness, regard them as game;
You must be committed and true before you shoot.

Withdrawing, hide yourself and efface your traces;
Advancing, go out into the world and court favor.
Reject the hard and seek the gentle,
Adopt reverence and respect and quietly honor [your duties].
Clearly comprehend glory yet keep to humility,
Unless you follow the way of Heaven, how will you succeed?

1.12 *Fu* on Living in Idleness (fragment)

How solitary I am!
Distant from friends and fellows, with no companions.
Going out, I have no chance to cheer my mood,
Coming in, I have no joy with which to dispel care.

How the years and months are like a full gallop!
And people's lives are ephemeral.

感陽春之發節
聊輕駕而遠翔

登高丘以延企
時薄暮而起雨
仰歸雲以載奔
遇蘭蕙之長圃
冀芬芳之可服
結春蘅以延佇
入虛廓之閒館
步生風之廣廡
踐密邇之脩除
即蔽景之玄宇
翡鳥翔於南枝
玄鶴鳴於北野
青魚躍於東沼
白鳥戲於西渚

遂乃
背通谷
對淥波
藉文茵
翳春華

Moved by sunny spring's seasonal start,
For a while I take a light carriage and meander afar.

Ascending a high hill, I crane my neck and stand on tiptoe,
The time is near sunset, and it begins to rain.
I look up at the retreating clouds racing along,
Come upon a long garden of thoroughwort and sweet basil.
Hoping the sweet-smelling fragrances can be worn,
I stand there for a long time plaiting asarum.
I enter an empty and spacious leisure lodge,
And pace a windswept broad portico.
I tread a silent long stairway
And reach a dark room that blocks the sunlight.
Kingfishers glide about southern branches,
Hooded cranes call in the northern fields.
Black carp leap in the eastern pond,
White birds play on a western islet.

And so,
I turn away from an open vale,
And facing green waves,
Sit on a tiger-skin carriage cushion,
Shaded by spring blossoms.

丹轂更馳
28 羽騎相過

1.13 慰子賦

彼凡人之相親
小離別而懷戀
況中殤之愛子
4 乃千秋而不見
入空室而獨倚
對孤幃而切嘆
痛人亡而物在
8 心何忍而復觀
日晼晚而既沒
月代照而舒光
仰列星以至晨
12 衣沾露而含霜
惟逝者之日遠
愴傷心而絕腸

Carriages with cinnabar-hued hubs speed along in succession,
Cavalry of the Feathered Forest pass in escort.

1.13 *Fu* on Condolence for a Departed Child

The way ordinary people are when attached to one another,
If they are apart for even a short time, they are filled with longing.
How much more in the case of a beloved child who dies young[1]
And so will not be seen in a thousand autumns?
One enters the empty room and leans there alone,
Faces the lonely bed-curtain and softly sighs.
It hurts that the other is gone yet the objects remain –
How can one's heart bear to see them again?
The sun is aslant and already going down,
The moon takes its place and spreads light.
Looking up at the ranged stars until dawn,
Clothes become soaked with dew and rimed with frost.
Thinking of the days of the departed growing distant,
Grief breaks the heart and rends one's bowels.

1 The term used here for dying young is *zhongshang* 中殤, which should refer to the death of a young person between twelve and fifteen *sui*.

1.14 敍愁賦

時家二女弟，故漢皇帝聘以為貴人。家母見二弟愁思，故令予作賦。曰：

嗟妾身之微薄
信未達乎義方
遭母氏之聖善
奉恩化之彌長
迄盛年而始立
脩女職於衣裳
承師保之明訓
誦六列之篇章
觀圖像之遺形
竊庶幾乎英皇
委微軀於帝室
充末列於椒房
荷印紱之令服
非陋才之所望
對床帳而太息
慕二親以增傷
揚羅袖而掩涕
起出戶而彷徨

1.14 *Fu* on Expressing Sorrow (fragment)

At that time, our family had two younger daughters, and the quondam emperor of the Han engaged them as Honorable Ladies. My mother saw the anxiety of the two sisters and therefore had me write this *fu*. It says:

O, in our personal insignificance and inferiority,
We truly have not yet fully comprehended the ways of duty.
We encountered a mother wise and good,
Received her favor and transforming influence for a long time.
Reaching the prime of life, only then were we appointed;[1]
We practiced women's duties with regard to apparel.
We received the clear instruction of teachers,
Recited the chapters and sections of the Six Categories.[2]
Perusing the handed-down figures in the pictures,[3]
We hope to correspond to Nüying and Ehuang.[4]
Consigning our insignificant selves to the imperial house,
We will fill inferior positions in the Pepper Chambers.[5]
Assuming fine raiment of seals and seal-cords,
Is not something our lowly talents expected.
Facing the bed curtains, we heave long sighs,
And think of our two parents' added distress.
Raising gauze sleeves, we cover our faces and weep,
Rise and go out the door, walking back and forth.

1 The "prime of life" 盛年 was fifteen to twenty *sui* for young women.

2 This may refer to the first six parts of the book *Categorized Biographies of Women* 列女傳, attributed to Liu Xiang 劉向 (79–8 BCE), but see *Additional Notes*.

3 This refers to illustrations accompanying *Categorized Biographies of Women*.

4 On Ehuang and Nüying, see **2.3** (line 95) and **5.7** (line 3).

5 The Pepper Chambers were rooms in the women's quarters whose walls were painted with a colorant containing Sichuan peppercorns, or fagara. The symbology is of warmth, fragrance, and many seeds (punning on "many children").

顧堂宇之舊處
悲一別之異鄉

1.15 秋思賦

四節更王兮秋氣悲
遙思惝怳兮若有遺
原野蕭條兮煙無依
雲高氣靜兮露凝衣
野草變色兮莖葉稀
鳴蜩抱木兮鴈南飛

歸室解裳兮步庭前
月光照懷兮星依天
居一世兮芳景遷
松喬難慕兮誰能仙
長短命也兮獨何愆

Looking back on our family's old place,
We are sad that once parted, we will be in different lands.

1.15 *Fu* on Autumn Thoughts

The four seasons reign by turns, and the aura of autumn is sad;
My faraway thoughts are deeply depressed, as though something were missing.
The clouds are high, the air still, dew condenses on my coat.
The plains country is barren and bleak, with nothing to support man's smoke;
Wild grasses change color, leaves on their stems are sparse;
Singing cicadas hold fast to trees, wild geese fly south.

Returning to my quarters and removing garb, I pace in the forecourt;
Moonlight illuminates my breast, stars cling to the sky;
We live a generation, then youth's sweet-scented scenes move on.
Red Pine and Wang Qiao are hard to emulate – who is able to transcend?[1]
Long life or short is due to fate – how can one exceed it?

1 On Master Red Pine and Wang Qiao, see the note to line 44 of **3.1**.

1.16 九愁賦

嗟離思之難忘
心慘毒而含哀
踐南畿之末境
越引領之徘徊
眷浮雲以太息
願攀登而無階
匪徇榮而愉樂
信舊都之可懷

恨時王之謬聽
受奸枉之虛辭
揚天威以臨下
忽放臣而不疑

登高陵而反顧
心懷愁而荒悴
念先寵之既隆
哀後施之不遂

雖危亡之不豫
亮無遠君之心
刈桂蘭而秣馬
舍餘車於西林

1.16 *Fu* on Nine Sorrows

O, feelings at parting are hard to dismiss;
The heart is anguished and resentful and full of grief.
I tread the farthest border of the southern region,
Craning my neck more and more, I loiter and linger.
I turn my gaze to the floating clouds and heave a long sigh;
I wish to clamber up but there is no stairway.
It is not that I seek glory or joyful pleasure,
But in truth, our old capital is worth longing for.

I hated that the one who was king then believed in falsehoods,
And accepted the empty words of the treacherous and crooked.[1]
He wielded his heavenly might to govern those below;
Suddenly he exiled me, not having any doubts.

Ascending a high barrow, I turn and look back –
My heart feels sorrowful and is anxious and distressed.
Recalling that former favor had been grand,
I lament that later bestowals were not fulfilled.

Although danger and ruin cannot be foretold,
I truly never strayed far from my lord's mind:
I cut down cinnamon and thoroughwort to feed the horses,
Halt my carriage in the western woods.

---

1 This *fu* is inspired by poems from the *Chu ci* 楚辭 (*Lyrics of Chu*). In addition to similarities of style and content, the number 9 appears in the titles of multiple sets of poems in that collection.

願接翼於歸鴻
嗟高飛而莫攀
因流景而寄言
24 響一絕而不還

傷時俗之趨險
獨惆悵而長愁
感龍鸞而匿迹
28 如吾身之不留
竄江介之曠野
獨眇眇而泛舟

思孤客之可悲
32 愍予身之翩翔
豈天監之孔明
將時運之無常
謂內思而自策
36 算乃昔之愆殃
以忠言而見黜
信無負於時王

俗參差而不齊
40 豈毀譽之可同
競昏瞀以營私

I wish to fly wing-to-wing with a swan-goose heading back;
O, to fly high and not have to clamber.
To this gliding shadow I would entrust my words,
But all at once its echo ceases, and it does not return.

I am distressed how the common world inclines to deceit;
I alone, downcast and despondent, am ever woeful.
I am sensible of even dragons and simurghs hiding their traces,
Just as I myself may not remain;
I will conceal myself in broad fields on the edge of the Yangzi,
And alone, dimly distant, drift by boat.

Thinking of how piteous is a solitary wanderer,
I am dismayed by my own aimless peregrinations.
Is Heaven's oversight really very clear,
Or is time's fate arbitrary?
If I ponder within and examine myself,
I suppose indeed it was my former errors and misdeeds.
Because of loyal advice, I was demoted,
But truly there was no betrayal of the one who was king then.

Common people are erratic and inconsistent,
How could their praise and blame have been the same?
They vied in stupidity and ignorance to seek their self-interest,

害予身之奉公
共朋黨而妒賢
44 俾予濟乎長江

嗟大化之移易
悲性命之攸遭

愁慊慊而繼懷
48 怛慘慘而情悗
曠年載而不回
長去君乎悠遠

御飛龍之蜿蜒
52 揚翠霓之華旌
絕紫霄而高騖
飄弭節於天庭
披輕雲而下觀
56 覽九土之殊形
顧南郢之邦壤
咸蕪穢而倚傾
駗盤桓而思服
60 仰御驤以悲鳴
紆予袂而收涕
僕夫感以失聲

Feared my own serving the public good.
Combining into cliques and spiteful of the worthy,
They caused me to cross over the Yangzi.

O, the alteration wrought by this great transformation,
I was saddened by what my life encountered.

Sorrow and discontent persist in my heart;
Constantly worried and depressed, my feelings are disordered.
For extended years I did not return,
Long apart from my ruler in a far-off place.

Guiding the wriggling and writhing of flying dragons,
I raise aloft a brightly-hued rainbow as my vibrant banner.
Quitting the purple empyrean, I gallop on high;
Gliding along I halt the pace in Heaven's courtyard.
I sweep away the light clouds and look below,
View the disparate forms of the nine lands.[1]
I look back on the territory of southerly Ying,[2]
All rank and weedy, leaning and listing.
The trace-horses paw and hesitate with longing,
They look up, tossing their heads at the driver, and sadly neigh.
Bending my sleeve, I gather my tears;
The driver is so touched he loses his voice.

1 "Nine lands" is synonymous with "Nine Provinces" 九州, which refers to the legendary nine provinces into which "China" was divided in remote antiquity.

2 Ying was a capital of the state of Chu in the Spring and Autumn and Warring States periods. Its location seems to have been in southern modern Hubei province.

履先王之正路
豈淫徑之可遵
知犯君之招咎
恥干媚而求親
顧旋復之無軌
長自棄於遐濱
與麇鹿而為群
宿林藪之葳蓁
野蕭條而極望
曠千里而無人
民生期於必死
何自苦以終身
寧作清水之沈泥
不為濁路之飛塵

踐蹊徑之危阻
登岩嶢之高岑
見失群之離獸
覿偏棲之孤禽
懷憤激以切痛
若回刃之在心

愁慼慼其無為
遊綠林而逍遙

If one treads the proper road of former kings,
How could one follow evil ways?
I know that to offend the ruler incurs blame,
But I am ashamed to be ingratiating to curry favor.
Reflecting that there is no way back for me,
I forever cast myself upon a distant shore.
I take the deer to be my herd,
Dwell in the overgrowth of woodland and marsh.
The wilderness is desolate and drear as far as you can see,
Stretching for a thousand *li* there are no people.[1]
People's lives have a date with certain death,
Why look for trouble all your days?
I would rather be sunken mud in clear water,
Not become the flying dust of a muddy road.

I have trod the perils and obstacles of this trail,
Ascended tall and towering lofty crags,
Seen stray animals who have lost their herds,
Observed lone birds roosting singly.
Full of indignation, I am acutely distressed,
As though a blade were twisted in my heart.

Sorrowful, worried, there is nothing I can do,
I roam to the green woods and wander there.

---

1 A *li* was the most common measure of distance. In Cao Zhi's time, the length of a *li* was a little less than half a kilometer.

臨白水以悲嘯
猿驚聽而失條
亮無怨而棄逐
88 乃餘行之所招

1.17 娛賓賦

感夏日之炎景兮
游曲觀之清涼
遂衎賓而高會兮
4 丹幃曄以四張
辦中廚之豐膳兮
作齊鄭之妍倡
文人騁其妙說兮
8 飛輕翰而成章
談在昔之清風兮
總賢聖之紀綱

欣公子之高義兮
12 德芬芳其若蘭
揚仁恩於白屋兮
踰周公之棄餐

At the edge of the white water, I give a long whistle;
A gibbon, startled at hearing it, slips from a branch.
I truly have no resentment over being exiled,
38 Since it was my own behavior that invited it.

1.17 *Fu* on Entertaining Guests (fragment)

Stirred by a summer day's scorching sunlight,
We wander to a corner gate-tower's refreshing coolness.
Then to please the guests, a grand feast is laid;
4 The cinnabar curtains are resplendent, set up on all sides.
Bountiful viands from the palace kitchen have been prepared,
Alluring entertainers from Qi and Zheng perform.
Men of letters indulge in subtle talk,
8 And quick brushes flying, they complete compositions.
We converse about the melodious poems of days past,
And survey the guiding standards of the worthies and sages.

We delight in the lofty principles of the young lord,[1]
12 His virtue as fragrant as thoroughwort.
He extends benevolence and kindness to simple homes,
Surpasses the Duke of Zhou's foregoing food.[2]

1 Cao Zhi's elder brother Cao Pi is the young lord referred to here.

2 The Duke of Zhou served as regent while King Cheng of Zhou 周成王 (r. 1042/35–1006 BCE) was too young to rule. He was noted for, among other things, his desire to recruit men of talent. He reported that he had to squeeze out his hair three times in every washing and spit out his food three times in the space of eating a single meal in order to meet with such people out of fear of missing someone worthy. It is also told that he went into humble homes in search of talented men.

聽仁風以忘憂兮
16 美酒清而肴乾

1.18 愍志賦

或人有好鄰人之女者，時無良媒，禮不成焉。彼女遂行適人。有言之於予者，予心感焉，乃作賦曰：

竊托音於往昔
迨來春之不從
思同遊而無路
4 情壅隔而靡通

哀莫哀於永絕
悲莫悲於生離
豈良時之難俟
8 痛余質之日虧

登高樓以臨下
望所歡之攸居

Hearkening to his humane influence, we forget care;
6 The fine wine is pure and the delicacies dried.[1]

1.18 *Fu* on Compassionate Thoughts (fragment)

There was someone who was in love with his neighbor's daughter, but at the time he lacked a good matchmaker, so the betrothal rites were not completed by him. In due course, that girl married someone else. There was someone who told me about this, and my heart was moved by it, so I wrote a *fu* saying:

"I had someone convey my words in the past,
But by the following spring, they were not accepted.
We longed to be companions but had no path,
4 Our feelings were obstructed and we could not interact."[2]

"There is no grief greater than the grief of permanent separation,
There is no sadness greater than the sadness of parting in life.
Is a wedding day really so hard to await?
8 But I deplore that my body wanes by the day.

Ascending the tall pavilion and looking down,
I gaze upon the place where my love lives.

---

1 This is an allusion to the *Record of Rites* (*Li ji* 禮記). A section of that book speaks of the archery ceremony that was part of missions between states and of the qualities of the archers, who were superior men with a strong sense of righteousness. It says that even though the wine on offer might be pure and the archers thirsty, they did not venture to drink, and though the meat was dried and the archers hungry, they did not venture to eat. Perhaps the best way of understanding this line is to see the comparison to the present banquet implied by the allusion to the provision of food in a canonical book as a form of praise for the Cao Pi, the host.

2 The speaking parts of this *fu* can be parsed in different ways. Here lines 1–4 are spoken by the man, but some might read 1–2 as the man's words and 3–4 as the man and woman speaking together. Again, here 5–14 are translated as though spoken by the woman, but 5–6 could be the man's voice, or the voice of the poet.

去君子之清宇
歸小人之蓬廬
欲輕飛而從之
迫禮防之我拘

[妾穢宗之陋女
蒙日月之餘輝
委薄軀於貴戚
奉君子之裳衣]

1.19 歸思賦

背故鄉而遷徂
將遙憩乎北濱
經平常之舊居
感荒壞而莫振
城邑寂以空虛
草木穢而荊蓁

嗟喬木之無陰
處原野其何為
信樂土之足慕
忽并日之載馳

To leave the pristine house of the gentleman,
And go in marriage to the thatched hovel of that lesser man –
I wish to fly swiftly to go to him,
But I am held back by the strictures of propriety that restrain me."

["I am the lowly daughter of a vile lineage,
But I encountered the afterglow of the sun and moon,
Consigned my insignificant self to a noble family,
And attended to a gentleman's clothing."][1]

1.19 *Fu* on Homeward Thoughts (fragment)

Putting my old home behind me, I go away;
I will come to rest far off in the northern marches.[2]
Passing through the former site of my past life,
I was moved that it is overgrown and in ruins and has not recovered.
Cities and towns are hushed and empty,
Grasses and trees are rank and dense.

O, the tall trees have no shade –
Living in plains country, what would you do?
Truly, our idyllic land is worth yearning for,[3]
Swiftly let us day and night gallop there.

1 The bracketed lines are appended to the piece by Ding. They are from *Beitang shuchao*, and Ding suggests they are lines that were lost from the beginning of the *fu*. See *Additional Notes*. The last line of this addendum means that she was married to the gentleman.

2 Cao Zhi was going to Ye from Qiao.

3 The "idyllic land" is Ye.

1.20 靜思賦

夫何美女之爛妖
紅顏曄而流光
卓特出而無匹
呈才好其莫當
性通暢以聰惠
行孊密而妍詳

蔭高岑以翳日
臨綠水之清流
秋風起於中林
離鳥鳴而相求
愁慘慘以增傷悲
予安能乎淹留

2.1 感婚賦

陽氣動兮淑清
百卉鬱兮含英
春風起兮蕭條
蟄蟲出兮悲鳴
顧有懷兮妖嬈
用搔首兮屏營
登清臺以蕩志

1.20 *Fu* on Stilling Desire (fragment)

This beautiful woman so elegant and charming;
Her rosy face radiant, emitting light.
Outstanding and unique, she has no peer;
The gifts she displays may have no rival.
By nature she is understanding and intelligent and wise;
Her behavior is calm and composed, serene and mild.

I hide amid tall crags, taking shelter from the sun,
Draw near a pure current of clear water.
An autumn wind rises from the woods,
Scattered birds call and seek each other.
Sorrow and distress increase my pain and sadness;
How can I stay here long?

2.1 *Fu* on Fretting about Marriage (fragment)

Warm air moves, immaculately pure;
A hundred plants densely grow, about to bloom.
A spring breeze rises, quiet and calm;
Hibernating insects emerge, sadly chirring.
Thinking of the comely, charming lass filled with longing,
I scratch my head, pacing to and fro.
I ascend the peaceful terrace to clear my mind,

8 伏高軒而遊情
悲良媒之不顧
懼歡媾之不成
慨仰首而嘆息
12 風飄飄以動纓

2.2 出婦賦

妾十五而束帶
辭父母而適人
以才薄而質陋
4 奉君子之清塵
承顏色而接意
恐踈賤而不親

悅新婚而忘妾
8 哀愛惠之中零
遂摧頹而失望
退幽屏於下庭
痛一旦而見棄
12 心忉怛以悲驚
衣入門之初服
背牀室而出征

Lean on the high balustrade to soothe my mood.
I am sad that a good matchmaker will not give me a look,
Fear that a happy marriage will not be brought about.
I ruefully raise my head and heave a sigh,
The wind flickers and flutters my hatstrings.

2.2 *Fu* on the Spurned Wife (fragment)

When I was fifteen, I tied up my sash,
Bade farewell to father and mother and married someone.
With meager ability and ill-favored appearance,
I attended upon your pure dust.[1]
Heeding your every expression, I catered to your wishes,
For I feared being estranged and scorned, no longer beloved.

Happy with your new wife, you have forgotten me;
I mourn that love and affection ended mid-course.
Thus, dejected and bereft of hope,
I will withdraw, hidden and screened in the lower courtyard.
It pains me that one morning I was cast aside,
My heart grief-stricken, I was both sad and shocked.
I put on the clothes I wore when I entered your door,
Turn my back on my bedchamber and set off on my journey.

1 "Pure dust" refers originally to the dust raised behind a carriage, with "pure" implying "distinguished" or "honorable." Here it is used to indicate the wife's devotion to serving her husband.

攀僕御而登車
16 左右悲而失聲

嗟冤結而無訴
乃愁苦以長窮
恨無愆而見棄
20 悼君施之不終

2.3 洛神賦

黃初三年，餘朝京師，還濟洛川。古人有言，斯水之神名曰宓妃。感宋玉對楚王說神女之事，遂作斯賦。其詞曰：

餘從京域
言歸東藩
背伊闕
4 越轘轅
經通谷

1 Many scholars have pointed out that the date given here is possibly incorrect – that it should say fourth year of the Huangchu reign period (223) – but see *Additional Notes*.

Catching hold of the driver, I get into the carriage,
Those in attendance so sad they are unable to speak.

O, choked with rancor, I have nowhere to complain,
So my sorrow and distress will last forever.
I resent that though without fault I was rejected,
Lament that your favor did not last to the end.

2.3 *Fu* on the Goddess of the Luo River

In the third year of the Huangchu reign period, I went to court at the capital, and on my return, I crossed the Luo River.[1] The ancients had a saying that the name of the goddess of this river was Fu Fei.[2] Inspired by the affair of the goddess that Song Yu spoke of in response to the king of Chu, I wrote this *fu*.[3] Its words say,

From the district of the capital,
I was returning to my eastern fief.[4]
I put Yique behind me,
Crossed Huanyuan,
Passed through Tong Valley,

2 Fu Fei, the deity of the Luo River, was believed by some to have been the daughter of the legendary culture hero Fu Xi 伏羲 (or Pao Xi 庖犧), who is credited with creating the eight trigrams that form the sixty-four hexagrams of the *Classic of Changes*.

3 Cao Zhi is referring to the encounter between a king of Chu and the goddess of Wushan (Shaman Mountain) related in "*Fu* on the Goddess," attributed to Song Yu, a figure of the third century BCE. Cao Zhi's piece does in places echo the language and imagery of "*Fu* on the Goddess."

4 Depending on the date of the poem, "eastern fief" here would mean either Juancheng (222) or Yongqiu (223).

陵景山
日既西傾
8 車殆馬煩
爾乃
稅駕乎蘅皐
秣駟乎芝田
容與乎陽林
12 流眄乎洛川

於是
精移神駭
忽焉思散
俯則未察
16 仰以殊觀
睹一麗人
於岩之畔

迺援御者而告之曰：爾有覿於彼者乎？彼何人斯，若此之艷也！御者對曰：臣聞河洛之神，名曰宓妃，然則君王之所見也，無乃是乎？其狀若何？臣願聞之。余告之曰：其形也，

Ascended Mount Jing.[1]
The sun was already leaning to the west,
The carriage was in peril and the horses were tired.
So then
I halted my rig by a marsh of asarum,
Fed my team in a field of mushrooms.[2]
Lingering leisurely in a sunny grove,
I cast a glance at the River Luo.

Thereupon,
My being was shaken and my spirit agitated,
Suddenly my thoughts were muddled.
Looking down, I yet spied nothing;
Looking up, I beheld a rare vision.
I glimpsed a beautiful woman
By the edge of a cliff.

Then I pulled my driver over and entreated of him, "Have you seen that over there? Who is that, that she be as ravishing as this?" The driver replied, "I have heard that the goddess of the River Luo is named Fu Fei, so is it possible that the one milord sees is she? What is her appearance like? I would like to hear of it." I told him, "As to her outer form,

1 Yique ("Gate-towers of the Yi") was south of Luoyang and was named for two mountains that stood like gate-towers on opposite sides of the river Yi. The Huanyuan Mountains are southeast of modern Yanshi county 偃師縣 in He'nan province. Tong Valley, south of Luoyang, is mentioned under its other name, Da gu 大谷, in **4.20**. Mount Jing also lay south of Yanshi county.

2 It is possible that this is a place name. A Mushroom Field Township (Zhitian zhen 芝田鎮) is located forty *li* southwest of modern Gong xian 鞏縣, He'nan. "Mushroom" here has been taken as a reference to divine (or numinous) mushrooms (*lingzhi* 靈芝), objects related to the quest for longevity or immortality and also employed as symbolic of virtue.

翩若驚鴻
20 婉若游龍
榮曜秋菊
華茂春松

仿佛兮若輕雲之蔽月
24 飄颻兮若流風之回雪

遠而望之
皎若太陽升朝霞
迫而察之
28 灼若芙蕖出淥波

穠纖得中
脩短合度
肩若削成
32 腰如約素
延頸秀項
皓質呈露
芳澤無加
36 鉛華弗御

雲髻峨峨
修眉聯娟

She is lightsome as a startled swan-goose,
As graceful as a roaming dragon;
Her lovely complexion outshines the autumn chrysanthemum,
Her radiance surpasses the springtime pine.

She is as nebulous as the moon concealed in light clouds,
Gracefully gliding, as snow spun by a flowing wind.

Gazing at her from afar,
She shines like the sun rising above the rosy mists of dawn;
Observing her close by,
She is as luminous as a lotus emerging from clear ripplets.

She fits the ideal between shapely and thin;
She matches the standard ’twixt tall and short.
Her shoulders are as though sculpted,
Her waist is like bound silk.
On her long neck and exquisite nape,
The gleaming flesh openly shows.
She does not apply fragrant oils,
She does not use ceruse powder.

Her cloud chignon is tall and upswept,
Her long eyebrows gently curve.

丹唇外朗
皓齒內鮮
明眸善睞
靨輔承權
瓌姿艷逸
儀靜體閑
柔情綽態
媚於語言

奇服曠世
骨像應圖
披羅衣之璀粲兮
珥瑤碧之華琚
戴金翠之首飾
綴明珠以耀軀
踐遠遊之文履
曳霧綃之輕裾
微幽蘭之芳藹兮
步踟躕於山隅

於是
忽焉縱體
以遨以嬉

Her cinnabar lips shine without,
Her gleaming teeth are brilliant within.
Her bright pupils are adept at sidelong glances,
Dimples caress her cheeks.
Her marvelous appearance is gorgeous and elegant,
Her demeanor is calm and her body composed.
With tender feelings and mild manner,
She charms by means of spoken words.

Her rare clothing is unique in our time,
The shape of her bone structure matches the portraits.
She is clad in the gleam and glitter of a gossamer gown,
Dangles ornate earrings of chalcedony and prase,
Wears hair ornaments of gold and kingfisher plumes,
Is studded with bright pearls to make herself sparkle.
She treads in Far Roaming patterned shoes,
Trails a light skirt of misty gauze.
Concealed by a fragrant lushness of thoroughwort,
She paces hesitatingly by a mountain nook.

Thereupon,
Suddenly she becomes less reserved,
Thereby to ramble, thereby to frolic.

左倚采旄
60 右蔭桂旗
攘皓腕於神滸兮
采湍瀨之玄芝
余情悅其淑美兮
64 心振蕩而不怡
無良媒以接歡兮
托微波而通辭
願誠素之先達兮
68 解玉佩而要之
嗟佳人之信脩兮
羌習禮而明詩
抗瓊珶以和予兮
72 指潛淵而為期
執眷眷之款實兮
懼斯靈之我欺
感交甫之棄言兮
76 悵猶豫而狐疑
收和顏而靜志
申禮防以自持

於是
洛靈感焉

On the left she leans on a colorful yak-tail pennant,
On the right she is shaded by a cassia banner.
She extends a gleaming wrist on the divine riverbank,
Picks the dark mushrooms of the racing rapids.
I passionately rejoice in her chaste beauty,
But my heart is agitated and I am not content.
Without a good matchmaker to unite us in pleasure,
I trust to small wavelets to convey my words.
Wanting my sincere feelings to be conveyed in advance,
I remove a jade pendant to make her a pledge.
O, excellent indeed is the fair one!
She is versed in ritual and understands poetry.[1]
She holds out a fine gem to requite me,
Points to the sunken depths as our trysting place.
The affection I hold is heartfelt and true,
But I fear this spirit's deceiving me.
Aware of the broken promise made to Jiaofu,[2]
Dejected, I am hesitant and doubtful.
Adopting an agreeable expression, I calm my mind,
And deploy the strictures of propriety to contain myself.

Thereupon,
The Luo divinity is touched by this,

1 This might also be understood to mean that she was versed in canonical ritual texts, like the *Record of Rites*, as well as the *Classic of Poetry*.

2 A parable about a man named Zheng Jiaofu 鄭交甫 says that one day he encountered two young women by the Han River. Not realizing they were river goddesses, he told his driver that he was going to ask for a pendant gem as a love token. After a brief exchange of banter, he was given a gem, which he happily tucked into his clothing, near his heart. After going just ten paces he went to look at it and found that it had disappeared, and when he looked back to see the women, they suddenly vanished.

徙倚彷徨
神光離合
乍陰乍陽
竦輕軀以鶴立
若將飛而未翔
踐椒途之郁烈
步蘅薄而流芳
超長吟以永慕兮
聲哀厲而彌長

爾乃
眾靈雜遝
命儔嘯侶
或戲清流
或翔神渚
或採明珠
或拾翠羽
從南湘之二妃
攜漢濱之遊女
嘆匏瓜之無匹兮
詠牽牛之獨處
揚輕袿之猗靡兮
翳脩袖以延佇

She moves back and forth, paces to and fro.
Her divine aura scatters and reunites,
First dark, then light.
Stretching her light body, she stands crane-like,
As though about to fly but yet to soar aloft.
She treads the redolence of a pepper-scented path,
Paces a patch of asarum, spreading its aroma.
Dispirited, long she sighs with eternal yearning,
The sound, mournful and piercing, lingers long.

And then,
Thronging spirits, a teeming mass,
Call to companions, whistle to peers.
Some frolic in the clear stream,
Some soar about a sacred holm,
Some gather bright pearls,
Some collect kingfisher feathers.
She accompanies the two consorts from the southerly Xiang,
Leads the roaming nymphs from the banks of the Han by the hand.[1]
She sighs that Gourd lacks a mate,
Keens o'er Oxherd's living alone.[2]
Her light mantle fanned out, riffles in the wind;
Shaded by her long sleeve, she stands craning her neck.

1 The Xiang consorts of line 95 are Ehuang 娥皇 and Nüying 女英, goddesses of the Xiang River who were said to be the daughters of the legendary sovereign Yao 堯 and the wives of Yao's successor Shun 舜. The women in line 96 are the deities mentioned in the note to line 75 above.

2 The asterism Gourd (made up of five stars in the constellation Delphinus) is also mentioned with the legend of Oxherd and Weaving Maid in a contemporaneous *fu* by Ruan Yu. However, the tradition behind the reference to Gourd's lack of a mate was already lost by Tang times. Oxherd (Altair) and Weaving Maid (Vega) were constellations separated by the Milky Way, astral lovers who could meet only once a year, on the seventh day of the seventh month.

體迅飛鳧
飄忽若神
淩波微步
羅襪生塵
動無常則
若危若安
進止難期
若往若還
轉眄流精
光潤玉顏
含辭未吐
氣若幽蘭
華容婀娜
令我忘餐

於是
屏翳收風
川后靜波
馮夷鳴鼓
女媧清歌
騰文魚以警乘
鳴玉鑾以偕逝
六龍儼其齊首

Her body is as swift as a duck in flight,
Gliding quickly, godlike.
With steps as delicate as skimming upon waves
Her silk gauze stockings stir up dust.
Her movements have no fixed pattern:
Now unsettled, now at ease.
Her advances and halts are hard to foresee:
Now she leaves, now returns.
Turning her glance and casting her eyes,
Bright and lustrous her fair complexion.
She holds in her words, not yet pouring them out,
But her breath is like hidden thoroughwort.
Her lovely appearance, graceful and delicate,
Makes me forget to eat.

Thereupon,
Pingyi stops the wind,
River Lord stills the waves,
Ping Yi sounds the drum,
And Nüwa sings melodiously.[1]
Striped flying fish leap to clear the way for her carriage;
Jade simurgh bells ring as all depart together.
The six dragon steeds neatly lift their heads together,

1 Pingyi was a wind god. River Lord might refer to Hebo 河伯 (River Earl), the god of the Yellow River, but Ping Yi is also identified with River Earl, so there is some uncertainty about these traditions. Cao Zhi has an "Encomium on Nü Wa" 女媧贊, in which he speaks of her invention of the syrinx and the fact that, as is often seen in representations of her, some people depicted her with a human head and serpent's body.

載雲車之容裔
鯨鯢踊而夾轂
水禽翔而為衛

於是
越北沚
過南岡
紆素領
回清陽
動朱唇以徐言
陳交接之大綱
恨人神之道殊
怨盛年之莫當
抗羅袂以掩涕兮
淚流襟之浪浪
悼良會之永絕兮
哀一逝而異鄉
無微情以效愛
獻江南之明璫
雖潛處於太陰
長寄心於君王
忽不悟其所舍
悵神宵而蔽光

Convey her cloud carriage slowly and serenely.
Whales breach alongside her wheel hubs,
24 Water fowl soar and form her guard.

Thereupon,
They transcend a northern islet,
Pass a southerly ridge,
She twists her white neck,
28 Turns her clear brow.
Moving vermilion lips, she speaks slowly,
Laying out the essential rule of intimate relations.
She regrets that the paths of humans and spirits are different,
32 Resents that in her prime she has no mate.
She lifts a gauze sleeve to hide her weeping;
Teardrops run streaming down her lapels.
She laments that our consummate union is forever finished,
36 Mourns that once we part, we shall be in different realms.
"I shall not show my love with slight affection
But offer you a bright earring from south of the Yangzi.
Although I live submerged in the Great Yin,
40 I forever entrust my heart to you, my prince."
Suddenly I do not know where she has gone,
And regret that the goddess has vanished and conceals her light.

於是
背下陵高
足往神留
遺情想像
顧望懷愁

冀靈體之復形
御輕舟而上泝
浮長川而忘反
思綿綿而增慕
夜耿耿而不寐
霑繁霜而至曙
命僕夫而就駕
吾將歸乎東路
攬騑轡以抗策
悵盤桓而不能去

2.4 愁霖賦

迎朔風而爰邁兮
雨微微而逮行
悼朝陽之隱曜兮
怨北辰之潛精

Thereupon,
Turning my back on the lowlands, I climb up high;
Though my feet advance, my spirit remains behind.
With abiding affection, I dwell on her image;
Gazing back, I am full of sorrow.

Hoping that her divine person might reappear,
I ply a skiff to go upstream.
Adrift on the long stream, I forget to return;
Thoughts unrelenting, unabating increase my yearning.
At night I am restless and do not sleep;
I arrive at dawn wet with heavy frost.
I order the driver to ready the equipage,
For I am going to return to the eastern road.
He takes up the traces and raises the whip,
But I linger in desolation and cannot leave.

2.4 *Fu* on Distress at the Downpour (fragment)

We face the north wind and go forth,
The rain is drizzling by the time we march off.
I lament that the morning sun hides its glare,
Hate that the Northern Dipper conceals its light.

車結轍以盤桓兮
馬躑躅以悲鳴

攀扶桑而仰觀兮
8 假九日於天皇
瞻沉雲之泱漭兮
哀吾願之不將

2.5 喜霽賦

禹身誓於陽盱
卒錫圭而告成
湯感旱於殷時
4 造桑林而敷誠

動玉輣而雲披
鳴鑾鈴而日陽
指北極以爲期
8 吾將倍道而兼行

The carts, becoming stuck in their tracks, linger and loiter;
The horses, hesitating, sadly neigh.

Let me climb the Fusang tree and look upward,
8 Borrow the nine suns from the Celestial Sovereign.[1]
Watching the vastness of the heavy clouds,
I mourn that my wish is not forthcoming.

2.5 *Fu* on Joy at the Clearing Sky (fragment)

Yu used his own body to make a pledge at Yangyu,
And at last he was given a scepter to announce his achievement.[2]
Tang was moved by a drought in the Yin dynasty,
4 So he went to Sanglin and displayed his good faith.[3]

The imperial coach began to move, and the clouds scattered;
The carriage bells began to jingle, and the sun grew bright.
Pointing toward the North Star to fix the appointed time,
8 I will double my speed and hasten my progress.

---

1 Fusang is the name of a mythical tree in the east that held ten suns, nine on its lower branches and one on its uppermost branch. One of the suns would traverse the sky, and when it returned, another would set out on its transit.

2 Yu is the legendary ancient culture hero who is said to have tamed the great deluge, dredging rivers and reclaiming the flooded land. The "Tribute of Yu" 禹貢 section of the canonical *Hallowed Documents* 尚書 catalogues his labors and mentions his receipt of the scepter.

3 After (Cheng 成) Tang, the reputed founder of the Yin (or Shang) dynasty, defeated the preceding Xia, there is said to have been a drought of seven years. In order to pray for rain to end the drought, he offered himself as a sacrifice at Shanglin.

2.6 登臺賦

從明后而嬉遊兮
登層臺以娛情
見太府之廣開兮
4 觀聖德之所營
建高門之嵯峨兮
浮雙闕乎太清
立中天之華觀兮
8 連飛閣乎西城
臨漳水之長流兮
望園果之滋榮
仰春風之和穆兮
12 聽百鳥之悲鳴
天功恆其既立兮
家願得而獲逞
揚仁化於宇內兮
16 盡肅恭於上京
雖桓文之為盛兮
豈足方乎聖明

休矣美矣
20 惠澤遠揚
翼佐我皇家兮

2.6 *Fu* on Ascending the Terrace

Following our enlightened lord we happily tour,
Ascend the tiered terrace to gladden our mood.
We see grand edifices started all around,
View all his sage virtue has built.
He constructed tall gates, lofty and steep,
Floated twin gate-towers in the empyrean,
Erected ornate pylons high into the sky,
Joined flying galleries to the west city-wall.
We look out over the Zhang River's long course,
Gaze upon the burgeoning glory of West Garden's fruit.
Lift our faces to the gentle serenity of the spring breeze,
Hear the sad calls of the many birds.
The constancy of the imperial enterprise is already established,
The success of your family's wishes has gotten to be realized.
You spread benevolent influence in the world,
Fulfill solemn reverence to the imperial capital.
Though Dukes Huan and Wen were most magnificent – [1]
How can they compare with your peerless wisdom?

O happy! O excellent!
Your kind favor wafts afar.
You aid our imperial house,

1 Dukes Huan of Qi 齊桓公 (r. 685–643 BCE) and Wen of Jin 晉文公 (r. 636–628 BCE) were commonly held to be model rulers.

寧彼四方
同天地之矩量兮
24 齊日月之輝光
永貴尊而無極兮
等年壽於東王

2.7 九華扇賦

昔吾先君常侍得幸漢桓帝時，賜尚方竹扇。其扇不方不圓，其中結成文，名曰九華扇。故為賦。其辭曰：

有神區之名竹
生不周之高岑
對淥水之素波
4 背玄澗之重深
體虛暢以立幹
播翠葉以成林

形五離而九析
8 蔑氂解而縷分
效虬龍之蜿蟬
法虹霓之氤氳
攄微妙以歷時

Pacify the four directions.
Your magnanimity equals heaven and earth,
Your brilliance matches the sun and the moon.
May you ever be honored and respected without limit,
And your lifespan equal the King of the East.[1]

2.7 *Fu* on the Many-Splendored Fan

Formerly, my great-grandfather, the Regular Attendant, received favor in the time of Emperor Huan [r. 146–168] of Han and was given a bamboo fan from the Imperial Manufactories. The fan was neither square nor round, its insides came together to form a pattern. It was called the Many-Splendored Fan. Therefore, I composed a *fu*. Its words say:

There is a famous bamboo from a divine district,
It grows on the high peaks of Buzhou Mountain.[2]
It faces a white spume of clear water,
Backs up to the doubled depths of a murky gill.
Its body is hollow and smooth for the stalk to stand straight,
It spreads its green leaves to create a grove.

Its form was five times splintered, nine times split;
Slips stripped to fine strands, parted into filaments.
They imitated the winding and writhing of the spirax and dragon,
Modeled the enveloping mists of a rainbow or iris,
Revealed delicate subtlety by taking their time,

1 The King of the East is a deity also called King Lord of the East, Eastern Father, and a variety of other names. He is associated with immortality and serves as a counterpart to the Queen Mother of the West in both texts and iconography of the Han and Three Kingdoms periods.

2 This was a mountain in the northwest. It is the mountain that Gonggong 共工 of myth butts out of place in his battle with Zhuan Xu.

12 絢九層之華文

爾乃浸以芷若
拂以江蘺
搖以五香
16 濯以蘭池

因形致好
不常厥儀
方不應矩
20 圓不中規
隨皓腕以徐轉
發惠風之微寒
時氣清以方厲
24 紛飄動兮綺紈

2.8 寶刀賦

建安中，家父魏王乃命有司造寶刀五枚，三年乃就，以龍、虎、熊、馬、雀為識。太子得一，余及余弟饒陽侯各得一焉。其餘二枚，家王自杖之。賦曰：

2 Adorned it with nine layers of decorative designs.
And then
They immersed it in angelica and pollia,
Rubbed it with lovage,
Wafted it with five fragrances smoke,
6 Rinsed it in a pond of thoroughwort.

Based on its appearance, it is the very best;
Extraordinary is its outward form.
In squareness it does not fit a carpenter's square;
10 In roundness it does not match a compass.
When it slowly turns with a gleaming wrist,
It sends forth a slight chill of gentle breeze:
The weather just then quickly grows cool
14 And a random gust ruffles brocade and silk.

2.8 *Fu* on Precious Sabers (fragment)

During the Jian'an period, our paterfamilias, the King of Wei,[1] ordered those in authority to manufacture five precious sabers. After three years, they were finished. They used a dragon, tiger, bear, horse, and bird as intaglios. The heir designate [Cao Pi] got one, and my younger brother the Marquis of Raoyang [Cao Lin] and I each got one of them.[2] As for the remaining two, our father the king kept those himself. The *fu* says:

1 Cao Cao became king of Wei in Jian'an 21 (216).

2 Cao Lin 曹林 (fl. 211–232) was one of Cao Zhi's many half-brothers. He was appointed Marquis of Raoyang in Jian'an 16 (211/212) and held this title until sometime in Jian'an 22 (217).

有皇漢之明后
思明達而玄通
飛文藻以博致
揚武備以禦凶

乃
熾火炎爐
融鐵挺英
烏獲奮椎
歐冶是營
扇景風以激氣
飛光鑑於天庭
爰告祠於太乙
乃感夢而通靈

然後
礪以五方之石
鑿以中黃之壤
規圓景以定環
攄神功而造象
垂華紛之葳蕤
流翠采之滉瀁

Our enlightened lord of august Han,[1]
His thoughts are insightfully comprehending, profoundly
knowledgeable,
He plies literary elegance to attract talents from afar,[2]
Brandishes armaments to ward off evil.

And so
With raging fire and blazing furnace,
They smelted iron ore and extracted the bloom.
Wu Huo wielded the hammer,
Ouye supervised.[3]
They fanned a great wind to speed the air,
The soaring light was reflected in the Celestial Court.[4]
Then they said a prayer to Grand Unity,[5]
Were enlightened by dream and communicated with spirits.

Afterwards,
They honed them with stones from the five regions,[6]
Polished them with loam of brown hematite,
Copied the full moon to shape the pommels,
Freed supernal skill to create the figures:
Strewing lush luxuriance of splendid profusion,
Streaming undulating ripples of halcyon hues.

1 I.e., Cao Cao.
2 Cao Cao is famous for the edicts he wrote to encourage the recruitment of talented men for official positions.
3 Wu Huo is mentioned in old texts as a strongman. Ouye was a legendary master swordsmith of antiquity.
4 Celestial Court was another name for Grand Tenuity, a celestial palace composed mostly of stars in the constellation Virgo.
5 Grand Unity was the supreme celestial deity.
6 North, south, east, west, and the center.

故其利
陸斷犀革
20 水斷龍角
輕擊浮截
刃不纖削

踰南越之巨闕
24 超西楚之太阿
實真人之攸御
永天祿而是荷

2.9 車渠椀賦

惟新碗之所生
于涼風之峻湄
采金光以定色
4 擬朝陽而發暉
豐玄素之煒曄
帶朱榮之葳蕤
縕絲綸以肆采
8 藻繁布以相追
翩飄颻而浮景

Therefore, their keen edges
On land can sever rhinoceros hide,
On water can sever dragon horns.
They nimbly strike and slickly cut,
And their blades suffer not the slightest wear.

They surpass Juque of Yue to the south,
Exceed Tai'e of Chu in the west.[1]
They assuredly are for the true man to use;
Wield these to perpetuate Heaven's blessings.[2]

2.9 *Fu* on a *Musāragalva* Bowl[3]

The origins of this bowl
Are on the verge of the crest of Liangfeng.[4]
It draws on the shine of gold to compose its hues,
Imitates the morning sun in emitting radiance.
It is replete with a bright resplendence of black and white,
Striated with a gorgeous riot of vermilion blossoms.
Tangled silk fishing lines spread their colors;
Ornate patterns scatter profusely as though pursuing each other.
Lightly swirling and whirling like floating shadows,

1 Juque was one of Goujian's 勾踐 (r. 496–465 BCE) swords. Tai'e was a sword said to have been made by Ouye for the king of Chu. See *Additional Note* to lines 7–8, 23–24.

2 The "true man" of line 25 is Cao Cao. The term "Heaven's blessings" refers to blessings and emoluments bestowed by Heaven, but it was also a metaphor for rulership. Here it must refer to Cao Cao's status as king of Wei.

3 On the term "*musāragalva*," see *Additional Notes*.

4 Liangfeng, also Langfeng 閬風, was a mountain abode of transcendent beings in the Kunlun Range.

若鷩鶵之雙飛
隱神璞於西野
12 彌百葉而莫希

于時乃有
篤厚神后
廣被仁聲
夷慕義而重使
16 獻茲寶於斯庭
命公輸使制匠
窮妍麗之殊形
華色粲爛
20 文若點成
鬱蓊雲蒸
蜿蟬龍征
光如激電
24 影若浮星
何神怪之巨偉
信一覽而九驚
雖離朱之聰目
28 猶炫耀而失精

何明麗之可悅
超群寶而特章

Resembling startled swans flying off in a pair.
Hidden was its divine matrix in the western wilds,
For more than a hundred ages, no one valued it.

And now there is
A wise and generous divine ruler
Who broadly extends his reputation for humaneness.
Foreigners admired his righteousness and sent an important envoy,
Who presented this treasure at our court.
He ordered an artisan with the skills of a Gongshu[1]
To make the most of its alluringly beautiful distinctive appearance.
Its flowery hues glitter and glow,
Its patterns seem touched up.
Thick and dense, rising cloud-like,
Winding and writhing, moving like dragons,
As bright as a flash of lightning,
As effulgent as the floating stars.
How astounding is this divine curiosity!
Truly, with just one look one is totally stunned.
Even the sharp eyes of a Li Zhu
Would be dazed and dazzled and go blind.[2]

How delightful are its brightness and beauty!
Surpassing all treasures, it is uniquely striking.

1 Gongshu is Gongshu Ban 公輸般 (or 公輸班), a master artisan of the Zhou period.

2 Li Zhu is another name for the sharp-eyed Li Lou 離婁 of *Mengzi* 4A.1.

俟君子之閒宴
酌甘醴於斯觥
既娛情而可貴
故求御而不忘

2.10 迷迭香賦

播西都之麗草兮
應青春而發暉
流翠葉於纖柯兮
結微根於丹墀
信繁華之速實兮
弗見雕於嚴霜
芳暮秋之幽蘭兮
麗崑崙之英芝
既經時而收采兮
遂幽殺以增芳
去枝葉而持御兮
入綃縠之霧裳
附玉體以行止兮
順微風而舒光

Attending the young lord's private feast,[1]
We pour sweet ale from this jorum.
It both delights the senses and is precious,
So, may it always be used and not forgotten.

2.10 *Fu* on *Midie*[2]

A beautiful plant sown in a city to the west,
In verdant spring it sends forth a radiance,
Spreads blue-green leaves on slender stems,
Fastens diminutive roots in red courtyard earth.
Truly the profuse blossoms quickly form fruits;[3]
They will not be withered by severe frost.
They are as fragrant as late autumn's secluded thoroughwort,
As beautiful as Kunlun's blossoming angelica.
After a time, they gather and pluck them,
Then dry them in a shaded spot to increase their fragrance.
Discarding stems and leaves, they are held for use,
And put in misty skirts of fine gauze.
Staying with one's jade-like body in motion or at rest,
It spreads fragrance abroad with the gentlest breeze.

1 The "young lord" is Cao Pi.

2 *Midie* is the word for "rosemary," but see *Additional Notes*.

3 If this plant is rosemary, it is worth noting that rosemary does have "fruits," which are generally called "nutlets."

2.11 大暑賦

炎帝掌節
祝融司方
羲和按轡
南雀舞衡
暎扶桑之高熾
燎九日之重光
大暑赫其遂蒸
玄服革而尚黃
蛇折鱗於靈窟
龍解角於皓蒼

遂乃温風赫羲
草木垂幹
山坼海沸
沙融礫爛
飛魚躍渚
潛黿浮岸
鳥張翼而遠栖
獸交逝而雲散

於時
黎庶徙倚

2.11 *Fu* on a Heat Wave (fragment)

The Fiery Emperor governs the season,
Zhu Rong oversees the region,[1]
Xihe handles the reins,[2]
The Bird of the South dances on the scale beam.[3]
Ashine with the towering blaze of the Fusang tree,
Afire with the redoubled rays of the nine suns,[4]
The heat is fierce and rises like steam,
Dark clothing is changed, yellow is preferred.
Snakes slough their scales in mysterious dens,
Dragons shed their horns in the bright cerulean sky.

Then the warm wind turns sweltering,
Plants and trees dip their stems,
Mountains split, seas boil,
Sand melts, gravel turns to mush.
Flying fish leap onto the islets,
Submerged turtles drift onto the banks,
Birds spread their wings and roost afar,
Beasts leave in unison and scatter like clouds

Thereupon,
The common people pace up and down,

1 The Fiery Emperor and Zhu Rong are deities associated with heat, fire, and the South. The Fiery Emperor is the god of the South. Zhu Rong was a tutelary spirit of the South and was thought to have become the Spirit of Fire after he died.

2 Xihe was the charioteer of the sun.

3 The Bird of the South is the Vermilion Bird 朱鳥, and according to one tradition, summer was regulated by the beam of a scale.

4 See **2.4**, lines 7–8.

棋布葉分
機女絕綜
農夫釋耘
背暑者不羣而齊跡
向陰者不會而成羣

於是大人
遷居宅幽
綏神育靈
雲屋重構
閑房肅清
寒泉涌流
玄木奮榮

積素冰於幽館
氣飛結而爲霜
奏白雪於琴瑟
朔風感而增涼

[壯皇居之瑰瑋兮
步八閎而爲宇
節四運之常氣兮
踰太素之儀矩]

Dispersed like chess pieces, strewn like leaves;
Weaver women leave behind their heddles,
Farmers abandon their weeding.
Those leaving the heat are not in a group but their pace is the same;
Those heading for shade are not meeting but they gather in groups.

Thereupon, the Great Man[1]
Moves his dwelling to a secluded place
To calm his spirits and nourish his psyche.
The cloud-high house is built in tiers,
The lateral rooms are quiet and cool.
Cold springs bubble and flow,
Dark trees vigorously bloom.

By storing white ice in a secluded lodge,
When the air stirs, it congeals and forms frost.
By performing "White Snow" on zither and zithern,[2]
The north wind responds and adds to the coolness.

[Magnificent the rare beauty of the imperial dwelling:[3]
They paced off the Eight Bounds to make the grounds,[4]
Regulated constant temperatures during the four seasons,
Exceeded the standards and norms of the Great Plainness.][5]

1 The Great Man is Cao Cao.

2 "White Snow" was the title of a tune that the Grand God (or God in Heaven) had Plain Girl 素女 play on a fifty-string zither.

3 These four lines appear by themselves in one source and may have originally come from somewhere near the beginning of this *fu*.

4 These were regions far beyond the Nine Provinces of ancient China.

5 The Great Plainness refers to a stage in the formation of the cosmos when matter first appears.

3.1 神龜賦

龜壽千歲。時有遺余龜者，數日而死，肌肉消盡，唯甲存焉。余感而賦之。曰：

嘉四靈之建德
各潛位乎一方
蒼龍虯於東岳
白虎嘯於西岡
玄武集於寒門
朱雀棲於南鄉
順仁風以消息
應聖時而後翔

嗟神龜之奇物
體乾坤之自然
下夷方以則地
上規隆而法天
順陰陽以呼吸
藏景耀於重泉

餐飛塵以實氣
飲不竭於朝露
步容趾以俯仰

3.1 *Fu* on the Divine Turtle

The longevity of the turtle is a thousand years. Once someone gave me a turtle, and after several days it died. Its flesh completely disappeared till only the carapace was left. Moved, I wrote a *fu* about it, which says:

Let us praise the established virtue of the four numina,
Each concealing its position in a direction.
Bluegreen Dragon coils on the eastern mountain,[1]
White Tiger roars on western ridges.
Dark Warrior settles at Coldgate,
Vermilion Bird roosts in southern climes.[2]
They wax or wane in accord with benevolent winds,
Come forth only in response to a sage.

Ah, a rare creature the divine turtle;
It embodies the naturalness of heaven and earth:
Beneath it is flat and square to pattern the earth,
On top it is round and domed to model the sky.
Breathing in accord with *yin* and *yang*,
It hides from the sun's glare in deep springs.

It eats floating dust to replenish its vital force,
Drinks unendingly of the morning dew.
It paces with leisurely gait, head moving up and down,

---

1 I.e., Mount Tai (Taishan 泰山).

2 These are the names of the four numina and the directions to which they correspond. Dark Warrior was a turtle. Hanmen (Coldgate) was said to be a mountain in the extreme north.

時鸞回而鶴顧
忽萬載而不恤
周無疆於太素
感白龍之翔翥
卒不免乎豫且
雖見珍於宗廟
罹刳剝之重辜
欲愬怨於上帝
將等愧乎遊魚
懼沉泥之逢殆
赴芳蓮以巢居
安玄雲而好靜
不淫翔而改度
昔嚴周之抗節
援斯靈而托喻
嗟祿運之屯蹇
終遇獲於江濱
歸籠檻以幽處
遭淳美之仁人
晝顧瞻以終日
夕撫順而接晨
遘淫災以隕越
命勦絕而不振

At times circling like a simurgh or canting its head like a crane.
Indifferent to myriad years, it worries not;
It has perfected infinitude like the Great Plainness.[1]
It is sensible of the soaring ascent of the white dragon,
Which in the end could not escape from Yu Ju:[2]
Although treasured in the ancestral temple,
It encountered dismemberment through gutting and flaying.
Were it to lodge a complaint with the High God,
He would rank its mortification with the swimming fish.
It fears the perils it would meet by submerging in the mud,
So goes to fragrant lotuses to make its nest:
It finds comfort in their dark clouds and enjoys the quiet,
Does not ramble recklessly and change its ways.
Of old the unyielding integrity of Yan Zhou[3]
Invoked this numen to draw an analogy.[4]
Ah, the hardships and difficulties of fortune and fate!
It finally met capture on a river bank.
Put in a cage to dwell in isolation,
It encountered a guileless and good kindly person.
In daytime he looked after and watched it all day;
At night he stroked and soothed it till dawn.
It met with drastic disaster and passed away,
Its life was cut short, not to be saved.

---

1 See **2.11**, last line.

2 There are different versions of the Yu Ju story, involving the capture of either a turtle or a dragon that had turned itself into a fish. In the dragon/fish version, the fish is shot in the eye by Yu Ju and complains to the High God, who points out that it was his own fault for changing into a fish. See *Additional Note*.

3 Yan Zhou is Zhuang Zhou 莊周 (Zhuangzi). The name was likely changed to avoid using the given name, Zhuang, of Emperor Ming of Han 漢明帝 (r. 58–75).

4 Zhuangzi was fishing one day when the King of Chu sent envoys to offer him control of the state. "Zhuangzi held his pole and, without turning to look at them, said, 'I have heard that Chu has a divine turtle that has already been dead for 3,000 years and that the king stores it in the ancestral temple, covered in a cloth inside a bamboo box. As for this turtle, would it rather have died to leave behind its bones and be prized, or would it rather have been alive and dragging its tail in the mud?' The two officials said, 'It would rather have been alive and dragging its tail in the mud.' Zhuangzi said, 'Begone! I will drag my tail in the mud.'"

天道昧而未分
神明幽而難燭
黃氏沒於空澤
松喬化於扶木
蛇折鱗乎平皋
龍脫骨於深谷
亮物類之遷化
疑斯靈之解殼

3.2 白鶴賦

嗟皓麗之素鳥兮
含奇氣之淑祥
薄幽林以屏處兮
蔭重景之餘光
挾單巢於弱條兮
懼衝風之難當
無沙棠之逸志兮

The ways of Heaven are obscure and unclear,
Divine illumination is hidden and hard to shed light on:
The Yellow Emperor sank in an empty marsh,
Whereas Red Pine and Wang Qiao transformed at the Fu Tree.[1]
Snakes lose their scales by level shores,
Dragons shed their bones in deep valleys.
In truth, all things are transformed by death;
But I wonder if this numen has been liberated by means of its shell.[2]

3.2 *Fu* on a White Crane

O, whitest bird of luminous beauty,
Harboring an excellent auspice of extraordinary vital force.
It drew near dark woods to dwell concealed,
Took shelter from the immoderate rays of excessive sunlight.
It hid its lone nest midst tender branches,
Fearing that buffeting winds are hard to weather.
It had no special yearning for [roosting in] crabapple,[3]

1 The revisionist idea that the Yellow Emperor sank into a body of water instead of mounting to immortality on a dragon is seen in the work of the Late Han independent thinker Wang Chong 王充 (27–ca. 100 CE). Red Pine (Chisongzi 赤松子) and Wangzi Qiao 王子喬 are the names of legendary figures who became immortals. Chisongzi is said to have been the rain master of the legendary culture hero Shen Nong, the Divine Farmer. Wangzi Qiao is often referred to as Wang Qiao or, as here, just Qiao. He is said to have been the heir-apparent Jin 晉 of King Ling of Zhou 周靈王 (r. 571–545 BCE). On the Fu Tree, see **3.9**, lines 7–8.

2 This asks whether although the turtle may have appeared to die, it may actually have transcended death, leaving its shell behind as a sign, as Daoists sometimes left behind swords or staffs or other objects as residues of their translation.

3 The *shatang* 沙棠, here translated as "crabapple," was a fabled tree from the Kunlun Mountains. It was said to have yellow flowers and red fruit that tasted like plum but had no pit. Eating it prevented drowning.

欣六翮之不傷
承邂逅之僥倖兮
得接翼於鸞皇
同毛衣之氣類兮
信休息而同行
痛美會之中絕兮
遘嚴災而逢殃
并太息而祗懼兮
抑吞聲而不揚

傷本規之違迕兮
悵離群而獨處
恆竄伏以窮栖
獨哀鳴而戢羽

冀大網之解結
得奮翅而遠遊
聆雅琴之清韻
託六翮之末流

Was content that its six quills were not injured.
But it received the good fortune of a chance encounter,
And got to link wings with simurgh and phoenix.
Sharing in the temperament of the feather-clad,
Truly their rest and repose were as one.
It grieves that this beautiful union was broken halfway,
That it met grave misfortune and encountered disaster.
It simultaneously heaves a great sigh and feels only dread,
Stifles and swallows its voice, making no outcry.

It grieves at this departure from original plans,
Is distressed over leaving the flock and dwelling alone.
Always concealed and hidden in its poor roost;
Alone it mournfully calls and folds its wings.

It hopes for the untying of the knots of the great net,
To get to beat its wings and roam afar,
To heed the pure euphony of the elegant zither,[1]
Seek a place among the lower six-quilled classes.

1 The poet here alludes to the connection between the proper music produced by the *qin* (zither) and the gentleman's ability to control his behavior.

3.3 蟬賦

惟夫蟬之清素兮
潛厥類乎太陰
在盛陽之仲夏兮
4 始遊豫乎芳林
實澹泊而寡慾兮
獨怡樂而長吟
聲曒曒而彌礫兮
8 似貞士之介心

內含和而弗食兮
與眾物而無求
棲高枝而仰首兮
12 漱朝露之情流

隱柔桑之稠葉兮
快閑居以遁暑
苦黃雀之作害兮
16 患螳蜋之勁斧
冀飄翔而遠托兮
毒蜘蛛之網罟
欲降身而卑竄兮
20 懼草蟲之襲予

3.3 *Fu* on the Cicada

The cicada, pure and unsullied,
Lies hidden with its kind in the Great Yin.[1]
In the middle month of summer, when the sun is at its fullest,
It begins to rollick in the fragrant woods.
Truly pleased and content, its desires are few;
Uniquely cheerful and merry, it steadily sings.
The sound is shrill, growing ever higher,
Like the upright heart of a principled man.

Harboring inner harmony, it does not take food;
It associates with all creatures but seeks nothing.
Perched on a high limb, it lifts its head,
Rinses its mouth with the pure fluid of morning dew.

Secreted among dense leaves of tender mulberry,
It lives happily and placidly, escaping the heat.
"I worried about the harm posed by sparrows,
Was troubled by the mighty axe of the mantis.
I hoped to swiftly fly upwards, seek refuge far away,
But I loathed the spider's web;
I wanted to move myself down and lie low,
But I dreaded the grasshopper's ambushing me.

1 Great Yin, or great darkness, refers to the ground. Cicada nymphs spend most of their existence in the earth.

免眾難而弗獲兮
遙遷集乎宮宇
依名果之茂陰兮
托修幹以靜處
有翩翩之狡童兮
步容與於園圃

體離朱之聰視兮
姿才捷於獼猿
條罔葉而不挽兮
樹無榦而不緣
翳輕軀而奮進兮
跪側足以自閑
恐余身之驚駭兮
精曾睨而目連
持柔竿之冉冉兮
運微黏而我纏
欲翻飛而愈滯兮
知性命之長捐
委厥體於膳夫
歸炎炭而就燔

Avoiding all sorts of dangers without getting caught,
I moved from afar and settled at a palace.
Relying on the lush foliage of rare fruit trees,
I took refuge on a tall tree trunk to dwell in peace.
There was a graceful, raffish lad
Strolling nonchalantly in the garden.

He embodied the sharp vision of a Li Zhu,[1]
In aptitude more agile than a macaque or gibbon.
No leaf on the branches did he leave unturned,
No trunk of a tree did he not climb.
Concealing his lithe body, he would suddenly advance;
Kneeling on one leg, he would screen himself.
Afraid lest my person be startled and take fright,
His eyes kept peering around till his sight made contact.
Holding a pliant pole that drooped downwards,
He used its slight stickiness to entangle me.
I was going to fly away but got more stuck
And knew that my life was forever forfeit."
He gave its body to the food steward,
Who returned to his fiery charcoal and roasted it.

1 Li Zhu is another name for the sharp-eyed Li Lou 離婁 of *Mengzi*.

秋霜紛以宵下
晨風烈其過庭
氣憯怛而薄軀
足攀木而失莖
吟嘶啞以沮敗
狀枯槁以喪形

亂曰
詩歎鳴蜩
聲嘒嘒兮
盛陽則來
太陰逝兮
皎皎貞素
侔夷節兮
帝臣是戴
尚其潔兮

The autumn frost is heavy, falling by night;
The dawn wind is biting as it passes the courtyard.
The air is brutal and foreboding and presses on their bodies;
As their feet crawl up trees, they slip from the stems.
Their singing grows hoarse and thus ceases and fails;[1]
Their appearance wizens and withers and thus they meet their end.

Envoi:
The *Poetry* praises the singing cicadas,
Their sound goes chirr chirr.
When the sun is at its fullest they come,
With the Great Yin they depart.[2]
Immaculate their rectitude and purity,
Equal to the integrity of Yi.[3]
The emperor's officials wear these
Esteeming their purity.[4]

1 Cicadas, of course, do not actually sing, nor do they stridulate in the same way crickets and other insects do. Rather they produce their sound with structures called tymbals on their abdomens.

2 In this line, Great Yin means "winter."

3 Yi is the archetypal figure Bo Yi 伯夷. Bo Yi and his younger brother Shu Qi 叔齊 went into seclusion on Shouyang Mountain. Their father wanted Shu Qi to be his heir, and Bo Yi fled so that Shu Qi could accept. But Shu Qi could not bear displacing his elder brother as rightful heir, so he, too, fled. In the end, they starved to death because they would not eat the grain of the state of Zhou, whose ruler, King Wu, they considered unprincipled.

4 Cicada ornaments were worn on the caps of certain military and court officials.

3.4 鸚鵡賦

美洲中之令鳥
越衆類而殊名
感陽和而振翼
4 遁太陰以存形

遇旅人之嚴網
殘六翮而無遺
身掛滯於重籠
8 孤雌鳴而獨歸
豈予身之足惜
憐衆雛之未飛
分糜軀以潤鑊
12 何全濟之敢希

蒙含育之厚德
奉君子之光輝
怨身輕而施重
16 恐往惠之中虧
常戢心以懷懼
雖處安其若危
永哀鳴以報德
20 庶終來而不疲

3.4 *Fu* on the Parrot

More beautiful than the finest birds of the central region,
Surpassing all others, unusually named.[1]
Feeling spring's warmth, it beats its wings,
Flees the great cold to preserve its body.

It meets a steward's tight mesh net,
Its six quills mangled till none remain.
Its body is suspended and stranded in a tiered cage,
Its lonely hen calls but returns alone.
"It is not that I myself was worth caring about,
But I lamented that my fledglings had yet to fly.
I was reconciled to being pulverized and boiled alive,
How dared I hope to save myself intact?

I have received the generous favor of being cherished and nurtured
And serve my lord's bright radiance.
I deplore that though personally trivial, I have been shown great kindness,
But I fear past benevolence at some point will cease.
I am always chary and full of dread:
Though I dwell in peace, it seems like peril.
I shall forever call mournfully to repay favor;
May I at all times toil without tiring.

1 The parrot is said here to be "unusually named" because most birds had monosyllabic names, whereas the parrot has the disyllabic name *yingwu*.

3.5 鶡賦

鶡之為禽猛氣，其鬬終無勝負，期於必死，遂賦之焉。

美遐圻之偉鳥
生太行之嵓阻
體貞剛之烈性
亮乾德之所輔
戴毛角之雙立
揚玄黃之勁羽
甘沈隕而重辱
有節士之儀矩

降居擅澤
高處保岑
遊不同嶺
棲必異林

若有
翻雄駭游
孤雌驚翔

3.5 *Fu* on the Brown Eared Pheasant

As birds go, brown eared pheasants have fierce temperaments, and when they fight there after all is no winning or losing – they pin their expectations on fighting to the death. Consequently, I have thus composed a *fu* about them.

Beautiful this majestic bird from a distant place,
Born in the cliffs and defiles of the Taihang mountains.[1]
It embodies a staunch and indomitable fiery nature,
Clearly backed by robust power.
It sports feathery tufts standing up in a pair,
Displays strong wings of black and yellow.
It finds dying sweet and humiliation unbearable,
Has the principles and standards of a man of integrity.

Dwelling down low, it claims a marshland;
Staying up high, it possesses a peak.
Moving about, it will not share a ridge;
At roost, it must have its own woods.

Should
A winging cock roam affrightingly by,
Or a lone hen soar startlingly up,

---

1 The Taihang mountains extend north to south for some 400 kilometers in Shanxi, Hebei, and He'nan provinces.

則
長鳴挑敵
鼓翼專場
踰高越壑
雙戰隻僵

階侍斯珥
俯耀文墀
成武官之首飾
增庭燎之高暉

3.6 離繳雁賦

余遊於玄武陂中，有雁離繳，不能復飛，顧命舟人追而得之，故憐而賦焉。

憐孤雁之偏特兮
情惆焉而內傷
尋淑類之殊異兮
稟上天之休祥
含中和之純氣系
赴四節而征行
遠玄冬於南裔兮
避炎夏於朔方

Then
With a long cry it challenges the rival,
16 Drums its wings to dominate the field.
Over heights, across ravines,
The pair fights till one falls dead.

The guards at the palace steps stick these tail feathers in their caps;
20 When they bow, the plumes shimmer on the figured steps.
Become the headdress of military officers,
They increase the grand radiance of the courtyard torches.

3.6 *Fu* on a Wild Goose Who Encountered an Arrow Cord

I was on an outing on Xuanwu Reservoir, and there was a wild goose who was caught by an arrow cord and could no longer fly. I looked back and ordered the boatman to catch up to it and get it. Thus, I have composed a *fu* about it out of pity.

Pity the lonesomeness of the solitary wild goose,
Its mood despondent, hurting inside.
It inherits the singular otherness of its excellent kind,
4 Is endowed with good auspice from heaven above.
Harboring the pure pneuma of balance and harmony,
It heeds the four seasons and travels afar,
Stays far from dark winter at the southern frontier,
8 Escapes fiery summer in the northern quarter.

白露淒以飛揚兮
秋風發乎西商
感節運之復至兮
12 假魏道而翱翔
接羽翮以南北兮
情逸豫而永康

望范氏之發機兮
16 播纖繳以凌雲
掛微軀之輕翼兮
忽頽落而離群
旅朋驚而鳴逝兮
20 徒矯首而魔聞

甘充君之下廚
膏函牛之鼎鑊
蒙生全之顧復
24 何恩施之隆博
於是
縱軀歸命
無慮無求
飢食稻粱
28 渴飲清流

The white dew turned chilly and upward it flew,
Autumn winds began to blow from the west.[1]
Sensing that the turning of the seasons had come again,
It took advantage of the way through Wei and soared aloft.
Pinion-to-pinion the flock headed south,
The mood was carefree and happy, ever peaceful.

"I blame Mr. Fan for pulling the crossbow's trigger,
Loosing the slender corded arrow to climb to the clouds.
It snagged a fleet wing on my insignificant body,
And suddenly I fell, leaving the flock.
My companions were alarmed and cried out as they departed,
In vain I raised my head but none could hear.

I was ready to add to my lord's lesser cuisine,
And season a cauldron or cookpot big enough for an ox.
But I received care and attention that preserved my life –
How liberal and inclusive are your favor and kindness!
So,
I abandoned my body, surrendered to fate,
Worried about nothing, sought nothing.
When hungry I eat of rice and millet
When thirsty I drink from a clear stream.

---

1 Literally, "from the western *shang*" 於西商. *Shang* is the name for a note in the Chinese pentatonic scale that is associated with autumn and the direction west.

3.7 鷂雀賦

鷂欲取雀雀自言
雀微賤
身體些小
肌肉瘠瘦
所得蓋少
君欲相噉
實不足飽

鷂得雀言
初不敢語
頃來轗軻
資糧乏旅
三日不食
略思死鼠
今日相得
寧復置汝

雀得鷂言
意甚怔營
性命至重
雀鼠貪生

3.7 *Fu* on the Sparrow Hawk and Sparrow (fragment)

A sparrow hawk was about to seize a sparrow. The sparrow said,
"A sparrow is lowly and humble:
Its body a little bit small,
Its flesh lean and scrawny,
What you get will surely be too little.
If you're going to devour me,
I'm really not enough to fill you up."

When the sparrow hawk heard the sparrow's words,
At first it did not dare to speak.
"Lately it's been rough –
A journey of short provisions.
For three days I haven't eaten,
And I've been sort of wanting some dead rat.
Today I've gotten you.
How can I let you go again?"

When the sparrow heard the sparrow hawk's words,
Its mind was very panic-stricken.
"Life is the most important thing,
Even sparrows and rats greedily cling to life.

君得一食
我命隕傾
皇天降監
賢者是聽

鷂得雀言
意甚怛惋
當死弊雀
頭如顆蒜
不早首服
捩頸大喚
行人聞之
莫不往觀

雀得颻言
意甚不移
依一棗樹
藂蕽多刺
目如擘椒
跳蕭二翅
我當死矣
略無可避

You may get a single meal,
But my life will be lost.
When August Heaven turns his gaze downward,
Only the worthy does it hear."

When the sparrow hawk heard the sparrow's words,
Its mind was very sad and upset.
That stupid sparrow's as good as dead,
Its head is like a garlic bulb.
Instead of quickly giving up,
It twists its neck and loudly screeches.
Passers-by hear it,
And none but comes to take a look.

When the sparrow heard the sparrow hawk's words,
Its mind was even more steadfast.
It sought refuge in a jujube tree,
Lush and dense with many thorns.
Its eyes were like split peppercorns,
And it thrashed its two wings.
"I ought to have died,
There was no way for me to escape."

40 鷂乃置雀
良久方去

二雀相逢
似是公嫗
44 相將入草
共上一樹
仍敘本末
辛苦相語
48 向者近出
為鷂所捕
賴我翻捷
體素便附
52 說我辨語
千條萬句
欺恐舍長
令兒大怖
56 我之得免
復勝於兔
自今徙意
莫復相妬

The sparrow hawk then relinquished the sparrow
And after a long time left.

Two sparrows met,
They seemed to be male and female.
They led each other into the brush,
And together they flew up a tree.
Then he recounted all that had happened,
Told the other of his hardship:
"Just now I went out near here
And was caught by a sparrow hawk.
I counted on the speed of my moves,
And I've always been glib and ingratiating.
I stated my arguments,
A thousand clauses, myriad phrases.
By being deceptive I may have abandoned my good points
And made you very afraid.
But since I was able to escape,
I'm after all better off than a rabbit.
From now change your opinion,
And never be suspicious of me again.

3.8 蝙蝠賦

吁何奸氣
生玆蝙蝠
形殊性詭
每變常式
行不由足
飛不假翼

明伏暗動
□□□□[1]

盡似鼠形
謂鳥不似
二足為毛
飛而含齒
巢不哺鷇
空不乳子

不容毛群
斥逐羽族
下不蹈陸
上不憑木

3.8 *Fu* on the Bat (fragment)

Geez! What fell pneuma
Makes these bats?
Strange in shape, weird in nature,
In all things they transmute the norm.
Walking they don't use feet,
Flying they don't employ wings.

They hide by day and move at night
. . . .

They look exactly like a rat in shape.
Call them birds? They're not the same:
Their two feet are hairy,
They fly but have teeth,
They don't feed fledglings in a nest,
They don't nurse young in a den.

They cannot stand the hairy horde,
They drive away the feathered tribe.
Below they do not tread on land,
Above they do not depend on trees.

---

1 The rhyming shows that some amount of text is missing here.

3.9 芙蓉賦

覽百卉之英茂
無斯華之獨靈
結脩根於重壤
泛清流而擢莖

竦芳柯以從風
奮纖枝之璀璨

其始榮也
皦若夜光尋扶木
其揚暉也
晃若九陽出暘谷
芙蓉蹇產
菡萏星屬
絲條垂珠
丹榮吐綠
焜焜韡韡
爛若龍燭
觀者終朝
情猶未足

3.9 *Fu* on the Lotus (fragment)

Looking at the lovely blossoms of all of the plants,
None compares with the unique magic of this flower.
They fasten long rhizomes in deep mud,
4 Floating on the clear current, thrust out their stems.

They lift up their fragrant stalks to catch the wind,
Raise the gleam and glitter of their slender sprigs.

When they first begin to bloom,
8 They are as candent as the moon seeking out the Fu Tree;
When they display their radiance,
They are as fulgent as the nine suns emerging from the Valley of the Sun.[1]
The blossomed lotuses bend and bow,
12 Those yet to blossom gather like stars.
The silky stamens dangle pearls,
The cinnabar-red blossoms send forth a greenery.[2]
Dazzling and glowing, gorgeous and glossy,
16 Glistening like candle dragons.[3]
Those looking at them spend a whole morning
And their interest is still not satisfied.

1 The mythical Fu Tree was located in the east by the Valley of the Sun and was the place from which the nine suns arose.

2 The "pearls" of line 11 are most likely anther appendages, while the "greenery" of line 12 refers to the seed pod.

3 A mythical creature that held a candle in its mouth. It may sometimes refer to a candleholder with a dragon motif.

於是
狡童媛女
20 相與同遊
擢素手於羅袖
接紅葩於中流

3.10 酒賦

余覽揚雄酒賦辭甚瑰瑋頗戲而不雅聊作酒賦粗究其終始賦曰

嘉儀氏之造思
亮茲美之獨珍
仰酒旗之景曜
4 協嘉號於天辰
穆生以醴而辭楚
侯嬴感爵而輕身
諒千鐘之可慕
8 何百觚之足云

1 Wine Pennant was a group of three stars representing the heavenly official in charge of wine.

2 Mu Sheng did not like wine 酒, so whenever Prince Yuan of Chu 楚元王 held a feast, he always served ale 醴 to Mu Sheng. But the prince's successor forgot about the previous arrangement and didn't serve him the ale. Mu Sheng took this as a slight and left the princedom.

Thereupon,
A raffish lad and pretty girl
Come drifting along together.
She extends a white hand from a gauze sleeve,
And takes a red flower from mid-stream.

3.10 *Fu* on Wine (fragment)

I have read Yang Xiong's [53 BCE–18 CE] "*Fu* on Wine." Its words are quite rare and precious, but it is too waggish and inelegant. For the time being, I have composed "*Fu* on Wine" to roughly delve into the ins-and-outs of the subject. The *fu* says:

Excellent, Master Yi's inventiveness!
Evident, the unique rarity of this delicious thing!
I look up to the bright shining of Wine Pennant,[1]
Finding confirmation of its admirable reputation in the asterism.
Mu Sheng took leave of Chu over ale,[2]
Hou Ying, out of gratitude for a cup, placed little value on his life.[3]
Truly, a thousand flagons is admirable,
But how is a hundred beakers worth mentioning?[4]

---

3 Hou Ying was a recluse in Wei 魏 in the Warring States period. He was 70 and poor and served as a gate guard at Yimen Gate 夷門 of Da Liang 大梁. Wuji 無忌, heard of him and, wanting to honor him, held a big feast, showing great deference to Hou Ying and offering him a toast for long life. Later Hou Ying presented Wuji with a plan to rescue Zhao 趙, which was surrounded by Qin 秦. Then, presumably out of loyalty to Wuji and to make sure the plan stayed secure, he committed suicide by cutting his own throat. It is this suicide that is meant by "placed little value on his life."

4 A passage in *Kongcongzi* 孔叢子 contains what it purports to be an old saying: "Yao and Shun could drink a thousand flagons of wine and Confucius a hundred beakers" 堯舜千鍾孔子百觚.

其味有□□亮沂
久載休名
宜城醪醴
蒼梧縹清
或秋藏冬發
或春醖夏成
或雲沸潮涌
或素蟻浮萍

爾乃
王孫公子
遊俠翺翔
將承歡以接意
會陵雲之朱堂
獻酬交錯
宴笑無方

於是
飲者並醉
縱橫歡嘩
或揚袂屢舞
或叩劍清歌
或顰噈辭觴

Its flavor has ...[1]
Long has it had a splendid reputation:
Yicheng's sweet ale,
Cangwu's light-green pure.[2]
Some are put by in autumn and ready in winter,
Some are fermented in spring and done in summer,
Some roil like clouds and surge like tides,
In some, white "ants" like floating duckweed.[3]

And then,
Young princes and lords –
These roving heroes wandering at whim –
Ready to be amusing in order to curry favor,
Assemble in a cloud-surmounting vermilion hall.
Host and guests pledge and toast back and forth,
Feasting and laughing without restraint.

Thereupon,
The drinkers all get drunk
And raise a racket all over the place,
Some wave their sleeves and dance over and over,
Some knock their swords and sing unaccompanied,
Some knit their brows and refuse a chalice,

---

1 There is an obvious problem with the text at this point that extends across editions. Not only is there a lacuna, the two words 亮沂 seem inexplicable, as noted by Yan Kejun, Zhao Youwen, and others.

2 Yicheng and Cangwu are place names, the first to the south of modern Yicheng in Hubei Province, and the latter in the southeastern part of modern Guangxi Province. A poem by Zhang Hua, who was born in the year Cao Zhi died, has these lines (in Wang Ping's translation): "Cangwu has Bamboo-leaf Pure, / Yicheng has Nine-brewed Ale" 蒼梧竹葉清 / 宜城九醖醝.

3 On the "ants," see **1.6**, line 35.

28 或奮爵橫飛
或歎驪駒既駕
或稱朝露未晞

於斯時也
質者或文
32 剛者或仁
卑者忘賤
窶者忘貧

於是
矯俗先生聞之而歎曰噫夫言何容易此乃淫荒之源非作者之事
若耽于觴酌流情縱逸先王所禁君子所斥

A [嗟麴蘖之殊味]

B [穆公酣而興霸
漢祖醉而蛇分]

1 This is an allusion to a farewell poem entitled "Black Colt" that was sung by departing guests and is supposed to have been one of the so-called "lost odes" from the *Classic of Poetry.*

Some hoist their cups and fly about wildly,
Some chant that the black colt is harnessed,[1]
Some declare the morning dew is not yet dry.[2]

At such a time,
The unsophisticated sometimes grow refined,
The intractable sometimes become humane,
The lowly forget their humble state,
The poor forget their poverty.

Thereupon,
Mr. Do-gooder heard this and sighed, saying, "Ai! What you say is way too slapdash!
This drinking is the root of debauchery and profligacy, and is not what a worthy person does. As to being addicted to drink and being as uninhibited as one wants, former rulers prohibited this, and it is what a gentleman condemns.

[Ah! The incomparable flavors of ferment and malt.][3]

[Duke Mu provided drink and was hegemon,
The Han Founder got drunk and the snake was cut in two.][4]

---

2 A *Classic of Poetry* poem (*Mao shi* 174/1) has these lines (in Bernhard Karlgren's translation): "Soaking is the dew, without the sun it will not dry; peacefully we drink in the night, without becoming drunk we do not go home" 湛湛露斯, 匪陽不晞. 厭厭夜飲, 不醉無歸.

3 These bracketed lines are appended to the *fu* by Ding. See *Additional Notes*.

4 These lines refer to two famous incidents. In the first, in the mid-seventh century BCE, Duke Mu of Qin lost a fine horse. It was found and eaten by a group of 300 men. When they were caught, rather than punishing them, Duke Mu provided them with wine and pardoned them. Later they came to his rescue when he was in distress. The second incident is even more famous. The Han dynasty founder Liu Bang 劉邦 (r. 206–19 BCE), also known by his temple name Gaozu 高祖, began his path to the Han throne when he was leading a band of conscript laborers to report for duty. Many had run away, so he decided to release the rest and go his own way. Some of the men stayed with him and they encountered a great snake in a swamp. Liu Bang, drunk at the time, drew his sword and cut the huge serpent in two.

C [和睚眥之宿憾
雖怨讎其必親]

D [敘嘉賓之歡會
惟耽樂之既闋
日晻暗於桑榆兮
命僕夫而皆逝]

E [安沉湎而為娛
非往聖之所述
闢酒誥之明戒
同元凶於三季]

3.11 槐賦

羨良木之華麗
爰獲貴於至尊
憑文昌之華殿
4 森列峙乎端門
觀朱榱以振條
據文陛而結根
暢沈陰以博覆

[It calms the long-standing resentments of those who stare angrily,
Even hated enemies may become close.]

[Speaking of the happy gathering of fine guests,
When their indulgence in pleasure has come to an end,
And the sun grows dark in mulberry and elm,
They order their drivers and all depart.]

[How can one wallow in wine to make merry,
Deny the teachings of former sages,
Repudiate the clear injunction of the "Proclamation on Alcohol,"[1]
And conform to the arch villains of the Three Ages?][2]

3.11 *Fu* on the Pagoda-tree (fragment)

I admire the resplendent beauty of these fine trees,
They are valued by the Most Revered.[3]
They verge on the magnificent palace of Wenchang,
4 Densely stand arrayed at its main gate.
Beholding the vermilion rafters, they lift up their branches;
Nearby the sculpted steps, they fasten their roots.
They unfurl deep shade to cover widely,

1 The second and third lines of E, with their references to the former sages and the "Proclamation on Alcohol" point to the *Hallowed Documents*. The "Proclamation on Alcohol" in that canonical work is China's oldest injunction against the use of alcoholic beverages.

2 The last line of E refers to the "bad last rulers" of the Xia, Shang, and Zhou dynasties: Jie 桀, Zhou 紂, and King You 幽王.

3 "Most Revered" here refers to Cao Cao.

似明后之垂恩
在季春以初茂
踐朱夏而乃繁
覆陽精之炎景
散流耀以增鮮

3.12 橘賦

有朱橘之珍樹
于鶉火之遐鄉
稟太陽之烈氣
嘉杲日之休光
體天然之素分
不遷徙于殊方

播萬里而遙植
列銅爵之園庭
背江洲之暖氣
處玄朔之肅清
邦換壤別
爰用喪生
處彼不雕
在此先零

Like our enlightened lord dispensing favor.[1]
In the last month of spring, they begin to flourish;
Reaching red-hot summer, they are lush.
They shield the blazing light of the essence of *yang*,[2]
Scatter the streaming radiance to enhance their sheen.

3.12 *Fu* on the Sourpeel Tangerine

There is a precious tree of vermilion tangerines,
In the far-off land of Quail Fire.[3]
It receives the great *yang*'s scorching heat,[4]
Delights in the glinting sun's lovely light.
Embodying its natural original attributes,
It does not move or migrate to different places.

Transported myriad *li* and planted far from home,
Set out in a courtyard of Bronze Bird Garden,
Turning away from the warm air of the islets of the Yangzi,
It lives in the austere chill of the dark north.
Its country changed, the soil different –
Thus it loses its life.
Living there it does not wither,
But in this place it perishes before its time.

1 Again, this refers to Cao Cao.
2 "Essence of *yang*" is the sun.
3 Quail Fire was the name of a Jupiter Station. In the system of astral-geography 分野, it is associated with the south.
4 The "great *yang*" is, of course, the sun.

朱實不啣
焉得素榮

惜寒暑之不均
嗟華實之永乖
仰凱風以傾葉
冀炎氣之所懷
颺鳴條以流響
晞越鳥之來棲

夫靈德之所感
物無微而不和
神蓋幽而易激
信天道之不訛
既萌根而弗幹
諒結葉而不華
漸玄化而弗變
非彰德於邦家
拊微條以嘆息
哀草木之難化

If the vermilion fruit will not be borne,
How shall we get the white flowers?

I regret that cold and heat are not balanced,
Sigh that its flower and fruit will always disoblige.
Looking up to balmy southern breezes it tilts its leaves,
Expecting the fiery air for which it longs;
It waves rustling branches to spread its sound,
Hoping a bird from Yue will come to roost.

Wherever numinous benevolence is felt,
There is nothing so small that it does not conform.
The spirit may be hidden but it is easily understood;
In truth the way of heaven does not deceive.
It sprouted roots but they will not support it,
It does form leaves but does not flower.
Immersed in profound influence, it still does not change,
And does not show off its merits in our realm.
I touch its thin branches and heave a sigh,
Grieve that plants and trees find adapting so hard.

3.13 述行賦

尋曲路之南隅
觀秦政之驪墳
哀黔首之罹毒
4 酷始皇之爲君
濯余身於神井
偉湯液之若焚

[恨西夏之不綱]

3.13 *Fu* Recounting a Journey (fragment)

I followed the southern fork of a winding road,
Viewed the Mount Li tomb of Zheng of Qin.[1]
I pity the way the black-haired ones encountered tragedy,[2]
Detest the way the First Emperor was as ruler.
I washed my body in its divine well;[3]
Extraordinary how the hot liquid is as though afire.

[I regret that western Xia is not under control.][4]

---

1 Zheng was the name of the First Emperor of Qin (r. 221–210 BCE), whose famous tomb is located just east of Xi'an at Mount Li.

2 "Black-haired ones" was the name the First Emperor of Qin applied to the populace. Cao Zhi is no doubt thinking about the cruelty and harshness associated with Qin rule when he speaks of tragedy, but more immediately he must have been considering the huge costs in conscripted labor and loss of resources borne by the people as a result of the construction of the First Emperor's mausoleum.

3 A tradition had it that the waters had curative powers.

4 This bracketed line appears by itself in a seventh-century commentary, where it is identified as coming from this *fu*. Xia here essentially means "China."

4.1 公宴

公子愛敬客
終宴不知疲
清夜游西園
飛蓋相追隨
明月澄清景
列宿正參差
秋蘭被長坂
朱華冒綠池
潛魚躍清波
好鳥鳴高枝
神飈接丹轂
輕輦隨風移
飄颻放志意
千秋長若斯

4.2 侍太子作

白日曜青天
時雨靜飛塵
寒冰辟炎景
涼風飄我身

https://doi.org/10.1515/9781501507038-002

Shi

4.1 Lord's Feast

The young lord cherishes and respects his guests;[1]
Throughout the feast he does not feel fatigue.
In the pristine night we tour West Garden,[2]
Our flying canopies follow each other.
The bright moon bathes us in its pristine rays,
The arrayed constellations now scatter-strewn.
Autumn thoroughwort blankets the long slopes,
Vermilion blossoms cover the green pond.
Submerged fish leap in the clear ripples;
Fine birds sing from high boughs.
A prodigious gust catches our cinnabar wheel-hubs,
And the light handcarts shift with the wind.
Wafted along we do as we please;
May a thousand autumns always be this way!

4.2 Seated in Attendance on the Heir Designate

The white sun glares in the azure sky,
Timely rain settles the flying dust.
Cold ice dispels the scorching sunlight,
A cool breeze blows against my body.

1 The "young lord" here is the poet's brother Cao Pi.
2 This was Bronze Bird Garden west of the Wenchang Palace in Ye.

清醴盈金觴
肴饌縱橫陳
齊人進奇樂
歌者出西秦
翩翩我公子
機巧忽若神

4.3 元會

初歲元祚
吉日惟良
乃爲佳會
讌此高堂
尊卑列敍
典而有章
衣裳鮮潔
黼黻玄黄
清酤盈爵
中坐騰光
珍膳雜遝
充溢圓方
笙磬既設
箏瑟俱張
悲歌厲響

Pure ale fills golden chalices,
Delicacies and choice dishes are arrayed at every turn.
Players from Qi offer wondrous music,
The singers come from western Qin.[1]
Graceful is our young lord,
Keen and clever as though divine.

4.3 New Year's Audience

The year's beginning commences good fortune,
The auspicious first day is nothing but perfect.
The court holds an elegant gathering,
And we feast in this lofty hall.
The high and low sit by rank;
By prescript there are protocols.
Upper and lower garments are fresh and immaculate,
Their zigzag and meander motifs are black and yellow.
Clear young ale fills the cups,
The eyes of the feasters sparkle with light.
Rare viands are chockablock,
They fill and overflow round and square vessels.
Once pipes and chimes are arranged,
The cithers and zitherns are set up.
The sad songs shrilly resound,

1 Early texts indicate that these states were noted for the quality of their performers. Their mention here is a form of praise for the banquet and its host.

16 咀嚼清商
俯視文軒
仰瞻華梁
願保茲喜
20 千載爲常
歡笑盡娛
樂哉未央
皇家榮貴
24 壽考無疆

4.4 送應氏（其一）

步登北邙坂
遙望洛陽山
洛陽何寂寞
4 宮室盡燒焚
垣牆皆頓擗
荊棘上參天
不見舊耆老
8 但覩新少年
側足無行徑
荒疇不復田
遊子久不歸
12 不識陌與阡

We ruminate on the pure *shang* mode.[1]
Looking down, we see patterned railings,
Looking up, we view ornate rafters.
We want to preserve this joy,
For a thousand years to be the norm.
Laughing merrily, we are wholly delighted;
Happy indeed! and not yet finished.
The imperial house is glorious and noble –
Long life without end!

4.4 Seeing off Mr. Ying, No. 1

Afoot I climb the slopes of Beimang;[2]
Afar I gaze on the hills of Luoyang.
Luoyang – how silent and still!
The palaces completely burned down.[3]
Fences and walls all collapsed and broken,
Thorns and brambles reach up to the sky.
I do not see any of the bygone elderly,
But only notice the new youths.
I step sideways, for there are no walkways;
The overgrown fields have not been tilled again.
The wanderer has not returned for such a long time
He no longer knows the field paths.

1 The *shang* mode of the pentatonic scale is associated with autumn and sadness.
2 Beimang is the name of the string of low hills north of Luoyang.
3 The destruction and neglect described in the poem are the result of the depredations of Dong Zhuo 董卓 (d. 192), who captured the city in 190 and soon razed it.

中野何蕭條
千里無人煙
念我平生親
16 氣結不能言

4.5 送應氏（其二）

清時難屢得
嘉會不可常
天地無終極
4 人命若朝霜
願得展嬿婉
我友之朔方
親昵並集送
8 置酒此河陽
中饋豈獨薄
賓飲不盡觴
愛至望苦深
12 豈不愧中腸
山川阻且遠
別促會日長
願爲比翼鳥
16 施翮起高翔

The countryside – how bleak and desolate!
For a thousand *li* no sign of man.
Thinking of those I was close to in life,
My breath chokes and I cannot speak.

4.5 Seeing off Mr. Ying, No. 2

Idyllic times are hard to come by often;
A happy gathering cannot last forever.
Heaven and earth have no end,
But human life is like a morning frost.
I hope I can express my tender affection,
For my friend is going to the northern quarter.
Relatives and friends gather together to see him off,
Set out wine here on the river's north bank.
The provisions are by no means meager,
But the guests drink without draining the chalices.
Where love is perfect, hope runs exceedingly deep:
How could I not feel ashamed in my innermost being?
The mountains and rivers are rugged and distant;
Parting hastens and our reunion is far off.
I wish that we were linked-wing birds,
Spreading our wings to rise and soar aloft.

4.6 雜詩

高臺多悲風
朝日照北林
之子在萬里
江湖迥且深
方舟安可極
離思故難任
孤煙飛南遊
過庭長哀吟
翹思慕遠人
願欲托遺音
形景忽不見
翩翩傷我心

4.7 雜詩（其二）

轉蓬離本根
飄颻隨長風
何意迴飈舉
吹我入雲中
高高上無極
天路安可窮
類此遊客子
捐軀遠從戎

4.6 Unclassified Poem, No. 1

On the high terrace there is much sad wind,
The morning sun shines on the northern woods.
That man is a myriad *li* away,
And the rivers and lakes are distant and deep.
How can my doubleboat reach all the way there?
Feelings of parting are surely hard to bear.
A lone wildgoose flies wandering south;
Passing the courtyard, it gives a long mournful cry.
I lift my head, worried, yearning for the one far away;
I wish to ask the wildgoose to convey a message.
But its silhouette suddenly disappears,
Its swift flight breaking my heart.

4.7 Unclassified Poem, No. 2

The tumbleweed leaves its native roots,
Whirling and swirling in ceaseless winds.
How could I know a whirlwind would rise
And blow me into the clouds?
Higher and higher, up without limit;
The road in the sky – how can one reach its end?
Like unto this is the wanderer,
Who lays down his life far away in the army.

毛褐不掩形
薇藿常不充
去去莫復道
沉憂令人老

4.8 雜詩（其三）

西北有織女
綺縞何繽紛
明晨秉機杼
日昃不成文
太息終長夜
悲嘯入青雲
妾身守空閨
良人從軍行
自期三年歸
今已歷九春
飛鳥遶樹翔
噭噭鳴索羣
願爲南流景
馳光見我君

Woolens and burlap don't cover his body,
Wild beans and bean leaves often are scarce.
Away, away, I'll say no more!
Such deep distress makes men old.

4.8 Unclassifed Poem, No. 3

In the northwest is a weaving woman,
Her tabby-weave and undyed silks – how profuse!
At daybreak she takes up the shuttle,
But when the sun declines, she has not completed a pattern.
She sighs heavily throughout the long night;
Her sad wailing enters the clouds in the blue.
"I keep to my empty chamber,
My good man has gone off to serve in the army.
He expected to return in three years,
Now it has already been nine springs.
A flying bird circles round the tree,
Calling dolefully seeking its flock.
I wish I were southward streaming rays,
Speeding like light to see my husband."

4.9 雜詩（其四）

南國有佳人
容華若桃李
朝遊江北岸
夕宿瀟湘沚
時俗薄朱顏
誰爲發皓齒
俯仰歲將暮
榮曜難久恃

4.10 雜詩（其五）

僕夫早嚴駕
吾行將遠遊
遠遊欲何之
吳國爲我仇
將騁萬里塗
東路安足由
江介多悲風
淮泗馳急流
願欲一輕濟
惜哉無方舟
閒居非吾志
甘心赴國憂

4.9 Unclassified Poem, No. 4

In a southern kingdom there is a lady fair,
The beauty of her countenance like peach and plum.
At daybreak she wanders the Yangzi's north bank,
In the evening she stays on an islet of the clear Xiang.
The taste of the time disdains a rosy face;
To whom will she reveal her gleaming teeth?
In no time the year draws to an end,
Radiant beauty is hard to rely on for long.

4.10 Unclassified Poem, No. 5

The driver hitches the carriage early,
I am about to travel afar.
Travel afar but where do I go?
The kingdom of Wu is our foe.
I shall gallop a trail of ten thousand *li*;
The eastern road – how is that worth taking?
Along the Yangzi there is much sad wind,
The Huai and Si run with swift currents.
I want to cross easily over at once,
A pity I have no doubleboat.
Staying idly at home is not my ambition,
I gladly hasten to respond to the kingdom's troubles.

4.11 雜詩（其六）

飛觀百餘尺
臨牖御櫺軒
遠望周千里
朝夕見平原
烈士多悲心
小人偷自閒
國讎亮不塞
甘心思喪元
撫劍西南望
思欲赴太山
弦急悲聲發
聆我慷慨言

4.12 喜雨

天覆何彌廣
苞育此羣生
棄之必憔悴
惠之則滋榮
慶雲從北來
鬱述西南征

4.11 Unclassified Poem, No. 6

The soaring gate-tower is over a hundred feet high,
I look down from a window, leaning on the latticed railing.
I gaze afar, a thousand *li* in all directions,
Morning and evening I watch the level plain.
A man of honor is often sad-hearted,
The enemies of the country are clearly unchecked,
While lesser men snatch leisure for themselves.
Willingly I intend to give up my head.
I stroke my sword and gaze southwest,
In my mind I want to go to Mount Tai.[1]
When the strings are tight, sad sounds emerge;
Hear my impassioned words.

4.12 Welcome Rain

Heaven's mantle – how vast and broad!
It enfolds and nourishes all of these living things.
If it abandons them, they must waste and wither;
If it favors them, then they grow and flourish.
Felicitous clouds came from the north,
Wreathing upwards and marching towards the southwest.

1 Mount Tai 泰山 is in modern Shandong province in eastern China. It is one of the Five Sacred Mountains 五嶽: Mount Tai in the east; Mount Hua 華山 in the west; Mount Heng 衡山 in the south; Mount Heng 恆山 in the north; and Mount Song 嵩山 in the center. Mount Tai is the holiest of these mountains. The sacrifices Emperor Wu made on Mount Tai in 110 B.C. were mainly to the Yellow Emperor, who was connected in the minds of the time with immortality, but here Cao Zhi is expressing his willingness to die.

時雨中夜降
8 長雷周我庭
喜種盈膏壤
登秋必有成

4.13 離友 （其一）

鄉人有夏侯威者、小有成人之風、余尚其爲人、與之昵好。王師振旅、送予於魏邦、心有眷然、爲之隕涕、乃作離友之詩。其辭曰、

王旅遊兮背故鄉
彼君子兮篤人綱
媵予行兮歸朔方
4 馳原隰兮尋舊疆
載車奔兮馬繁驤
涉浮濟兮泛輕航
迄魏都兮息蘭房
8 展宴好兮惟樂康

Welcome rain fell in the middle of the night,
Long peals of thunder encircled the courtyard.
Good seed fills the fertile soil,
In autumn there will surely be a crop.

4.13 Parting from a Friend, No. 1

Among the people from my native place is one Xiahou Wei. When he was young, he already had the air of an adult. I admire him as a person and am friendly with him. When the royal army withdrew, he escorted me to Ye. In my heart I did not wish to part from him, and shedding tears over him, I composed the poem "Parting from a Friend." Its words say:

The royal army, returning in triumph, left my hometown behind;[1]
That gentleman, devoted to human relationships,
Came along accompanying me to return to the North.
Galloping plains and lowlands, we made our way toward my old haunts;
The carriages raced headlong, the horses ran en masse.
Drifting across the River Ji, we floated on light boats;[2]
Reaching the capital of Wei, we rested in scented rooms,[3]
Set out a feast party and were happy and at ease.

1 His "hometown" was Qiao, in modern Bo county, Anhui province. It was not where he was born or where he lived, but it was considered his family's ancestral home.

2 The source of the River Ji was in modern He'nan province. The river ultimately flowed into the Yellow River. The route from Qiao, where Xihou Wei joined Cao Zhi, to Ye would have them cross the Ji on the way north.

3 The capital of Wei was Ye.

4.14 離友（其二）

涼風肅兮白露滋
木感氣兮條葉辭
臨淥水兮登重基
4 折秋華兮采靈芝
尋水歸兮贈所思
感離隔兮會無期
伊鬱悒兮情不怡

[日匿景兮天微陰
經迴路兮造北林]

4.15 應詔

肅承明詔
應會皇都
星陳夙駕
4 秣馬脂車

命彼掌徒
肅我征旅
朝發鸞臺
8 夕宿蘭渚
芒芒原隰

4.14 Parting from a Friend, No. 2

The chilly wind is harsh, white dew spreads;
The trees sense the air, leaves bid farewell to branches.
Looking out over the clear river, I climb a high mountain,
Break off autumn flowers, pick numinous mushrooms.
Since he will soon go home afar, I give them to the one I cherish.
I am moved by our parting and separation, no reunion in sight,
I feel depressed, and my mood is somber.

[The sun hides its light and the sky slightly darkens,
Passing along the road back, we reach the northern wood.][1]

4.15 Responding to an Edict

I respectfully received your wise edict,
And came in response to attend court in the imperial capital.
Beneath the starry array, I harnessed up early,
Fed the horses, greased the carriage.

I ordered the foreman
To alert my military escort.
At dawn I set out from Simurgh Terrace,
At dusk I halted at Thoroughwort Holm.[2]
Broad and boundless the plains and fens,

---

1 The lines in brackets may not be from this poem, and the poem itself is not in all editions of Cao's works. See *Additional Notes.*

2 These names are not meant to refer to real places, but such names serve two functions: they conjure up the distinctive nature of the emperor's lands; and, along with the dawn-and-dusk formula seen here, they recall the urgent quest for an understanding ruler undertaken by the poet-protagonist of the famous allegorical poem "Li sao" ("Encountering Sorrow").

祁祁士女
經彼公田
12 樂我稷黍

爰有樛木
重陰匪息
雖有餱糧
16 飢不遑食

望城不過
面邑不游
僕夫警策
20 平路是由

玄駟藹藹
揚鑣漂沫
流風翼衡
24 輕雲承蓋

涉澗之濱
緣山之隈
遵彼河滸
28 黃阪是階

Teeming with men and women.
Passing through those official fields,
12 I rejoiced at our foxtail millet and broomcorn millet.

And there were trees with down-curving branches,
But in their dense shade, I did not rest.
Although I had dried rations,
16 Even starving I had no time to eat.

I gazed at towns but did not go through them,
I faced toward cities but paid them no visit.
My driver used the whip,
20 The smooth roads, those we followed.

My team of four black horses was hale and hearty,
They strained at their bits and spewed foam.
The streaming wind buttressed the crossbar,
24 Light clouds held up the canopy.

We crossed over stream banks,
Skirted mountain bends,
Followed along the river's edge,
28 The loess slopes, those we climbed.

西濟關谷
或降或升
鋋驂倦路
載寢載興

將朝聖皇
匪敢晏寧
弭節長騖
指日遄征
前驅舉燧
後乘抗旌
輪不輟運
鸞無廢聲

爰暨帝室
稅此西墉
嘉詔未賜
朝覲莫從

仰瞻城閾
俯惟闕庭
長懷永慕
憂心如酲

Westward we traversed passes and valleys,
Now descending, now ascending.
When the team tired of travel,
We slept and rose again and again.

I was going to have an audience with the sage sovereign,
So I dared not be tranquil and calm.
If the pace slowed, we then galloped a long way;
Checking the itinerary, we hastened our journey.
The vanguard held torches,
The rear carriages hoisted banners.
The wheels never stopped turning,
The carriage bells never ceased ringing.

Reaching the imperial abode,
I stayed by the western wall.
A favorable edict has not yet been bestowed,
A court audience I cannot bring about.

Looking up I see threshold of the palace walls,
Looking down I contemplate the court.
Ever longing, ever yearning,
My worried mind is as though hungover.

4.16 贈徐幹

驚風飄白日
忽然歸西山
圓景光未滿
眾星燦以繁
志士營世業
小人亦不閒
聊且夜行遊
遊彼雙闕間
文昌鬱雲興
迎風高中天
春鳩鳴飛棟
流猋激櫺軒
顧念蓬室士
貧賤誠足憐
薇藿弗充虛
皮褐猶不全
慷慨有悲心
興文自成篇
寶棄怨何人
和氏有其愆

4.16 Presented to Xu Gan

A hard wind whirls away the white sun,
And it suddenly returns to the western hills.
The light of the radiant orb is not yet full,[1]
The sundry stars are sparkling and profuse.
The man of ambition strives for achievements for the ages,
Nor is a lesser man like me idle.[2]
For now, I go roaming in the night,
And roam between twin gate-towers.
Cultural Splendor rises like a dense cloud,
Windgreeter is as high as mid-sky.[3]
Spring doves coo among the towering ridgepoles,
Stray gusts buffet the latticed railing.
I think about that thatched hut scholar,
Poor and humble, truly worthy of pity.
Wild beans and bean leaves do not fill his emptiness,
Even his short leather coat is not whole.
Impassioned, he has a sad heart;
Moved to write, he completes his works for himself.
When a gem is rejected, who is to blame?
Mr. He made his mistakes.[4]

---

1 I.e., the moon.

2 The "man of ambition" in line 5 is Xu Gan.

3 The Palace of Cultural Splendor was the principal palace in Ye. Cao Zhi alludes to the Lodge of Greeting the Wind elsewhere in his works, but while the location of Cultural Splendor is indicated on reconstructed maps of Ye, it is not clear where in the city Windgreeter was located.

4 Lines 19–20 draw on the famous story of Bian He 卞和, who presented a piece of raw jade to his king. According to *Han Fei zi*, when He offered the jade to King Li of Chu, an expert said it was just a rock, and the king had He's left foot cut off. When the king died, He offered the jade to his successor. The jade was again not recognized for its worth, and he lost his right foot. Afterwards, he cried until he wept blood at the foot of the mountains, and when asked why, he replied, "It is not that I am sad because my feet have been amputated. I am sad because a precious jade is labeled a mere rock and a man of integrity is called a cheat." Only after the new, third king heard this was the jade polished and its great value revealed. In the poem, of course, Cao Zhi is likening Xu Gan to the jade and himself to Bian He, who initially failed in getting the jade recognized.

彈冠俟知己
知己誰不然
良田無晚歲
膏澤多豐年
亮懷璵璠美
積久德愈宣
親交義在敦
申章復何言

4.17 贈丁儀

初秋涼氣發
庭樹微消落
凝霜依玉除
清風飄飛閣
朝雲不歸山
霖雨成川澤
黍稷委疇隴
農夫安所獲
在貴多忘賤
為恩誰能博
狐白足禦冬
焉念無衣客
思慕延陵子

To flick the dust from your cap requires a good friend,[1]
Of your good friends, who is any different?
Good fields are not harvested late,
Enriching rain brings many bumper crops.
When one truly harbors the beauty of jade,
Over time his virtue stands out more.
A good friend's duty is to encourage;
Having presented this poem, what more can I say?

4.17 Presented to Ding Yí

Early autumn, cold air arises;
Courtyard trees faintly waste and wither.
Thick frost rests on jade-white steps;
Fresh breezes buffet the soaring gallery.
Morning clouds do not return to the mountains;
Incessant rains create rivers and marshes.
Broomcorn and foxtail millet lie abandoned in the fields;
How can the farmers harvest anything?
The noble mostly forget the lowly:
In practicing charity, who can do it all?
When your white fox furs suffice to stave off winter,
Would you be mindful of strangers lacking clothes?
I think of and admire Yanlingzi,

1 Flicking the dust from one's cap is a metaphor for taking up an official position.

寶劍非所惜
子其寧爾心
親交義不薄

4.18 贈王粲

端坐苦愁思
攬衣起西遊
樹木發春華
清池激長流
中有孤鴛鴦
哀鳴求匹儔
我願執此鳥
惜哉無輕舟
欲歸忘古道
顧望但懷愁
悲風鳴我側
羲和逝不留
重陰潤萬物
何懼澤不周
誰令君多念
自使懷百憂

Ungrudging of his precious sword.[1]
You may set your mind at rest:
6 Your close friend's loyalty is undiminished.

4.18 Presented to Wang Can

Sitting erect, I am troubled by sorrowful thoughts,
Gathering up my robe, I rise and wander west.[2]
The trees put forth their spring blossoms,
4 The clear pond stirs a steady current.[3]
In the middle is a lone mandarin duck
Mournfully calling in search of its mate.
I want to befriend this bird,
8 A pity I have no light craft!
I wish to go back but have forgotten the way I came;
When I look back, I feel only sorrow.
A sad wind soughs by my side,
2 Xihe goes and will not stay.[4]
But the layered clouds moisten all things:
Why fear their favor will not extend all around?
Who causes you to brood so much?
6 You make yourself harbor these hundredfold worries.

---

1 Yanlingzi is a name referring to Ji Zha 季札, who lived in the sixth century BCE and was the youngest son of the King of Wu. Accounts say that when Ji Zha passed through the state of Xu, the ruler of Xu greatly desired the precious sword that Ji Zha wore but didn't say anything. Ji Zha could see what was on the Xu ruler's mind but could not offer him the sword, because he was traveling as an envoy to the major state of Jin. He planned to give the sword to the Xu ruler on his way back. But by then the Xu ruler had died, so Ji Zha hung the sword on a tree in front of the Xu ruler's grave, then left. Because of this, there was a song in Xu that said, "Yanling Jizi did not forget old friends, / He took off a sword worth a thousand in gold and strung it by the tomb."

2 This is usually understood to mean that he goes to visit Ye's Western Garden.

3 This is probably a reference to the Xuanwu Reservoir in the Western Garden.

4 Xihe was the charioteer of the sun.

4.19 贈丁儀王粲

從軍度函谷
驅馬過西京
山岑高無極
涇渭揚濁清
壯哉帝王居
佳麗殊百城
員闕出浮雲
承露槩泰清
皇佐揚天惠
四海無交兵
權家雖愛勝
全國為令名
君子在末位
不能歌德聲
丁生怨在朝
王子歡自營
歡怨非貞則
中和誠可經

4.19 Presented to Ding Yí and Wang Can

Accompanying the army, we crossed Hangu;
Spurring our horses, we passed the western capital.[1]
Mountains and peaks were infinitely high;
The Jing and the Wei shown turbid and clear.[2]
O magnificent! this home of emperors and kings!
Its fine beauty exceeds a hundred cities.
The Round Gate-towers emerge from drifting clouds,
Dew collectors scrape Grand Clarity.[3]
The imperial assistant spreads celestial favor,[4]
And within the four seas there is no clash of arms.
Although a military tactician loves victory,
Taking a state in one piece makes a good name.
You are in low-ranking positions
And cannot extol his virtuous reputation.
Mr. Ding is resentful at court,
Master Wang is elated to make his own plans.
But elation and resentment are not the right standards;
Moderation and harmony truly can serve as a guide.

---

1 Hangu was the name applied in Han times to a strategic pass northeast of modern Tiemen county 鐵門縣, He'nan province. "Western capital" refers to the old Han capital at Chang'an.

2 Of the two rivers, the Jing runs muddy, and the Wei is clear.

3 "Grand Clarity" can be understood here simply to mean "high heaven." "Round Gate-towers" and the dew collectors both refer to structures built during the reign of Emperor Wu of Han (r. 140–87 BCE) at the Jianzhang Palace in Chang'an. The twin pylons of the Round Gate-towers were capped with bronze phoenixes and were said to be over one hundred fifty feet high. The dew collector was held aloft by a statue of an immortal atop a pillar. A pan held by the immortal, which contained a cup for collecting dew, was said to be over two hundred feet in diameter.

4 The "imperial assistant" is Cao Cao.

4.20 贈白馬王彪

黃初四年五月，白馬王、任城王與餘俱朝京師，會節氣。到洛陽，任城王薨。至七月，與白馬王還國。後有司以二王歸藩，道路宜異宿止，意毒恨之！蓋以大別在數日，是用自剖，與王辭焉，憤而成篇。

謁帝承明廬
逝將歸舊疆
清晨發皇邑
日夕過首陽
伊洛廣且深
欲濟川無梁
汎舟越洪濤
怨彼東路長
顧瞻戀城闕
引領情內傷

其二
大谷何寥廓
山樹鬱蒼蒼
霖雨泥我途
流潦浩從橫

4.20 Presented to Biao, Prince of Baima

In the fifth month of Huangchu 4 [223], the Princes of Baima and Rencheng and I all went to attend court at the capital and gather for [the ritual of welcoming] the solar term.[1] After we arrived in Luoyang, the Prince of Rencheng died. When it got to be the seventh month, the Prince of Baima and I were going to return to our princedoms together. But later someone in charge thought that we two princes returning to our fiefdoms should en route separately stop for the night, and in my mind, I deplored and resented it. Because our big parting was likely to be in a few days, I used these poems to unburden myself and bid farewell to the Prince with them. I wrote the poems out of anger.

I paid my respects to the emperor at Chengming Lodge,
And am about to return to my old realm.[2]
In the clear dawn, I set out from the imperial city,
At sunset I pass Mount Shouyang.
The Yi and the Luo are wide and deep,
I want to cross them but there's no bridge.
Going by boat, I pass over huge waves,
Complain that road east is long.
Looking back, I long for the gate-towers of the capital;
Craning my neck, my emotions are painful within.

II.
Grand Valley – how vast and empty!
The trees on its hillsides a mass of grey-green.
Incessant rain muddies my road,
And the runoff overflows all around.

1 Cao Biao (195–251) was Cao Zhi's younger half-brother. The Prince of Rencheng was Cao Zhi's elder brother Cao Zhang (d. 223). Welcoming the solar term (or seasonal ether) was a Han observance that was continued under the Wei. That year the Autumn's Beginning was on the twenty-fourth day of the sixth month (August 8, 223)

2 At the time, Cao Zhi was Marquis of Juancheng 鄄城.

中逵絕無軌
改轍登高崗
脩阪造雲日
我馬玄以黃

其三

玄黃猶能進
我思鬱以紆
鬱紆將何念
親愛在離居
本圖相與偕
中更不克俱
鴟梟鳴衡軛
豺狼當路衢
蒼蠅間白黑
讒巧令親疏
欲還絕無蹊
攬轡止踟躕

其四

踟躕亦何留
相思無終極
秋風發微涼

Crossroads are cut off and the track is gone,
So I change my route and climb a high ridge.
Its long slope reaches as far as the clouds and sun,
And my horses are dark and sallow.[1]

III.
Dark and sallow yet they still can go on,
But my thoughts are tangled with gloom.
Tangled with gloom – what is troubling me?
We loved ones are to stop in separate lodgings.
We originally planned to be alongside each other,
But things changed midway – we could not be together:
Owls hooted on the crossbar and yoke,
Dholes and wolves blocked the roads and thoroughfares,[2]
Blue flies debased black and white,
Slanderers and flatterers caused relatives to be estranged.
I want to go back but am cut off without a path;
Pulling the reins, I stop and hesitate.

IV.
Hesitate, but why tarry?
My longing for you has no end.
The autumn wind brings a slight chill,

---

1 This is an allusion to the *Classic of Poetry*: "I ascend that high ridge, / My horses are dark and sallow." The traditional interpretation is that "dark and sallow" means the dark (i.e., black) horses have turned sallow due to being afflicted with fatigue.

2 The owls and the dholes and wolves, like the flies in the next line, are metaphors for those who were hostile to Cao Zhi and spoke ill of him.

寒蟬鳴我側
原野何蕭條
白日忽西匿
歸鳥赴喬林
翩翩厲羽翼
孤獸走索群
御草不遑食
感物傷我懷
撫心長太息

其五

太息將何為
天命與我違
奈何念同生
一往形不歸
孤魂翔故域
靈柩寄京師
存者忽復過
亡歿身自衰
人生處一世
去若朝露晞
年在桑榆間
影響不能追

Cold cicadas chirr by my side.
How desolate the countryside!
The white sun suddenly hides in the west.
A returning bird heads for the tall woods,
Darting along, swiftly flapping its wings.
A lone beast scurries seeking its herd,
No time to eat the grass in its mouth.
Being moved by these things wounds me to the core;
Putting hand to heart, I heave a long sigh.

V.
Heave a long sigh, but for what?
Heaven's fate is against me.
Why dwell on my full brother?
Once gone a body does not return.
His lone soul soars to his old realm,
While his coffined remains stay on in the capital.
We survivors will quickly pass away as well;
Departed, the body naturally dissolves.
A human life inhabits just one age;
It goes like morning dew drying in the sun.
My years are at the time of mulberry and elm,[1]
Light and sound cannot keep pace.

1 "Mulberry and elm" signify evening or lateness in life. Two explanations for this usage exist. One is that the setting sun shines on the tops of the mulberry and elm trees. The other is that Mulberry and Elm were the names of two asterisms in the western sky between which the sun set.

自顧非金石
咄唶令心悲

其六
心悲動我神
棄置莫復陳
丈夫志四海
萬里猶比鄰
恩愛苟不虧
在遠分日親
何必同衾幬
然後展殷勤
憂思成疾疹
無乃兒女仁
倉卒骨肉情
能不懷苦辛

其七
苦辛何慮思
天命信可疑
虛無求列仙
松子久吾欺
變故在須臾

As I look on myself, neither metal nor stone,
In a gasp it makes my heart sad.

VI.
My heart being sad disturbs my spirit;
I'll dispense with this and tell no more.
A true man sets his mind on the world at large,
A myriad *li* is like his next-door neighbor.
If our loving affection does not diminish,
Though far apart our affection will daily grow closer.
What need to share a quilt and bedcurtains
Before extending earnest regard?
If anxious thoughts were to turn into illness,
Would not that be an adolescent infatuation?
Of a sudden such feelings of flesh and blood,
Can I not harbor bitter anguish?

VII.
In bitter anguish, what do I brood over?
Heaven's fate is truly untrustworthy.
Absurd to seek the various immortals,
Master Pine has long deceived us.[1]
Catastrophe lies a moment away,

1 This refers to the legendary immortal Master Red Pine.

百年誰能持
離別永無會
76 執手將何時
王其愛玉體
俱享黃髮期
收淚即長路
80 援筆從此辭

4.21 贈丁廙

嘉賓填城闕
豐膳出中廚
吾與二三子
4 曲宴此城隅
秦箏發西氣
齊瑟揚東謳
肴來不虛歸
8 觴至反無餘
我豈狎異人
朋友與我俱
大國多良材
12 譬海出明珠
君子義休偫
小人德無儲

Who can last a hundred years?
Once parted, we shan't meet for an eternity,
When are we ever going to clasp hands?
May you take care of your precious self
And both of us enjoy days of grizzled hair.
Stemming my tears, drawing near the long road,
I take up my brush and bid henceforth farewell.

4.21 Presented to Ding Yì

Fine guests fill the town,
Choice viands emerge from the central kitchen.
But I and a few others,
Feast privately in a nook of the city-wall.
A Qin cither sends forth a western air,
A Qi zithern performs an eastern song.
Delicacies come and don't go back for nothing;
Chalices arrive and return without a drop.
Why would I mingle with strangers?
Intimate friends are together with me.
Our great state has many talented men,
Just as the sea produces bright pearls.
A gentleman's decency is perfect and amply cached;
Lesser men have no reserves of virtue.

積善有餘慶
榮枯立可須
滔蕩固大節
世俗多所拘
君子通大道
無願為世儒

4.22 朔風

仰彼朔風
用懷魏都
願騁代馬
倏忽北徂
凱風永至
思彼蠻方
願隨越鳥
翻飛南翔

四氣代謝
懸景運周
別如俯仰
脫若三秋
昔我初遷
朱華未希

Amassing good deeds brings a surfeit of blessings,
Through ups and downs one can stand by and wait.
Magnanimously hold to what's most important –
Ordinary people are too bound by convention.
The gentleman comprehends the Great Way,
And has no desire to be an ordinary scholar.[1]

4.22 Boreal Wind

I lift my face to that boreal wind,
And, so, long for Wei's capital.
I yearn to gallop a horse from Dai[2]
And swiftly and speedily head north.
When balmy winds come from afar,
I long for that Man region,[3]
Yearn to follow a bird from Yue
And flittering and flying soar to the south.

The four seasons wane in turn,
And the suspended luminaries move in cycles.[4]
Parting was as sudden as a glance up and down,
But our separation has been like three autumns.
Back then when I was first transferred,
Vermilion blossoms were not yet scarce,

1 The term "ordinary scholar" is notably used by Wang Chong, who considers the work of those who compose their own works, or "literary scholars" 文儒, superior to that of ordinary scholars (common pedants), who discourse on the classics and sages.

2 Dai commandery was in the north of modern Shanxi province and was noted for producing good horses.

3 "Man region" means the South.

4 The sun and moon.

今我旋止
素雪云飛

俯降千仞
仰登天阻
風飄蓬飛
載離寒暑
千仞易陟
天阻可越
昔我同袍
今永乖別

子好芳草
豈忘爾貽
繁華將茂
秋霜悴之
君不垂眷
豈云其誠
秋蘭可喻
桂樹冬榮

絃歌蕩思
誰與銷愁

Now as I return,
White snow flies.

Downward descending a thousand fathoms,
Upward ascending a sky-high fastness,
Tossed by wind the tumbleweed flies,
Successively encountering cold and heat.
A thousand fathoms are easily climbed,
A sky-high fastness can be got over,
But from my close companions of former days,
Now forever parted.

You were fond of fragrant plants.
Would I forget to gift you some?
But just as the riotous blooms were about to peak,
Autumn frost withered them.
Though milord no more grants me kind concern,
How could I go back on my loyalty to him?
Autumn thoroughwort may serve as a metaphor,
Or the cinnamon tree's flowering in winter.

Singing to strings washes worry away,
But who will dispel sorrow with me?

臨川慕思
何為泛舟
豈無和樂
游非我憐
誰忘汎舟
愧無榜人

4.23 矯志

芳桂雖香
難以餌魚
尸位素餐
難以成居

磁石引鐵
於金不連
大朝舉士
愚不聞焉

抱璧途乞
無為貴寶
履仁遘禍
無為貴道

By the river, I pine and long –
Who will ply a boat for me?
Is there really no one to harmonize with?
My companions are not those I love.
Who would not think to take a boat?
I am ashamed I have no boatman.

4.23 Resolve

Sweet the smell of fragrant cassia,
But it's hard to bait a fish with it;
In a sinecure with unearned pay,
It's hard to establish a permanent household.

Lodestone attracts iron
But doesn't fasten to bronze;
Great courts appoint gentlemen,
But dullards are not known therein.

If holding a jade disc one begs by the road,
It will not be considered a valued treasure;
If by being humane one encounters disaster,
It will not be seen as a valued path.

鴛雛遠害
不羞卑棲
靈虯避難
不恥污泥

都蔗雖甘
杖之必折
巧言雖美
用之必滅

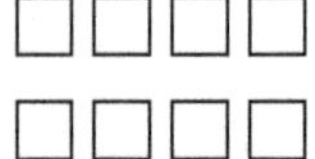
濟濟唐朝
萬邦作孚

逢蒙雖巧
必得良弓
賢主雖智
必得英雄

螗螂見嘆
齊士輕戰
越王軾蛙
國以死獻

The *yuanchu*-bird keeps far from harm,
It's not ashamed of humble roosts.
The numinous spirax avoids trouble,
It's not embarrassed by filthy mud.

Sugar cane may be sweet,
But a staff of it will surely break;
Glib words may be pretty,
But following them must lead to ruin.

. . . .
. . . .[1]
Imposing was the court of Tang,[2]
The myriad states trusted it.

Though Pengmeng was skilled,
He had to obtain a good bow.[3]
Though a sage ruler be wise,
He has to obtain outstanding men.

A mantis was praised,
And the soldiers of Qi looked lightly on war.[4]
The King of Yue bowed to a frog from his chariot,
And men offered their lives for the state.[5]

---

1 The rhyme scheme in Chinese shows that there must be at least two lines missing.

2 Tang is the legendary sage ruler Yao.

3 Pengmeng was a protégé of the mythical archer Yi 羿.

4 An anecdote says that Duke Zhuang of Qi 齊莊公 (r. 553–548 BCE) was out hunting when a praying mantis tried to grab the wheel of his chariot. He praised its bravery and backed up the chariot so as not to harm it. As a result, brave men flocked to his service.

5 A similar anecdote says that Goujian stood at his chariot's grab-bar and bowed to an angry frog in order to inspire a spirit of sacrifice in his soldiers for a coming battle with the state of Wu.

道遠知驥
世偽知賢
□□□□
□□□□

覆之幬之
順天之矩
澤如凱風
惠如時雨

口為禁闥
舌為發機
門機之闓
楛矢不追

4.24 閨情

攬衣出中閨
逍遙步兩楹
閒房何寂寥
綠草被階庭
空穴自生風
百鳥翩南征
春思安可忘

If the road is long, know your steed;
If the age is fraudulent, know the worthy.
. . . .
. . . .[1]

Overspreading, overlaying,[2]
Follow Heaven's norms.
Let favor be like a balmy wind,
Beneficence like a timely rain.

The mouth is a palace door,
The tongue is a crossbow trigger.
Once door and trigger are pulled open,
The thornwood arrow cannot be recalled.

4.24 Boudoir Feelings, No. 1

Gathering up my robe, I leave the inner apartments,
Wander between two pillars.
The vacant rooms, how silent and still!
Green grass blankets steps and courtyard.
Spaces and gaps naturally bring on a breeze,
All the birds soar migrating south.
Spring thoughts, how can they be forgotten?

---

1 There must be at least two lines missing here. See *Additional Notes*.

2 This line alludes to a passage in "On the Practice of the Mean" 中庸 that speaks to the all-encompassing nature of Heaven.

憂戚與君并
佳人在遠道
妾身單且煢
歡會難再逢
芝蘭不重榮
人皆棄舊愛
君豈若平生
寄松為女蘿
依水如浮萍
齎身奉衿帶
朝夕不墮傾
儻願終顧盼
永副我中情

4.25 閨情（其二）

有一美人
被服纖羅
妖姿豔麗
蓊若春華
紅顏韡曄
雲髻嵯峨
彈琴撫節
爲我弦歌

My cares and worries are the same as yours.
My good man is on a distant road,
While I am alone and unaided.
A happy reunion will be hard to chance on again –
Thoroughwort and angelica do not bloom twice.
Men always spurn old loves,
How could you remain as you used to be?
I was the lichen attached to the pine,
Like duckweed floating on water.
I devoted myself to you, attended to your collar and sash –
Morning and evening they did not sag or slant.
If you wish always to regard me fondly,
It will forever match my truest feelings.

4.25 Boudoir Feelings, No. 2

There is a beautiful woman,
Dressed in sheer gauze.
Her enchanting appearance and seductive beauty
As lush as springtime blossoms.
Her rosy face is radiant and striking,
And her cloud-like chignon juts upward.
She plucks the zither and beats the time,
Plays and sings for me.

清濁齊均
既亮且和
取樂今日
遑恤其他

4.26 三良

功名不可為
忠義我所安
秦穆先下世
三臣皆自殘
生時等榮樂
既沒同憂患
誰言捐軀易
殺身誠獨難
攬涕登君墓
臨穴仰天歎
長夜何冥冥
一往不復還
黃鳥為悲鳴
哀哉傷肺肝

The clear and turbid sounds are balanced,
Are both bright and harmonious.
Enjoying myself on this day,
How can I worry about other things?

4.26 Three Good Men

"Merit and fame cannot be made,
Loyalty and duty are what content us."
Duke Mu of Qin departed the world first,
Then three subjects all slew themselves.[1]
While he lived, they were equal in glory and joy;
Once he died, they shared grief and suffering.
Who says sacrificing one's life is easy?
To kill oneself is truly hard.
Shedding tears, I ascend your tumulus,
Approaching the vault, look to Heaven and sigh.
That eternal night, how dark, dark!
Once gone, we never come back.
The yellow bird sadly calls for them,
Alas! It wounds my innermost heart.

1 This poem was inspired by an event that took place in 620 BCE. Duke Mu of Qin died that year, and, according to one account, one hundred seventy-seven people went to their deaths with him, including the Three Good Men, who committed suicide out of a sense of obligation. The *Classic of Poetry* poem (*Mao shi* 131) "Yellow Bird," or "Oriole" 黄鳥, is supposed to have been composed to mourn them.

4.27 責躬（有表）

臣植言：臣自抱釁歸藩，刻肌刻骨。追思罪戾，晝分而食，夜分而寢。誠以天網不可重罹，聖恩難可再恃。竊感相鼠之篇，無禮遄死之義。形影相弔，五情愧赧。以罪棄生，則違古賢夕改之勸；忍垢苟全，則犯詩人胡顏之譏。伏惟陛下德象天地，恩隆父母，施暢春風，澤如時雨。是以不別荊棘者，慶雲之惠也；七子均養者，鳲鳩之仁也；舍罪責功者，明君之舉也；矜愚愛能者，慈父之恩也。是以愚臣徘徊於恩澤而不敢自棄者也。前奉詔書，臣等絕朝，心離志絕，自分黃耇永無執圭之望。不圖聖詔，猥垂齒召。至止之日，馳心輦

4.27 Blaming Myself (with memorial)[1]

Your servant Zhi states:

From the time that I returned to my fief bearing my guilt, it has been engraved upon my flesh and bones. When I recall my crimes, it is noon before I can eat and midnight before I can sleep. I honestly realize that I cannot again run afoul of the laws of the state; it would hardly be possible to rely on your sage mercy again. Your subject is sensible of the poem "See the Rat" – the implication that one who lacks propriety should quickly die.[2] My form and shadow commiserate with each other, and my five emotions blush with shame. If because of my crime, I forfeit my life, then I violate the injunction of the ancient worthy to "reform in the evening;" if I endure disgrace and somehow or other preserve my life, then I risk the poet's ridicule "What face!"[3] In my humble opinion, Your Majesty's beneficence is like Heaven and Earth, Your kindness surpasses that of a father and mother; Your goodwill flows as freely as the spring wind; Your generosity is like timely rain. Therefore, not discriminating against thorns and brambles, such is favor of felicitous clouds; nurturing equally its seven chicks, such is the benevolence of the cuckoo;[4] pardoning offenses and demanding performance, such is the behavior of an enlightened ruler; pitying ignorance and cherishing ability, such is the kindness of an affectionate father. Therefore, this ignorant servant is one who lingers on in your kindness and generosity and does not dare to give up on himself. Formerly, when

1 The memorial and poem, as well as poem **4.15**, are addressed to Cao Pi, who was emperor of Wei. They were written in the fourth year of the Huangchu reign period (223).

2 This is an allusion to lines from a *Classic of Poetry* poem (*Mao shi* 52/3): "See the rat, it has limbs. / A man without propriety, / A man without propriety, / Why doesn't he hurry up and die" 相鼠有體，人而無禮，人而無禮，胡不遄死.

3 Confucius' disciple Zengzi must be the "ancient worthy" Cao Zhi had in mind. Zengzi is reported to have said, "If someone errs in the morning but corrects it in the evening, then praise him; if someone errs in the evening but corrects it in the morning, then praise him." It is not as clear what might have been the source for the words "What face! "

4 This is an allusion to these lines from another *Classic of Poetry* poem: "The cuckoo in the mulberry / Has seven chicks." The commentary to these lines says that the cuckoo treats all of its chicks equally.

轂。僻處西館，未奉闕庭。踊躍之懷，瞻望反側，不勝犬馬戀主之情。謹拜表，並獻詩二首。詞旨淺末，不足采覽，貴露下情，冒顏以聞。臣植誠惶誠恐，頓首頓首，死罪死罪。

於穆顯考
時惟武皇
受命于天
4 寧濟四方
朱旗所拂
九土披攘
玄化滂流
8 荒服來王

超商越周
與唐比蹤
篤生我皇
12 奕世載聰

I received the edict that Your servant and the others were cut off from court, the heart went out of me and my will was broken.[1] I thought that until I was old and gray I would have no hope of holding a scepter of office. I did not expect that an imperial edict would come down to appoint me to official rank. From the day I arrived and halted in the capital, my heart has sped toward Your Highness. I am residing isolated in the west mansion and have not yet attended court. With a leaping and throbbing heart, I peer out and toss and turn. I am unable to contain my feelings, which are like those of a dog or horse for its master. I respectfully submit this memorial and at the same time present two poems. The words and import are shallow and trivial, and they are not worth selecting and reading closely. But I value expressing my lowly feelings, and I will risk Your displeasure to make them known to you. Your servant Zhi is truly terrified, truly afraid. I knock my head on the ground, I knock my head on the ground. I deserve death, I deserve death.

O, august our illustrious father,
This was the Martial Emperor.[2]
He received the mandate from Heaven,
Pacified and assisted the four quarters.
Where his vermilion flags waved,
The nine lands were swept clear.[3]
His profound influence spread extensively,
The wild zones came to pay allegiance.

He surpassed Shang and exceeded Zhou,
Matched Tang stride for stride.[4]
Blesséd born was our sovereign:
A sequent generation again astute.[5]

1 Cao Zhi is referring here in particular to his brothers Cao Zhang and Cao Biao, who were also sent away from court.

2 Cao Cao is the "illustrious father" and "Martial Emperor."

3 On the vermilion flags, see **1.1**, line 11.

4 Shang and Zhou are the dynasties by those names. Tang is the legendary ruler Yao.

5 Beginning with line 11, the poem shifts from praising Cao Cao to praising Cao Pi. The sense of line 12 is that both Cao Cao and Cao Pi were intelligent.

武則肅烈
文則時雍
受禪于漢
君臨萬邦

萬邦既化
率由舊則
廣命懿親
以藩王國

帝曰爾侯
君茲青土
奄有海濱
方周于魯
車服有輝
旗章有敘
濟濟雋乂
我弼我輔

伊予小子
恃寵驕盈
舉挂時網
動亂國經

In matters of war, he is solemn and intense;
In matters of culture, he is harmonious and concordant.
He received the abdication of the Han,
Governed as ruler the myriad states.

The myriad states having been transformed,
He follows the old rules.
He broadly ordered excellent kinsmen
To be a fence for his royal realm.

The Emperor said, "You, Marquis,
Rule this land of Qing,[1]
Completely covering the ocean shore,
Just the way Zhou was to Lu."[2]
My conveyances and clothing were resplendent,
My flags and ensigns had my rank.
Clustered were the virtuous and talented:
My aides and my assistants.

I, the little child,
Presumed on favor, was arrogant and complacent.
My behavior violated the ordinances of the time,
My actions disrupted the laws of the state.[3]

---

1 Qing refers to Qingzhou, in what is now northeastern Shandong. Its administrative seat was Linzi. Cao Zhi was appointed Marquis of Linzi in 214, but Cao Pi reappointed him and reassigned him to live there.

2 The Duke of Zhou, brother of the Zhou dynasty founder and himself one of the great icons of Chinese history, was the titular founder – a son of his was the actual founder – of the state of Lu. Like Qingzhou, Lu was in the Shandong region. Cao Zhi is drawing on the historical parallel offered by an important member of the Zhou ruling family having been installed in the Shandong region.

3 It is probable that lines 29–32 refer to an incident in 217 in which Cao Zhi got drunk and rode his carriage down the roadway that was reserved for the ruler's use and went out the Major's Gate, which was also reserved for the ruler. This greatly angered his father Cao Cao.

作藩作屏
先軌是隳
傲我皇使
犯我朝儀

國有典刑
我削我黜
將置于理
元凶是率

明明天子
時惟篤類
不忍我刑
暴之朝肆
違彼執憲
哀予小子

改封兗邑
於河之濱
股肱弗置
有君無臣
荒淫之闕
誰弼予身

I served as a fence, served as a screen,
But the former rules, those I destroyed.
I spurned my imperial envoy,
And violated my court etiquette.

The state has statutory punishments:
My benefice was reduced, I was demoted in rank.
I was about to be sent before the judge;
Major felon, thus was I classed.

The wise and perceptive Son of Heaven,
He was generous to his kind.
He could not bear my being punished,
To expose my corpse in court or market.
He went against those who enforce the laws,
Pitied me, the little child.

He changed my benefice to the seat of Yan,
On the banks of the Yellow River.[1]
Of trusted aides, none were provided;
I was a lord without officials.
With my fault of profligate excess,
Who was there to keep me straight?

---

1 Lines 29–56 deal with an incident in the second year of the Huangchu period that almost cost Cao Zhi his life. He got drunk and was insolent to the official who had been specifically assigned to watch him. Cao Zhi was sent to Luoyang, and seems only to have escaped death when his mother intervened with Cao Pi to save his life. His enfeoffment was soon changed to Marquis of Juancheng, which was in Yan. See the "Introduction," p. xxiv.

煢煢僕夫
于彼冀方
嗟予小子
乃罹斯殃

赫赫天子
恩不遺物
冠我玄冕
要我朱紱

光光大使
我榮我華
剖符授玉
王爵是加

仰齒金璽
俯執聖策
皇恩過隆
祗承怵惕

咨我小子
頑凶是嬰
逝慚陵墓
存愧闕庭

Alone and unaided,
I went to that land of Ji.
O, I, the little child,
Thus met this disaster.[1]

Illustrious and grand the Son of Heaven,
His kindness neglects no creature.
He capped me with a black official cap,
Placed vermilion ribbons about my waist.

Radiant was the great envoy,
I was granted honor, I was granted glory.
He split a tally, bestowed a jade;
The rank of prince, this was conferred.

Looking up, I accepted a metal seal;
Looking down, I held an imperial patent.
The sovereign's kindness was more than generous,
I received it respectfully, trembling with fear.

Ah, I, the little child,
Stubbornness and wickedness, these enmesh me.
To the departed, I am ashamed before his tumulus;
To the living, I am embarrassed before his court.

1 Lines 49–56 concern yet another time in the second year of Huangchu that Cao Zhi was in serious trouble. No record of this is found in his biography in the *Records of the Three States*, so the present memorial and poem, along with a command (*ling* 令) he wrote are the only sources. He was apparently accused by the officials Wang Ji and Cang Ji on specious charges and had to go to Luoyang again for adjudication. He was cleared and allowed to return to his benefice.

匪敢傲德
實恩是恃
威靈改加
76 足以沒齒

昊天罔極
生命不圖
常懼顛沛
80 抱罪黃壚

願蒙矢石
建旗東嶽
庶立毫氂
84 微功自贖

危軀授命
知足免戾
甘赴江湘
88 奮戈吳越

天啟其衷
得會京畿
遲奉聖顏

I dare not disdain Your beneficence,
For in truth I have relied on your kindness.
Your awesome sagacity has changed my fief and raised my rank,
And this will suffice till the end of my days.

Vast heaven has no bounds,
Human fate cannot be predicted.
I have always feared dropping dead,
And bearing my guilt to the yellow soil.

I wish to brave arrows and stones,
To plant our flag on the Eastern Peak.
I hope to establish some trifling merit,
The smallest deed to redeem myself.

I would endanger my body, offer up my life,
Content to have avoided punishment.
I would gladly go to the Jiang and Xiang,
Brandish a dagger-ax in Wu and Yue.

Heaven opened up Your innermost heart,
And I have obtained an audience in the capital domain.
I look forward to attending upon your sage countenance,

如渴如飢
心之云慕
愴矣其悲
天高聽卑
皇肯照微

4.28 情詩

微陰翳陽景
清風飄我衣
游魚潛綠水
翔鳥薄天飛
眇眇客行士
徭役不得歸
始出嚴霜結
今來白露晞
遊子嘆黍離
處者歌式微
慷慨對嘉賓
悽愴內傷悲

As though thirsting, as though starving.
How my heart yearns –
Despondent in its sadness.
Heaven is high yet hears the lowly,
The sovereign agrees to regard the humble.

4.28 Love Poem

A light overcast veils the sunlight,
A fresh breeze ruffles my clothes.
Swimming fish lie low in green water,
Soaring birds fly close to heaven.
Far, far away the wayfaring man;
On distant service, unable to return.
When first he left, severe frost had formed;
Now the white dew has dried.
The wanderer chants the poem "The Millet Hangs,"
The one at home sings the poem "No Use."[1]
With brave forbearance I face my fine guests;
Heartsore and heartsick, inside I am grieved and sad.

1 These two lines refer to *Shi jing* poems. "The Millet Hangs" is the lament of a careworn person incessantly on the move. On "No Use," see **1.10**.

4.29 妬

嗟爾同衾
曾不是志
寧彼冶容
安此妒忌

4.30 芙蓉池

逍遙芙蓉池
翩翩戲輕舟
南揚棲雙鵠
北柳有鳴鳩

4.31 雜詩

悠悠遠行客
去家千餘里
出亦無所之
入亦無所止
浮雲翳日光
悲風動地起

4.29 Jealousy (fragment)

Ah, you shared a quilt with me,
But you never remember this.
Instead of those attractive looks,
Whence this jealousy and spite?

4.30 Lotus Pond (fragment)

Carefree at the Lotus Pond,
Skimming along, having fun on a light boat.
By a poplar to the south, a pair of roosting swans;
On a willow to the north there is a calling dove.

4.31 Unclassified Poem

On and on, the long-distance traveler,
A thousand *li* and more from home.
When he leaves, he has nowhere to go;
When he comes, he has nowhere to stop.
Drifting clouds screen the sunlight,
Sad winds rise and shake the ground.

4.32 雜詩

美玉生磐石
寶劍出龍淵
帝王臨朝服
秉此威百蠻
□□歷見貴　[歷久不見貴]
雜糅□刀閒　[雜糅刀劍間]

4.33 言志

慶雲未時興
雲龍潛作魚
神鸞失其儔
還從燕雀居

4.32 Unclassified Poem (fragment)

Fine jade is born from slabs of stone,
A precious sword comes from Dragon Pool.[1]
If an emperor or king wears it to court,
Grasping this will awe the hundred Man.[2]
For a long time it has not been valued,
Is mixed among nondescript sabers and swords.

4.33 Stating My Aims (fragment)

Felicitous clouds have not arisen on time,
The cloudy dragon remains submerged feigning a fish.[3]
The divine simurgh has lost its kind,
And instead dwells with swallows and sparrows.

1 Dragon Pool is a place name here, but it was also the name of a famous sword in antiquity. It appears as such in Cao Zhi's famous "Letter to Yang Dezu" 與楊德祖書, and it also appears in earlier texts. The place known as Dragon Pool, or Dragon Springs 龍泉, in Xiping 西平 of Runan 汝南 had water that was good for tempering sabers and swords to make them hard and sharp.

2 "Hundred Man" is a term applied to non-Chinese peoples of the south.

3 Dragons were said to ride on clouds, and a submerged, or hidden, dragon became a metaphor for the worthy man whose talents were not being used in government.

4.34 七步詩

煮豆燃豆萁
漉豉以為汁
本是同根生
相煎何太急

4.35 離別詩

人遠精神近
寤寐夢容光

4.36 失題

雙鶴俱遨游
相失東海傍
雄飛竄北朔
雌驚赴南湘
棄我交頸歡
離別各異方
不惜萬里道
但恐天網張

4.34 Poem in Seven Paces

Boil beans by burning beanstalks,
Strain fermented beans to make a juice.
Beanstalks burn beneath the pot,
Beans in the pot weep,
We are born from the same root,
Why such hurry us to fry?[1]

4.35 Parting (fragment)

The man is far away but his spirit is near,
Awake or asleep, I dream of the radiance of his face.

4.36 Title Lost

A pair of cranes roamed together,
They lost each other by the eastern sea.
The male flew off and hid in the boreal north,
The female was frightened and hastened to the southern Xiang.
Forsaking our pleasure from crossing necks,
We part, each in a different direction.
I do not begrudge the myriad *li* road,
I only fear the spreading of the heavenly net.[2]

---

1 This poem is not authentic. Its first appearance is in *A New Account of Tales of the World* 世說新語, a work of the fifth century, where it is embedded in this anecdote: "Emperor Wen [Cao Pi] once ordered the King of Dong'e [Cao Pi] to compose a poem in the time it took to walk seven paces. Should he not complete it, the death penalty would be carried out. Immediately in response, he composed this poem [the poem quoted at this point differs slightly from the one above]. The emperor had a profoundly embarrassed expression."

2 "Heavenly net" may be understood to refer to the authority of the royal court.

5.1 箜篌引

置酒高殿上
親友從我遊
中廚辦豐膳
烹羊宰肥牛
秦箏何慷慨
齊瑟和且柔
陽阿奏奇舞
京洛出名謳
樂飲過三爵
緩帶傾庶羞
主稱千金壽
賓奉萬年酬
久要不可忘
薄終義所尤
謙謙君子德
磬折何所求
驚風飄白日
光景馳西流
盛時不再來
百年忽我遒
生存華屋處

https://doi.org/10.1515/9781501507038-003

Yuefu

5.1 Harp Lay

We hold a feast in a high hall,
And kith and kin join me in pleasure.
The inner kitchen prepares bountiful foods –
Boils a sheep, slays a fatted calf.
How impassioned the Qin cither!
Gentle and soft the Qi zithern.
Yang'e performs a marvelous dance,[1]
From capital Luo come famous songs.
Happily drinking, we exceed three beakers;[2]
Loosening our belts, we devour the many delicacies.
The host presents a thousand in gold,
The guests reply with a toast for long life.
Old friends may not be forgotten:
To let them down in the end is what loyalty condemns.
Modesty is the virtue of the princely man:
He seeks nothing by bowing humbly.
A hard wind whirls away the white sun,
And daylight speeds on its westerly course.
The prime of life does not come twice,
Within a century we suddenly come to an end.
When alive, we dwell in splendid homes,

---

1 Yang'e is a name associated with accomplished dancing. Since here it seems to refer to a place, in parallel with "capital Luo" in the next line, it likely alludes to Flying Swallow Zhao (Zhao Feiyan 趙飛燕, d. 1 CE), a beautiful singer and dancer who rose to be an empress. Her biography says that when Emperor Cheng 成帝 (r. 33–7 BCE) of the Han dynasty first saw her, she was in the household of the princess of Yang'e, where she had studied voice and dance.

2 The reference to exceeding three cups stems from a custom reflected in canonical texts that held three drinks to be the most one should have at such an event. Exceeding that number, of course, means that the feasters were enjoying themselves a great deal.

零落歸山丘
先民誰不死
24 知命復何憂

5.2 野田黃雀行

高樹多悲風
海水揚其波
利劍不在掌
4 結友何須多
不見籬間雀
見鷂自投羅
羅家得雀喜
8 少年見雀悲
拔劍捎羅網
黃雀得飛飛
飛飛摩蒼天
12 來下謝少年

5.3 七哀

明月照高樓
流光正徘徊
上有愁思婦
4 悲歎有餘哀

When we fall, we go to hilly graves.
Who in the past did not die?
Knowing fate, why worry any longer?

5.2 Ballad of the Sparrow in the Field

Tall trees abound with sad wind,
Ocean waters stir up their waves.
If a sharp sword is not in one's hand,
What is the need to make many friends?
Have you not seen sparrows in the hedge,
On seeing a sparrow hawk cast themselves into a bird-net?
The bird-netter is happy to get the sparrows,
A youth is sad to see the sparrows.
He draws his sword and cuts the net;
The sparrows get to fly, to fly.
To fly, to fly, and touch blue sky,
Coming back down to thank the youth.

5.3 Seven Sorrows

The bright moon shines on the tall pavilion,
Its streaming light lingers there.
Upstairs there is a wife with cheerless thoughts;
Her sorrowful sighs overflow with grief.

借問歎者誰
言是宕子妻
君行踰十年
8 孤妾常獨棲
君若清路塵
妾若濁水泥
浮沈各異勢
12 會合何時諧
願為西南風
長逝入君懷
君懷良不開
16 賤妾當何依

5.4 鬭雞

遊目極妙伎
清聽厭宮商
主人寂無爲
4 衆賓進樂方
長筵坐戲客
鬭雞觀閒房
羣雄正翕赫
8 雙翹自飛揚
揮羽激流風

May I ask, "Who is the one sighing?"
They tell me this is a wanderer's wife.
"My lord has been gone for over ten years,
And I, his unworthy handmaid, have always roosted alone.
My lord is like the dust of a clean path,
His handmaid is like the mud of turbid water.
Floating and sinking, each a different state;
On our reunion – when will we agree?
I wish I were a southwest wind,
Going a long way and entering your bosom.
If your bosom is not truly open,
On what shall your lowly handmaid rely?"

5.4 Cockfight

Roving eyes have perused all the marvelous dancers;
Keen hearing is sated with musical notes.
The host is silent, with nothing to do,
So the guests all offer a way to have fun.
Long bamboo mats seat the revelers
As they watch cockfights in a lateral room.
The flock of roosters are in a rage,
Their twin tail-feathers instinctively fly up.
Their beating wings stir up a brisk breeze,

悍目發朱光
觜落輕毛散
嚴距往往傷
長鳴入青雲
扇翼獨翱翔
願蒙狸膏助
長得擅此場

5.5 升天行（其一）

乘蹻追術士
遠之蓬萊山
靈液飛素波
蘭桂上參天
玄豹游其下
翔鶤戲其巔
乘風忽登舉
彷彿見眾仙

Their jutting eyes emit vermilion light.
Beaks fall and light feathers scatter,
Grim spurs wound again and again.
A long crow enters the clouds in the blue,
Fanning its wings a single bird struts about.
It wishes to receive raccoon-dog grease,[1]
And forever be able to dominate this pit.

5.5 Ascending to Heaven, No. 1

Sandal-borne, I seek the mages,[2]
Go afar to Mount Penglai.[3]
Numinous liquid flies from whitecaps,
Magnolia and cinnamon trees rise up and touch the sky.
Black leopards roam beneath them,
Soaring *kun*-fowl sport in their tops.[4]
Mounting the wind, I suddenly ascend and rise,
And dimly see the immortal throng.

---

1 Smearing raccoon-dog grease on a gamecock's head was thought to give it an advantage in a fight, apparently because it would intimidate a rival rooster.

2 "Sandal-borne" 乘蹻 was the term for a Daoist method of magical flight.

3 For Penglai, see **5.25**, line 6.

4 The *kun* is difficult to identify. It is often said to be a large bird akin to a swan or a crane. Sometimes it is said to be a kind of stork.

5.6 升天行（其二）

扶桑之所出
乃在朝陽谿
中心陵蒼昊
4 布葉蓋天涯
日出登東乾
既夕沒西枝
願得紆陽轡
8 回日使東馳

5.7 仙人篇

仙人攬六著
對博太山隅
湘娥拊琴瑟
4 秦女吹笙竽
玉樽盈桂酒
河伯獻神魚
四海一何局
8 九州安所如
韓終與王喬

---

1 On the Fusang tree, see **2.4**, lines 7–8.

2 The Fusang tree is normally associated with a place called Thermal Valley (Tang gu 湯谷), which appears together with it in the *Classic of Mountains and Seas.* The Gorge of the Rising Sun is mentioned in a nearby passage in the same book.

5.6 Ascending to Heaven, No. 2

The place where the Fusang grows,[1]
Is indeed the Gorge of the Rising Sun.[2]
Its central trunk climbs into the bright cerulean sky,
And its spreading leaves cover the ends of the earth.
When the sun comes out, it ascends the eastern bole;
When night falls, it sinks to a western limb.
I wish I were able to twist daylight's reins,
Turn round the sun and send it speeding east.

5.7 Transcendents

The transcendents hold the six sticks,[3]
And play *liubo* in a nook of Mount Tai.
The Fair Ones of the Xiang play zither and zithern,
The Daughter of Qin blows the reed pipes.[4]
Jade goblets brim with cinnamon wine,
The River Earl offers a sacred fish.[5]
The four seas – how cramped!
And where is there to go in the Nine Provinces?
Han Zhong and Wang Qiao

---

3 *Liubo* 六博 was a popular board game – one that transcendents were sometimes depicted playing. Although it is not known precisely how it was played, it appears that moves of game pieces were determined by tossing six sticks.

4 The fair ones of the Xiang were two goddesses named Ehuang and Nüying who were the daughters of the legendary ruler Yao and the wives of his successor Shun. The Daughter of Qin was the daughter of Duke Mu of Qin. She learned to play the flute (*xiao*) from her husband Xiao Shi. The couple in the end flew away with a pair of phoenixes.

5 I.e., the god of the Yellow River.

要我於天衢
萬里不足步
12 輕舉凌太虛
飛騰踰景雲
高風吹我軀
迴駕觀紫微
16 與帝合靈符
閶闔正嵯峨
雙闕萬丈餘
玉樹扶道生
20 白虎挾門樞
驅風遊四海
東過王母廬
俯觀五嶽間
24 民生如寄居
潛光養羽翼
進趨且徐徐
不見昔軒轅
28 升龍出鼎湖
徘徊九天上
與爾長相須

Invite me to the heavenly highway.[1]
Ten thousand *li* are less than a step,
Levitating, I mount the great void.
Flying rapidly upward I pass felicitous clouds,
Winds on high buffet my body.
I wheel around to view Purple Tenuity,
And match numinous tallies with God.[2]
The Celestial Portal stands in the middle, lofty and steep,
Its twin gate-towers over ten thousand *zhang*.[3]
Jade trees grow beside the road,
White Tiger surrounds the portal's Pivots.[4]
Driving the wind, I roam the four seas,
Eastward I pass the Queen Mother's hut.[5]
Looking down, I see all within the Five Sacred Peaks –
Human life is like a sojourn.
Hide your light, nurture feather and wing;[6]
Striving to advance, go slowly, slowly.
Not seeing the Yellow Emperor
Ride the dragon out of Cauldron Lake,[7]
I go back and forth above the Ninth Heaven,
"To join you I would wait forever."

---

1 On Wang Qiao, see **3.1**, line 44. Han Zhong was one of those sent by the First Emperor of Qin in 215 BCE to seek the drugs of deathlessness.

2 "God" translates *di* 帝, the term for the highest god, sometimes also translated as "Thearch" or "Theocrat." He dwelled in the heavens within a two-section circumpolar constellation of fifteen stars called the Wall of Purple Tenuity.

3 One *zhang* was about 2.31 meters.

4 Cao Zhi's use of the word "Pivots" here refers to Left and Right Pivot, two stars on opposite sides of the handle of the Big Dipper. Their apparent movement described the two arcs that form the Wall of Purple Tenuity around Polaris. White Tiger also has astronomical significance as the name of one of the four palaces into which the heavens were divided – the western equinoctial palace – and was a guardian spirit of the western heavens.

5 I.e., the Queen Mother of the West.

6 Wings and feathers are often features of transcendent beings in literature and art.

7 Xuanyuan, the Yellow Emperor, is said to have cast a tripod cauldron. When it was finished, a dragon appeared to him, and he – along with some seventy officials and consorts – soared off into the sky on the dragon. The place where this happened came to be called Tripod Cauldron Lake.

5.8 妾薄命

攜玉手喜同車
比上雲閣飛除
釣臺蹇產清虛
4 池塘靈沼可娛
仰泛龍舟綠波
俯擢神草枝柯
想彼宓妃洛河
8 退詠漢女湘娥

5.9 妾薄命 （其二）

日既逝矣西藏
更會蘭室洞房
華燈步障舒光
4 皎若日出扶桑

促樽合坐行觴
主人起舞娑盤
能者穴觸別端
8 騰觚飛爵闌干
同量等色齊顏
任意交屬所歡
朱顏發外形蘭

5.8 I Am Ill-Fated, No. 1

Holding a jade-white hand, I happily share a carriage.
Side-by-side we ascend the soaring stairs of a cloud-high pavilion.
Fishing Terrace is tall and towering, pristine and vacant,
Its pools and ponds and numinous basin delightful.[1]
Looking up, we drift in dragon boats on green waves;
Looking down, we pluck sprigs and stems of divine herbs.
I think of Fu Fei and the Luo River,
Returning I sing of the nymphs of the Han and the Beauties of the Xiang.[2]

5.9 I Am Ill-Fated, No. 2

The sun departs and hides in the west;
We gather again in redolent rooms and innermost chambers.
Ornate lanterns and windbreaks spread out light,
It gleams like a sun rising from the Fusang tree.[3]

Goblets to hand and seats close together, we offer toasts.
The host gets up to dance, whirling and twirling;
Guests who can dance tilt and touch, part and stand straight.
Lifted beakers and flying cups go back and forth;
Drinkers all, we equally redden, identically flush.
We freely consort with ones who delight us;
Flush-faced girls display graceful shapes.

---

1 A Fishing Terrace was located at the Xuanwu Reservoir built in 208 by Cao Cao near the northwest corner of Ye. This, too, was the location of Lingzhi (Numinous Mushroom) Reservoir built by Cao Pi in 222, to which line 4 may refer.

2 Fu Fei is the Goddess of the Luo who is the subject of **2.3**. On the Nymph of the Han and the Beauties of the Xiang, see **2.3**, lines 75 and 95–96.

3 On the Fusang tree, see **2.4**, line 7.

袖隨禮容極情
妙舞仙仙體輕
裳解履遺絕纓
俯仰笑喧無呈

覽持佳人玉顏
齊舉金爵翠盤
手形羅袖良難
腕弱不勝珠環
坐者歎息舒顏

御巾裛粉君傍
中有霍納都梁
雞舌五味雜香
進者何人齊姜
恩重愛深難忘

召延親好宴私
但歌盃來何遲
客賦既醉言歸
主人稱露未晞

Sleeves trailing, their postures convey the utmost feeling,
In wonderful dance, lithe and lissome, bodies buoyant.
With clothing loosened, shoes off, and broken cap strings,
Looking up and down, our laughing and shouting is unruly.

A man cradles and holds a fair lady's jade-white face,
In concert they lift the bronze cup, the halcyon-blue saucer.
For her hand to appear from the gauzy sleeve is quite difficult,
And her wrist is so frail it can hardly bear its pearl bracelet.
The seated guests sigh and grin.

A towel suffused with scented powders is offered by milord's side,
In it are betony and thoroughwort,
Clove, schizandra, and sundry fragrances.
Who offers them but a Jiang of Qi?[1]
The magnitude of milord's favor and depth of his affection are unforgettable.

He invites kith and kin to an informal party,
And all they sing out is "What's keeping the cups?"
When the guests declaim "We're drunk and going home,"
The host proclaims, "The dew is not yet dry."

---

1 This is an allusion to a poem in the *Classic of Poetry*: "Why in taking a wife must one have a Jiang of Qi?" The sense, of course, is that of a woman of beauty and rank.

5.10 白馬篇

白馬飾金羈
連翩西北馳
借問誰家子
幽并遊俠兒
少小去鄉邑
揚名沙漠垂
宿昔秉良弓
楛矢何參差
控弦破左的
右發摧月支
仰手接飛猱
俯身散馬蹄
狡捷過猴猿
勇剽若豹螭
邊城多驚急
虜騎數遷移
羽檄從北來
厲馬登高堤
長驅蹈匈奴
左顧陵鮮卑
棄身鋒刃端
性命安可懷

5.10 White Horse

A white horse outfitted with a golden bridle
Ceaselessly gallops toward the northwest.
"May I ask, whose son is this?"
"He's a roving hero from You-Bing.[1]
When young he left his old hometown,
And made a name on the desert frontier.
Long has he grasped a goodly bow;
His thornwood arrows – how bristling!
Drawing his bowstring, he smashes the left target;
Shooting right, he destroys a Yuezhi.[2]
Raising his hands, he hits a gibbon mid-air;
Bending his body, he scatters a horse-hoof butt.[3]
His deftness and agility surpass a monkey or gibbon;
He is as brave and as nimble as a leopard or wyverne.
Frontier forts have many alerts and emergencies,
For the caitiff riders often move.
When a feathered dispatch comes from the north,[4]
He spurs his horse to climb the high banks.
Racing afar, he tramples the Xiongnu;
Looking left, crushes the Xianbei.[5]
He would lay down his life at the point of a blade.
How could he cleave to life?

---

1 You-Bing refers to the old provinces of You and Bing in north and northwest China. They were associated with traditions of errantry.

2 Yuezhi 月支 was the name of a type of target. The name may stem from the Chinese name for a nomadic people located to the northwest of Han-dynasty China, and it has been speculated that the target was a likeness of a Yuezhi warrior.

3 A "horse-hoof" was a kind of archery target.

4 "Feathered dispatches" were used to summon troops. A bird feather was attached to the document to show urgency.

5 The Xiongnu, a confederation of ethnolinguistic groups on China's northern border, existed in a contentious and complex relationship with Chinese dynasties, most notably during the Han and early medieval periods. The two sides were often at war. The Xianbei, or Särbi, were originally from the steppe lands north-east of China proper. During Cao Zhi's time, they often fought against Cao Cao's forces at the end of Han and then later against the Cao's Wei dynasty.

父母且不顧
24 何言子與妻
名在壯士籍
不得中顧私
捐軀赴國難
28 視死忽如歸

5.11 名都篇

名都多妖女
京洛出少年
寶劍直千金
4 被服麗且鮮
鬬雞東郊道
走馬長楸間
馳騁未能半
8 雙兔過我前
攬弓捷鳴鏑
長驅上南山
左挽因右發
12 一縱兩禽連
餘巧未及展
仰手接飛鳶
觀者咸稱善

He does not even care about his parents,
Not to speak of his children and wife.
His name is on the roll of heroes;
He cannot consider personal matters.
He will sacrifice his body in rushing to the country's plight,
View death the same as going home.

5.11 Famous Cities

In famous cities are many enchanting women;
From the capital Luo come dashing youths.
Their precious swords worth a thousand in gold,
The clothes they wear are beautiful and bright.
They fight cocks along the eastern suburbs road,
Race horses between the long rows of catalpas.
Before the gallop can be half run,
A brace of hares crosses in front.
I grasp my bow and nock a whistling arrow,
Give a long chase up the southern hills.
I draw with my left hand then shoot to the right,
One shot and both game are impaled.
With other tricks yet to be shown,
I lift my hands and hit head-on a kite in flight.
Spectators all praise my prowess,

衆工歸我妍
我歸宴平樂
美酒斗十千
膾鯉臇胎鰕
炮鱉炙熊蹯
鳴儔嘯匹侶
列坐竟長筵
連翩擊鞠壤
巧捷惟萬端
白日西南馳
光景不可攀
雲散還城邑
清晨復來還

5.12 薤露行

天地無窮極
陰陽轉相因
人居一世間
忽若風吹塵
願得展功勤
輸力於明君
懷此王佐才
慷慨獨不群

Experts all admire my mastery.
We return and feast at Pingle,[1]
The excellent wine ten thousand a ladle.
Minced carp, braised roe shrimp,
Soft-shelled turtle roasted in clay, grilled bear paws.
Calling companions, shouting to mates,
The entire company fills a long mat.
Endlessly playing at football and pegs,[2]
Their skill and agility are of untold variety.
The white sun speeds southwest,
And daylight cannot be stayed.
Scattering like clouds, we return to the city,
In the clear dawn we will come back again

5.12 Dew on the Shallots

Heaven and earth have no end,
Yin and *yang* revolve one after the other.
A person lives but one age,
Just like windblown dust.
I wish I could manifest deeds of merit,
Offer my strengths to a wise ruler.
Harboring these king-helping talents,
In my strong forbearance I alone am not like others.

---

1 Pingle Lodge 平樂觀 is a name associated with both Chang'an and Luoyang.

2 This was a type of team football, originally associated with martial training, played with a leather ball filled with wool. What is translated here as "pegs" was a game using two pieces of wood. One piece was stuck into the ground at a distance of thirty or forty paces, and the object was to hit it by throwing the other piece.

鱗介尊神龍
走獸宗麒麟
蟲獸猶知德
何況於士人
孔氏刪詩書
王業粲已分
騁我徑寸翰
流藻垂華芬

5.13 豫章行

窮達難豫圖
禍福信亦然
虞舜不逢堯
耕耘處中田
太公未遭文
漁釣終渭川
不見魯孔丘
窮困陳蔡間
周公下白屋
天下稱其賢

Among things with scales and shells, we revere divine dragons;
Among gressile beasts, we honor the unicorn.
If even in creatures and beasts one perceives virtue,
How much more with regard to a gentleman!
Confucius edited the *Poetry* and *Documents*,
And royal achievements were clearly thereby explained.
I will give rein to my inch-round brush,
Spread eloquence and leave behind a flowery fragrance.

5.13 Yuzhang Ballad, No. 1[1]

Failure and success are hard to foretell;
Adversity and good fortune frankly are also like this.
Had Yu Shun not met Yao,
He'd have stayed tilling and weeding in the fields.[2]
Had Taigong not encountered Wen,
He'd have spent his life fishing and angling by the Wei River.[3]
Have you not seen Confucius of Lu,
Desperate and destitute between Chen and Cai?[4]
The Duke of Zhou went down into plain houses,
And the whole world praised his worthiness.[5]

---

1 Yuzhang (Camphor Tree) is the name of a mountain that lent its name to the title of a *yuefu* poem. It is possible to read this and the following poem as part of Cao Zhi's program to obtain a position in which he can be of service to the state.

2 For Yu Shun and Yao, see **2.3**, line 96.

3 For Taigong and King Wen, see **1.4**, line 12.

4 The state of Chu wanted to employ Confucius, and this worried the high officials of Chen and Cai. They had him surrounded in the countryside and kept him from moving so that his provisions were exhausted. Finally Chu sent troops to liberate Confucius.

5 These lines concern the Duke of Zhou's tireless search for talented people to serve in government, which led him to seek out even those who lived in humble homes. See also **1.17**, line 14.

5.14 豫章行 其二

鴛鴦自朋親
不若比翼連
他人雖同盟
骨肉天性然
周公穆康叔
管蔡則流言
子臧讓千乘
季札慕其賢

5.15 美女篇

美女妖且閑
采桑歧路間
柔條紛冉冉
落葉何翩翩
攘袖見素手
皓腕約金環
頭上金爵釵
腰佩翠琅玕

1 When King Wu of Zhou died, his brother, the Duke of Zhou, became regent for King Cheng. Brother Kang was the youngest brother of King Wu and the Duke of Zhou, but there were others, including Brother Guan and Brother Cai,

5.14 Yuzhang Ballad, No. 2

Mandarin ducks naturally partner as mates,
But that cannot compare to being joined by linked wings.
Although others may form alliances,
Flesh and bone relatives are innately so.
The Duke of Zhou was on good terms with Younger Brother Kang,
But Guan and Cai then spread rumors.[1]
Zizang relinquished a state of a thousand chariots,
And Ji Zha aspired to his worthiness.[2]

5.15 The Beautiful Woman

The beautiful woman is enchanting and refined;
She picks mulberry leaves at a fork in the road.
The tender branches are profuse and softly hanging,
How swiftly fly the falling leaves!
Turning up her sleeve, she shows her white hand,
The gleaming wrist encircled by a golden bracelet.
Atop her head, a golden bird hairpin;
Hanging from her waist, emerald green malachite.

---

who rebelled against what they saw as a usurpation. During Cao Zhi's time, the view of the Duke of Zhou as an altruistic culture hero was well established, and Cao Cao – as protector of the Han emperor – often enjoyed comparison to him.

2 Zizang was a member of the royal family of the state of Cao in the sixth century BCE. When the Cao nobility wanted to make him ruler, he refused out of a sense of integrity and fled to the state of Song. Ji Zha was the youngest son of King Shoumeng of Wu. The king wanted to make Ji Zha his successor, but Ji Zha declined in favor of his elder brother Zhufan. Later Zhufan wanted to abdicate in favor of Ji Zha, but Ji Zha refused, citing his wish to emulate the example of Zizang.

明珠交玉體
珊瑚間木難
羅衣何飄飄
輕裾隨風還
顧盼遺光采
長嘯氣若蘭
行徒用息駕
休者以忘餐
借問女何居
乃在城南端
青樓臨大路
高門結重關
容華耀朝日
誰不希令顏
媒氏何所營
玉帛不時安
佳人慕高義
求賢良獨難
衆人徒嗷嗷
安知彼所觀
盛年處房室
中夜起長歎

Bright beads entwine her jade body,
Coral interspersed with *munan*.[1]
Her gauze garment – how it flutters!
Her light skirt swirls with the breeze.
When she glances round, she leaves behind a radiance;
When she whistles loud and long, her breath is like thoroughwort.[2]
Because of her, travelers halt their carriages;
Due to her, those resting forget to eat.
"Where," may I ask, "does she live?"
"Just at the southern gate of the city-wall,
A blue mansion overlooking the main road,
A tall gate shut by multiple bars."
The beauty of her countenance outshines the morning sun;
Who would not admire her lovely face?
What have the matchmakers been doing
That jade and silk were not settled in timely fashion?[3]
The lady fair admires lofty principles,
But finding a worthy man is truly uniquely hard.
The crowd clamors in vain;
How could they know what would make her happy?
In the prime of her life she keeps to her room,
In the middle of the night rises and heaves long sighs.

1 *Munan* was the name of a green gemstone.
2 In early medieval times, a kind of whistling was a form of expression.
3 This is a reference to betrothal gifts.

5.16 豔歌

出自薊北門
遙望湖池桑
枝枝自相植
葉葉自相當

5.17 遊仙

人生不滿百
歲歲少歡娛
意欲奮六翮
排霧陵紫虛
蟬蛻同松喬
翻跡登鼎湖
翺翔九天上
騁轡遠行游
東觀扶桑曜
西臨弱水流
北極玄天渚
南翔陟丹丘

5.16 Prelude (fragment)

Going out the north gate of Ji,[1]
I gaze afar at mulberry trees by lakes and ponds.
Branch to branch, they naturally support one another;
Leaf to leaf, they naturally screen one another.

5.17 Roaming into Transcendence

Our lives are not a hundred years long;
Year after year less joy and delight.
I want to spread my six quills,
Push mists aside and surmount the purple void,
Husk off this cicada shell like Red Pine and Wang Qiao,
Alter my tracks and rise up from Tripod Lake,[2]
Wheel about above the Ninth Heaven,[3]
Slacken the reins and go roaming afar.
In the east I will view the sunlight of the Fusang,
In the west I will draw nigh the currents of Weak Water.[4]
In the north I will reach and climb the Dark Isle,
In the south I will soar and scale Cinnabar Hill.[5]

---

1 Ji was a city of the state of Yan 燕 in Zhou times. Located just on the southwest of modern Beijing, it was the earliest walled city in the Beijing sub-plain.

2 On Red Pine and Wang Qiao, see **3.1**, line 44. Tripod Lake is the place from which the Yellow Emperor is said to have ascended into the heavens to become immortal.

3 This was the highest heaven.

4 On Fusang, see See **2.4**, lines 7–8. Weak Water is the name of a river that is very often mentioned in accounts of the Western Regions and, in the lore of transcendence, is typically connected with Kunlun.

5 Dark Isle is mentioned in Zhang Heng's "Western Metropolis Rhapsody" in a section including allusions to haunts of transcendents. The term here translated as "dark" (*xuan*) is often connected with the boreal direction. Cinnabar Hill already appears in the "Far Roaming" poem of *Lyrics of Chu* as a place where ethereal, immortal "feathered persons" were to be found.

5.18 五遊詠

九州不足步
願得凌雲翔
逍遙八紘外
游目歷遐荒
披我丹霞衣
襲我素霓裳
華蓋芬晻藹
六龍仰天驤
曜靈未移景
倏忽造昊蒼
閶闔啟丹扉
雙闕曜朱光
徘徊文昌殿
登陟太微堂
上帝休西櫺
群后集東廂
帶我瓊瑤佩
嗽我沆瀣漿
踟躕玩靈芝
徙倚弄華芳
王子奉仙藥
羨門進奇方

5.18 Song of the Fifth Roaming

The Nine Provinces do not even amount to a step;[1]
I want to be able to mount the clouds and soar,
To wander beyond the Eight Cords,[2]
And let my eyes roam across the remotest wilderness.
I don my cinnabar aurora robe,
Put on my white rainbow skirt.
The fragrance from my floriate canopy is thick,
My six dragon steeds, looking heavenwards, dash on.
The Sparkling Numen has not yet moved a shadow,[3]
When suddenly I have reached the infinite azure.
The Celestial Portal opens its cinnabar doors,
The twin gate-towers shine with vermilion light.
I go to and fro in the Basilica of Cultural Splendor,
Ascend the Hall of Grand Tenuity.[4]
The High God leans on a western balustrade,
His vassal lords all gather in the eastern wing.
I attach my belt pendants of carnelian and chalcedony,
Rinse my mouth with a broth of midnight mists.[5]
Pacing to and fro, I relish the numinous mushrooms,[6]
Moving back and forth, I enjoy the flowers' fragrance.
Wangzi Qiao offers drugs of transcendence,
Xianmen presents wonderful formulas.[7]

---

1 See **4.11**, line 10.

2 The Eight Cords is the name of one of the regions well beyond the borders of the early Chinese oikoumene.

3 I.e., the sun.

4 The Basilica of Cultural Splendor was a cluster of stars in Ursa Major. On Grand Tenuity, see **2.9**, line 10.

5 See **5.27**, line 10 *Additional Note*.

6 Numinous mushrooms, or magic mushrooms, were among the substances ingested by seekers of long life or immortality.

7 On Wangzi Qiao, see **3.1**, line 44. Xianmen Gao 高, or Xianmen Zigao 子高, was the name of someone mentioned in early texts as a practitioner of the arts of magic and immortality.

服食享遐紀
24 延壽保無疆

5.19 梁甫行

八方各異氣
千里殊風雨
劇哉邊海民
4 寄身於草墅
妻子象禽獸
行止依林阻
柴門何蕭條
8 狐兔翔我宇

5.20 丹霞蔽日行

紂為昏亂
虐殘忠正
周室何隆
4 一門三聖
牧野致功
天亦革命
漢祖之興
8 階秦之衰

Taking elixirs, I will enjoy great age,
Extend my lifespan and preserve it forever.

5.19 Liangfu Ballad

The eight directions all vary in climate;
A thousand *li* means different wind and rain.
Wretched! the people by the sea,
Entrusting their bodies to grass huts.
Wives and children are like birds and beasts,
Stirring or still, they depend on the sylvan defiles.
How desolate the brushwood doors!
Foxes and hares scurry about our dwellings.

5.20 Vermilion Clouds Hide the Sun

Zhòu begat darkness and disorder,
He abused and brutalized the loyal and upright.[1]
The Zhou royal house, how did it triumph?
One family, three sages.[2]
At Muye they achieved the feat,
Heaven in turn changed the Mandate.
The rise of Han's progenitor
Stemmed from Qin's decline.[3]

---

1 Zhòu was the evil last ruler of the Shang dynasty. He was defeated by King Wu of Zhou at the battle of Muye.

2 The three sages were the Zhou founding kings Wen and Wu and the Duke of Zhou.

3 "Han's progenitor" refers to Liu Bang 劉邦 (Gaozu 高祖, r. 206–195 BCE), founder of the Han dynasty. Qin, of course, is the Qin dynasty.

雖有南面
王道陵夷
炎光再幽
忽滅無遺

5.21 怨歌行

為君既不易
為臣良獨難
忠信事不顯
乃有見疑患
周旦佐文武
金縢功不刊
推心輔王政
二叔反流言
待罪居東國
泣涕常流連
皇靈大動變
震雷風且寒
拔樹偃秋稼
天威不可干

---

1 This is a way of referring to emperors – in this case, the Han emperors.

2 This poem, which may or may not be by Cao Zhi (see *Additional Notes*), is based on famous traditions involving the Duke of Zhou, here referred to as Dan of Zhou, who is specifically mentioned or alluded to several times in the poems in this book. In

Although there was the one who faced south,[1]
The royal way withered and waned.
The fiery light went dark once more,
12 Suddenly extinguished without a trace.

5.21 Song of Resentment[2]

Being a ruler is not at all easy,
But being a subject is surely the hardest:
If your loyalty and sincerity are not obvious as you serve,
4 Then you will experience the misfortune of suspicion.
Dan of Zhou aided Wen and Wu,
And the deeds of the metal-bound casket are indelible.
He put his whole heart into helping the king's government,
8 But the two brothers nonetheless spread rumors.
Awaiting sentencing, he dwelled in the eastern capital,
The tears he wept often flowed freely.
The august numen wrought great havoc –[3]
12 Crashing thunder, wind and cold.
Uprooting trees, flattening the autumn crop –
Heaven's power cannot be defied.

---

short, the tradition says that when King Wu of Zhou died, his successor, the future King Cheng, was quite young, so the Duke of Zhou, who was one of King Wu's brothers, governed on the young king's behalf. But the Duke of Zhou's brothers mistrusted him and spread rumors about his intentions (see **5.14**, lines 5–6), and even launched an attempted coup against him. The Duke of Zhou fled to Luoyang. Earlier he had written out a prayer to his ancestors, offering to die in place of King Wu. The prayer was placed in a box and sealed with metal. After the rebellion, there was a disastrous storm, which led King Cheng and others to open the metal-bound casket to see what clues it might hold. They found the Duke of Zhou's offer to die in place of King Wu. King Cheng wept at the realization that Heaven had sent the storm to call his attention to the Duke of Zhou's virtue.

3 "The August Numen" here means god on high.

素服開金縢
16 感悟求其端
公旦事既顯
成王乃哀嘆

吾欲竟此曲
20 此曲悲且長
今日樂相樂
別後莫相忘

5.22 善哉行

來日大難
口燥脣乾
今日相樂
4 皆當喜歡
經歷名山
芝草翩翩
仙人王喬
8 奉藥一丸
自惜袖短
內手知寒
慚無靈輒
12 以報趙宣

In austere garments they opened the metal-bound casket;
6 Stirred to awareness, they sought the source.
Once Dan of Zhou's service became clear,
King Cheng then sorrowfully sighed.

I want to end this song,
10 This song is sad and everlasting.
Today, joy upon joy,
After we part, let us not forget one another.

5.22 Grand![1]

In days past, great hardship:
Mouths parched, lips dry.
Today we make merry together,
4 And all should be happy and glad.
I passed through successive famous mountains –
The numinous mushrooms fluttering.
The immortal Wang Qiao
8 Handed me one pill of a drug.
I regret that my sleeves are short;
As I draw back my hand, I notice the cold.
I am ashamed I have no Ling Zhe
12 To repay Zhao Xuan.[2]

1 This poem may not be by Cao Zhi (see *Additional Notes*).

2 Zhao Xuan is Zhao Dun. Once when he was out hunting, he encountered Ling Zhe, who was starving, and gave him food for himself and for his mother. Later, Ling Zhe saved Zhao Dun's life.

月沒參橫
北斗闌干
親友在門
飢不及餐

歡日尚少
戚日苦多
以何忘憂
彈箏酒歌
淮南八公
要道不煩
參駕六龍
游戲雲端

5.23 當來日大難

日苦短
樂有餘
乃置玉樽辦東廚
廣情故
心相於

The moon sinks, Triaster transits,[1]
The Northern Dipper lies across the sky.
Kith and kin are at the gate;
Though hungry, there's been no time to eat.

Merry days are still few,
Parlous days, far too many.
How can we forget our cares?
By playing the cither, and with wine and song.
To the eight dons of Huainan
The essential way was no problem:
Harness together six dragons,
And caper on the tips of the clouds.[2]

5.23 Great Hardship in Days Past, A Variation

The day is sadly short,
And we've merriment to spare,
So set out jade goblets and ready the eastern kitchen.
We make clear our innermost feelings,
And our hearts are close.

1 On Triaster see **5.30**, line 22.

2 Lines 21–24 allude to eight men who were experts in the esoteric arts at the court of Liu An 劉安, Prince of Huainan 淮南 (r. 164–122 BCE). According to tradition, the monumental book *Huainanzi* grew out of their discussions. Note that in a Daoist hagiographical account, Liu An, his household, and his domestic animals became immortal and rose into the heavens.

闔門置酒
和樂欣欣
8 遊馬後來
轅車解輪

今日同堂
出門異鄉
12 別易會難
各盡杯觴

5.24 君子行

君子防未然
不處嫌疑間
瓜田不納履
4 李下不整冠
叔嫂不親授
長幼不並肩
和光得其柄
8 謙恭甚獨難
周公下白屋
吐哺不及餐
一沐三握髮
12 後世稱聖賢

We shut the gate and hold a feast;
Harmonious and happy, joyful are we.
8 Walk the horses and bring them back later,
Thill the carriages and take off the wheels.[1]

Today we share this hall,
But once out the gate, we go to different places.
2 Parting is easy, coming together is hard,
Let everyone drain his cup.

5.24 Gentlemen[2]

A gentleman guards against what has yet to occur,
He does not dwell in doubt and uncertainty.
In a melon patch, you don't put on your shoe;
4 Under a plum tree, you don't straighten your cap.
A brother-in-law and sister-in-law don't let their hands touch in giving things;
An elder person and a younger one can't be side-by-side.
Merge with the brilliant to obtain its handle,
8 Being modest and respectful is especially hard.
The Duke of Zhou went down into plain houses,
He spat out his food and had no time to eat,
In one washing he would squeeze out his hair three times,
2 And later ages praise him as wise and worthy.

1 Lines 8–9 express the wish to detain the guests at the feast and keep them from going home. The meaning of "thill the carriages" is unclear, but one scholar has suggested that it means to raise the thills so that they are pointed straight up in the air.

2 Like **5.22**, the authorship of this piece is uncertain (see *Additional Notes*).

5.25 平陵東

閶闔開
天衢通
被我羽衣乘飛龍
乘飛龍
與仙期
東上蓬萊採靈芝
靈芝採之可服食
年若王父無終極

5.26 苦思行

綠蘿緣玉樹
光耀燦相輝
下有兩真人
舉翅翻高飛
我心何踊躍
思欲攀雲追
鬱鬱西嶽顛
石室青葱與天連
中有耆年一隱士
鬚髮皆皓然
策杖從我游
教我要忘言

5.25 East of Pingling

Heaven's Portal opens,
The Celestial Highway is clear.
I don my feather robe and mount a flying dragon.
Mount a flying dragon,
To rendezvous with a transcendent
And in the east ascend Penglai to gather the numinous mushroom.[1]
The numinous mushroom – gather it and it can be ingested,
And one's years, like the King Father's, will have no end.[2]

5.26 Painful Thoughts

A green vine climbs a jade tree;
Bright and sparkling, they glitter and illumine each other.
Beneath are two perfected ones,[3]
Lifting their wings, they flap them and fly up high.
How my heart bounds with joy!
In my mind I want to scale the clouds and follow them.
Lush the summit of the western sacred mountain,
Its grottoes blue-green, blending into the sky.
Among them is a recluse advanced in years,
Beard and hair both pure white.
Leaning on his staff, he goes roaming with me,
Teaches me that one must forget about words.

---

1 Penglai, like Fangzhang in the next poem, was one of the three mountainous island homes of transcendent beings off the east coast of China.

2 On the King Father, see **5.27** n. 5 and *Additional Notes*.

3 Perfected ones is a designation for persons who have attained the Dao. Although not originally tied to the quest to become a transcendent being or to gain immortality, that changed over time.

5.27 遠遊篇

遠遊臨四海
俯仰觀洪波
大魚若曲陵
承浪相經過
靈鼇戴方丈
神嶽儼嵯峨
仙人翔其隅
玉女戲其阿
瓊蕊可療飢
仰首吸朝霞
崑崙本吾宅
中州非我家
將歸謁東父
一舉超流沙
鼓翼舞時風
長嘯激清歌
金石固易弊
日月同光華
齊年與天地
萬乘安足多

5.27 Far Roaming

Far roaming I approach the four seas;
Up and down, I watch the immense waves.
Great fish like arching hills
Riding the billows pass one another.
A numinous sea turtle carries Fangzhang on its head:[1]
The sacred peak rises lofty and steep.
Transcendent beings soar about its crags,
Jade maidens play on its slopes.[2]
Carnelian stamens can appease my hunger;
Lifting my head, I sip the rosy mists of dawn.[3]
Kunlun was originally my dwelling,[4]
The central provinces are not my home.
I shall go back to visit the Eastern Father
And leap the Flowing Sands in a single bound.[5]
Beating my wings, I will dance upon a timely wind,
And whistling loud and long, break out in unaccompanied song.
Metal and stone are so easily ruined –
I shall equal the splendor of the sun and moon.
When one lives as long as heaven and earth,
What is there to praise in being the ruler of a large realm?

---

1 Fangzhang was one of the magical islands in the Eastern Sea said to be inhabited by transcendent beings who might virtually be immortal. It was borne on the head of a giant sea turtle.

2 Jade maidens are associated with the world of transcendents and deities of longevity.

3 Eating crushed carnelian stamens is associated with the search for prolonged life, as is imbibing the rosy dawn mist.

4 Kunlun is the name of a mountain range in the far west of China. Here it refers to a mythical mountain in that direction that was the abode of transcendents and the Queen Mother of the West.

5 Flowing Sands (or Quicksand) was reportedly at the base of Kunlun.

5.28 吁嗟篇

吁嗟此轉蓬
居世何獨然
長去本根逝
宿夜無休閒
東西經七陌
南北越九阡
卒遇回風起
吹我入雲間
自謂終天路
忽然下沉泉
驚飆接我出
故歸彼中田
當南而更北
謂東而反西
宕宕當何依
忽亡而復存
飄飄周八澤
連翩歷五山
流轉無恆處
誰知吾哭艱
願為中林草
秋隨野火燔

5.28 Alas!

Alas, this tumbleweed,
Living in the world all alone.
Forever separated from its native roots it goes,
Day and night it has no rest.
East to west it passes seven paths,
South to north it crosses nine trails.
I suddenly meet a whirlwind rising,
And it blows me into the clouds.
As soon as I think I have run out of road in the sky,
Suddenly I descend a deep abyss.
A fierce wind then lifts me out,
And so I return to fields.
Heading south, I am shifted north;
Expecting to go east, instead I turn west.
Adrift, on what should I rely?
Suddenly I am gone and then I appear again.
Tossing and tumbling, I circuit the Eight Marshes,[1]
Flittering and fluttering, I visit the Five Mountains.[2]
Drifting and wending, having no fixed abode,
Who knows my troubles and hardships?
I would rather be grass in the woods,
In autumn burned by wildfires.

1 This may be a reference to eight far distant wetlands beyond the heartland of early China. Alternatively, it could refer to the marshlands of specific Zhou dynasty states.

2 This refers to the Five Sacred Mountains. See **4.11**, line 10.

糜滅豈不痛
願與株荄連

5.29 鰕䱇篇

鰕䱇游潢潦
不知江海流
燕雀戲藩柴
安識鴻鵠游
世士誠明性
大德固無儔
駕言登五嶽
然後小陵丘
俯觀上路人
勢利惟是謀
高念翼皇家
遠懷柔九州
撫劍而雷音
猛氣縱橫浮
汎泊徒嗷嗷
誰知壯士憂

To be destroyed would surely hurt,
But I long to be attached to roots.

5.29 Shrimps and Eels

Shrimps and eels swim in pools and puddles,
They do not comprehend the currents of rivers and seas.
Swallows and sparrows sport about in hedges,
How can they grasp the wanderings of swans?
If a man of the world truly understands his nature,
Then his great virtue shall have no match.
Drive and ascend the Five Sacred Peaks,
Only afterwards will you consider a large hill small.
Look down and observe those taking the road,[1]
Power and profit – only those do they seek.
My highest hope is to aid the imperial house,
My most cherished ambition is to pacify the Nine Provinces.
Gripping my sword like the sound of thunder,
Fierce spirit sails forth in all directions.
Common idlers clamor in vain;
Who comprehends a brave man's distress?

1 This may be understood as referring to those embarking on an official career.

5.30 種葛篇

種葛南山下
葛藟自成陰
與君初婚時
結髮恩意深
懽愛在枕席
宿昔同衣衾
竊慕棠棣篇
好樂和瑟琴
行年將晚暮
佳人懷異心
恩紀曠不接
我情遂抑沈
出門當何顧
徘徊步北林
下有交頸獸
仰見雙棲禽
攀枝長歎息
淚下沾羅衿
良馬知我悲
延頸代我吟
昔為同池魚

5.30 Plant the Kudzu

Plant kudzu at the foot of the southern mountain,
Kudzu and liana naturally make shade.
When I first was wed with you,
We bound our hair together, and our love was deep.
Joy and love were present on pillow and mat,
And we always shared clothes and coverlet.
I admire the poem "Sweet-plum" –
Fondness and joy like zithern and zither.[1]
The years of my life are approaching late sunset,
And my beloved harbors an unfaithful heart.
Loving kindness has long been withdrawn,
So my mood is depressed and despondent.
Going out the door, where should I turn my sight?
Back and forth I pace the northern wood.
Below are animals with necks crossed,
Looking up I see pairs of roosting birds.
Clutching a branch, I heave a long sigh,
Tears fall and wet my gauzy lapels.
My fine horse knows that I am sad,
It stretches its neck and neighs for me.
Before we were fish in the same pond,

---

1 Lines 7–8 are an allusion to the *Classic of Poetry* poem "Sweet-plum," which speaks in part of familial concord.

今為商與參
往古皆懽遇
我獨困於今
棄置委天命
悠悠安可任

5.31 浮萍篇

浮萍寄清水
隨風東西流
結髮辭嚴親
來為君子仇
恪勤在朝夕
無端獲罪尤

在昔蒙恩惠
和樂如瑟琴
何意今摧頹
曠若商與參

茱萸自有芳
不若桂與蘭
新人雖可愛
不若故所歡

Now we are Shang and Triaster.[1]
In the old days we both were happy and got along,
But I alone am tormented by the present.
I give up and yield to Heaven's will;
On and on, how can I bear it?

5.31 Duckweed

Duckweed depends on clear water,
Drifting east or west with the wind.
I bound up my hair and took leave of my parents,[2]
Came to be your companion.
I was respectful and diligent day and night,
But for no reason suffered blame.

In the past I met affection and kindness,
We were harmonious and happy as zithern and zither.[3]
How could I imagine that now would be dashed,
And we'd be as distant as Shang and Triaster?[4]

Prickly ash naturally has fragrance,
But its not as good as cinnamon and thoroughwort;
Though a new someone may be loved,
She won't be as good as your old sweetheart.

---

1 Triaster was the group of three stars that in other traditions make up Orion's belt, and Shang is Scorpio. At opposite ends of the sky, they are often paired as a metaphor for separation or alienation.

2 Binding up the hair was a mark of entering adulthood and was done at age 20.

3 Line 8 is an allusion to the *Classic of Poetry* poem "Sweet-plum," which speaks in part of familial concord.

4 See see **5.30**, line 22.

行雲有反期
16 君恩儻中還

慊慊仰天歎
愁心將何愬
日月不恒處
20 人生忽若寓
悲風來入帷
淚下如垂露
散篋造新衣
24 裁縫紈與素

5.32 惟漢行

太極定二儀
清濁始以形
三光照八極
4 天道甚著明
為人立君長
欲以遂其生
行仁章以瑞
8 變故誡驕盈
神高而聽卑
報若響應聲

Moving clouds have their time of return;
Might your affection return mid-course?

Discontented, I look to the heavens and sigh;
To whom complain of my sorrowful heart?
The sun and moon do not stay in place;
Human life is just like a sojourn.
A sad wind comes and enters the curtains,
My tears come down like falling dew.
I'll rummage cases and make new clothes,
Cut and sew taffeta and plainsilk.

5.32 Han Ballad

The Grand Culmen established the Two Principles,
And the pure and the turbid began to take form.[1]
The three lights illuminated earth's eight endpoints,[2]
And the way of Heaven was exceedingly evident.
It set up rulers and leaders for the people,
Wanting thereby to let them live out their lives.
Practicing benevolence was marked by good omens,
Misfortune warned of pride and complacency.
The gods were high but heeded the lowly,
And their response was like an echo in reply to sound.

1 The Grand Culmen is the undifferentiated state of primal chaos before the formation of heaven and earth and the myriad things. It gave rise to the Two Principles (*yin* and *yang*), which in turn produced all things.

2 The three lights are the sun, moon, and stars.

明主敬細微
12 三季瞢天經
二皇稱至化
盛哉唐虞庭
禹湯繼厥德
16 周亦致太平
在昔懷帝京
日昃不敢寧
濟濟在公朝
20 萬載馳其名

5.33 門有萬里客

門有萬里客
問君何鄉人
褰裳起從之
4 果得心所親
挽裳對我泣
太息前自陳
本是朔方士
8 今為吳越民
行行將複行
去去適西秦[3]

Enlightened rulers respected the lowly and humble,
But the three ending reigns were blind to Heaven's norms.[1]
The two august ones were acclaimed for their perfect transforming influence,
Thriving, indeed, were the courts of Táng and Yú!
Yǔ and Tang continued their virtue,
And Zhou, in turn, brought about Great Peace.
In the past I yearned for the imperial capital,
When the sun slanted down dared not take repose.
Impressively imposing are those at court,
May ten thousand years spread their fame.

5.33 At the Gate There Is a Traveler of a Thousand *li*

At the gate there is a traveler of a thousand *li*,
May I ask, "Where's your home?"
Gathering my skirt, I rise and follow him;
I've finally found one near to my heart.
Tugging my robe, he faces me and weeps;
With a deep sigh, he comes forward and states:
"Originally I was a gentleman from the north,
Now I'm a commoner of Wu-Yue.[2]
Moving on and on, about to move on again;
Going away, away, bound for western Qin.

1 This refers to the last sovereigns of the Xia, Shang, and Zhou dynasties, who were considered bad rulers.

2 Wu and Yue are old names for the South. In Cao Zhi's time, of course, the state of Wu was an enemy.

3 Qin refers to the vicinity of the modern northwestern provinces of Shaanxi and Gansu.

5.34 桂之樹行

桂之樹
桂之樹
桂生一何麗佳
揚朱華而翠葉
流芳布天涯
上有棲鸞
下有蟠螭

桂之樹
得道之真人
咸來會講仙
教爾服食日精
要道甚省不煩
淡泊無為自然
乘蹻萬里之外
去留隨意所欲存
高高上際於眾外
下下乃窮極地天

5.34 Cinnamon Tree Ballad

Cinnamon tree, cinnamon tree,
How beautiful and fair grows the cinnamon![1]
It displays vermilion blossoms and turquoise leaves;
Its wafting fragrance spreads to the edge of the sky.
Atop is a roosting simurgh,
Beneath is a coiled wyverne.

Cinnamon tree,
Perfected persons who have attained the Dao,
All come gather to discuss transcendence.[2]
They will teach you to ingest essence of sun.[3]
The essential way is spare and not troublesome:
Contentment, inaction, naturalness.
Borne on sandals beyond ten thousand *li*,[4]
Go or stay, according to what your inclination might seek.
Higher, higher, going up till you reach beyond the multitude;
Lower, lower, till you've exhausted the limits of earth and heaven.

---

1 The cinnamon tree is associated with the search for long life and immortality. See the comment on the title in the Additional Notes.

2 A *xian* 仙 is a being who has transcended normal human existence and who, though not an immortal *per se*, lives a very long time. Like the concept of perfected persons in the previous line, this concept is an old idea and is closely associated with Daoism.

3 This is a technique for ingesting the rosy aurora 霞 of the dawn sun as part of the quest for transcendence.

4 See **5.5**, line 1.

5.35 當牆欲高行

龍欲升天須浮雲
人之仕進待中人
眾口可以鑠金
讒言三至
慈母不親
憒憒俗間
不辨偽真
願欲披心自說陳
君門以九重
道遠河無津

5.36 當欲遊南山行

東海廣且深
由卑下百川
五嶽雖高大
不逆垢與塵
良木不十圍
洪條無所因
長者能博愛

1 This poem is prosodically unusual. It has lines of varied length in two five-line groups, each rhyming on lines 1, 2, 3, and 5, with the same rhyme throughout.

5.35 Walls Need be High Ballad, A Variation[1]

If a dragon wants to ascend the sky, it needs floating clouds;
The progress of a man in office depends on insiders.
A mass of mouths can melt metal,
And if slanderous words thrice arrive,
Even a loving mother will be estranged.[2]
The muddleheaded common world
Does not distinguish false and true.
I wish to open my heart and set forth an explanation of myself,
But the ruler's gates are nine deep,
The road is far, and the river lacks a ford.

5.36 About to Roam the Southern Mountains Ballad, A Variation

The eastern sea is broad and deep,
By being low it brings down a hundred rivers.
Although the Five Sacred Peaks are tall and grand,
They don't reject dirt and dust.
If a good tree is not ten spans round,
Then huge limbs will have nowhere to adhere.
If the superior man can practice universal love,

---

2 A parable in the *Intrigues of the Warring States* 戰國策 says that when Confucius' disciple Zengzi 曾子 was living in Fei 費, a person with the same name committed murder. Someone told Zengzi's mother that he had killed a person, but she sat weaving and said he wouldn't do such a thing. Another person then came to tell her that Zengzi had killed someone, and again she kept on weaving and said he wouldn't do such a thing. But when a third person told her, she dropped her shuttle and ran away.

天下寄其身
大匠無棄材
船車用不均
錐刀各異能
何所獨卻前
嘉善而矜愚
大聖亦同然
仁者各壽考
四坐咸萬年

5.37 當事君行

人生有所貴尚
出門各異情
朱紫更相奪色
雅鄭異音聲
好惡隨所愛憎
追舉逐聲名
百心可事一君
巧詐寧拙誠

Then the people of the world will entrust themselves to him.
A great carpenter does not reject any wood,
For boats and carts call for different kinds.
Awls and knives each have different abilities,
How is it possible to reject or prefer one or the other?
Praise the good and pity the incapable,
The great sage, too, was just this way.[1]
May the benevolent each attain high old age,[2]
And those about them myriad years.

5.37 Serving the Ruler, A Variation

A person's life has things one values and esteems,
Away from home each has different inclinations.
Vermilion and purple compete to be the color,
Courtly music and that of Zheng are different musics.[3]
Like and dislike conform to what one is partial to or hates;
Seeking preferment, a man will pursue a false reputation.
Can a hundred hearts serve one ruler?[4]
Instead of shrewd mendacity, better artless honesty.

1 Line 13 is an allusion to the Confucian *Analects* 19.3, so the "great sage" of line 14 should be understood as a reference to Confucius.

2 This is an allusion to *Analects* 6.23.

3 Lines 3–4 are an allusion to *Analects* 17.18: "I hate the way purple has taken over from vermilion; I hate the way the sounds of Zheng have corrupted courtly music; I hate the fact that glib mouths overturn states and families."

4 "A hundred hearts" is the opposite, in effect, of undivided loyalty. *Kong Congzi* 孔叢子 has Yanzi 晏子 saying, "With one heart one may serve a hundred rulers, but with a hundred hearts one may not serve one ruler."

5.38 當車以駕行

歡坐玉殿
會諸貴客
侍者行觴
主人離席
顧視東西廂
絲竹與鞞鐸
不醉無歸來
明燈以繼夕

5.39 飛龍篇

晨遊太山
雲霧窈窕
忽逢二童
顏色鮮好
乘彼白鹿
手翳芝草
我知真人
長跪問道
西登玉堂
金樓複道
授我仙藥
神皇所造

5.38 The Carriages are Already Harnessed, A Variation

Happily seated in a jade hall,
The host has assembled all of his honored guests.
Those in attendance offer toasts,
The host leaves the mat [to toast in return].
Turning to look in the east and west chambers,
There are strings and woodwinds and drums and bells.
If you're not drunk, you shan't go home;
Light the lanterns to extend the night.

5.39 Flying Dragon

In the morning I roamed Mount Tai;[1]
The clouds and fog were dense and silent.
Suddenly I encountered two lads,
Their faces fresh and fair.
Mounted on this white deer,
Their hands screening numinous mushrooms.
I knew them to be perfected ones;
Kneeling formally, I asked about the Way.
In the west we ascended to a hall of jade,
Golden pavilions, and double-decked skywalks.
They gave me an immortality potion,
Made by a divine deity.

1 On Mount Tai, see **4.11**, line 10.

教我服食
還精補腦
壽同金石
16 永世難老

[芝蓋翩翩]

[南經丹穴
積陽所生
煎石流礫
品物無形]

5.40 盤石篇

盤盤山巔石
飄颻澗底蓬
我本泰山人
4 何為客淮東
蒹葭彌斥土
林木無芬重
岸巖若崩缺
8 湖水何洶洶
蚌蛤被濱涯
光采如錦虹

They taught me how to ingest doses
And to recycle essence to nourish the brain.[1]
My lifespan will equal metal and stone,
6 And forever and ever I will not grow old.

[The mushroom canopy fluttered and flapped.]

[In the south we passed Cinnabar Cave,
Where copious *yang* is produced;
It cooks the stones till they transform and melt
And objects have no form.][2]

5.40 Boulder

Massive, the mountaintop boulder;
Whirling and twirling, the canyon floor tumbleweed.
I am originally a man of Mount Tai,
4 Why am I sojourning east of the Huai?
Reeds spread across the saltlands,
The woods lack any lushness.
The shoreline ledges seem collapsed and broken;
8 The lake water – how it roars!
Mussels blanket the water's edge,
Their luster like a brocade rainbow.

1 This was a sexual practice associated with Daoism.
2 On these bracketed lines, see the *Additional Notes*.

高波淩雲霄
浮氣象螭龍
鯨脊若丘陵
鬚若山上松
呼吸吞船欐
澎濞戲中鴻
方舟尋高價
珍寶麗以通
一舉必千里
乘颸舉帆幢
經危履險阻
未知命所鍾
常恐沉黃壚
下與黿鼉同
南極蒼梧野
游盼窮九江
中夜指參辰
欲歸當定從
仰天長歎息
思想懷故邦
乘桴何所志
吁嗟我孔公

Tall waves surmount the clouded sky,
The drifting mists resemble wyverns.
Leviathans' spines are like hills;
Their barbels like pines on a mountain.
With a breath they swallow boats and skiffs,
Pounding and lashing they sport in the vasty deep.
The doubleboat seeks costly goods,
Precious treasures depend on it to circulate.
Once setting off, we must go a thousand *li*;
Catching a brisk wind, we hoist sail and mast.
We pass through danger, experience difficulty and hardship,
Never knowing what fate has in store.
I always fear sinking in the yellow earth,[1]
Going down to join the turtles.
We reach as far south as the wilds of Cangwu,
My drifting gaze exhausts Nine Rivers.[2]
In the middle of the night I point to Triaster and Chen;[3]
If I want to go home, I should set my course.
I look up to the sky and heave a long sigh,
Longing and yearning, I miss my old land.
What is the purpose of riding a raft?
Alas, Master Confucius![4]

---

1 The underworld, or death.

2 In this case Cangwu most likely refers to the commandery in the far south by that name that encompassed portions of modern Guangxi, Guangdong, and Hunan provinces. It is not clear whether "Nine Rivers" should be treated as a proper noun here rather than simply as "nine rivers," but I have done so in the translation because of the parallel with Cangwu. Nine Rivers was the name of a watery commandery encompassing modern Jiangxi province and parts of the provinces of Anhui, Henan, and Hubei. Its name in any case derived from the numerous rivers in the area.

3 These two asterisms are roughly equivalent to the constellations Orion and Scorpio, respectively.

4 In the *Analects*, Confucius says, "If the Way is not put into practice, I will take a raft and sail the seas." The speaker in the present poem so laments his own dislocation and thinks so much about the place he longs to be that he cannot accept Confucius' words.

5.41 驅車篇

驅車撣駑馬
東到奉高城
神哉彼泰山
五嶽專其名
隆高貫雲霓
嵯峨出太清
周流二六候
間置十二亭
上有涌醴泉
玉石揚華英
東北望吳野
西眺觀日精
魂神所系屬
逝者感斯征
王者以歸天
效厥元功成
歷代無不遵
禮祀有品程
探策或長短
唯德享利貞
封者七十帝
軒皇元獨靈

5.41 Driving the Carriage

Driving the carriage, I guide worn-out nags;
In the east arrive at Fenggao's city-wall.
Wondrous! that Mount Tai;[1]
Of the Five Sacred Mountains, its fame is unique.
Prominent and tall, it pierces cloud and rainbow;
Lofty and steep, it emerges in the empyrean.
Distributed around it are a dozen observation posts,
And twelve precinct houses are placed between them.
Above and below wellsprings of sweet water,
And jade rock displays splendid brilliance.
From the northeast one gazes on the wilds of Wu;
Peering from the west, one sees the quintessence of sunlight.
As the place to which souls and spirits are tied,
The departed are moved to journey here.
Rulers use it to give credit to Heaven,
And present the completion of their great deeds.[2]
Through successive dynasties none have not observed this custom,
And the rituals and sacrifices have standards and sequences.
Choose a divining stick, and it may say long life or short;
Only the virtuous will enjoy a favorable augury.
Seventy emperors have made the *feng* sacrifice;
The Yellow Emperor was first and alone was deified.

---

1 Fenggao was located not far from the foot of Mount Tai. On Mount Tai and the Five Sacred Mountains, see **4.11**, line 10.

2 This is a reference to the *feng* and *shan* sacrifices (see also line 21). As the poem indicates, the *feng* sacrifice was carried out on Mount Tai. The emperor thereby would announce his success and express his indebtedness to Heaven and, not incidentally, certify his legitimacy.

餐霞漱沆瀣
毛羽被身形
發舉蹈虛廓
徑庭升窈冥
同壽東父年
曠代永長生

5.42–46 鞞舞歌（有序）

漢靈帝西園鼓吹有李堅者，能鞞舞，遭亂西隨段煨。先帝聞其舊有伎，召之。堅既中廢，兼古曲多謬誤。異代之文未必相襲，故依前曲，改作新歌五篇。不敢充之黃門，近以成下國之陋樂焉。

5.42 聖皇篇

聖皇應曆數
正康帝道休
九州咸賓服
威德洞八幽
三公奏諸公
不得久淹留

By eating the aurora of dawn and rinsing his mouth with midnight mists,
Downy feathers covered his physical form.
He set forth and rose to tread the empty infinite,
Straightaway ascended the deep and obscure.
He matches longevity with the Eastern Father's years,[1]
Through vast ages he will forever prolong life.

5.42–46 Horseback War-drum Dance Songs [Preface]

Among Emperor Ling's [r. 168–189] Western Garden Musicians was one Li Jian, who could do the "Horseback War-Drum Dances." On encountering the chaos [near the end of the Eastern Han], he accompanied Duan Wei west. When the late emperor [Cao Cao] heard that Li Jian formerly possessed this skill, he summoned him. But Jian had already discontinued [dancing it]; in addition, the ancient music was rife with errors and mistakes. The libretti of different ages do not necessarily carry on from one to the other, so based on the former music, I have recreated five new songs. I dare not offer them to the imperial court, but nearer to hand one might form the inferior music of a vassaldom with them.

5.42 Sage Emperor

Our Sage Emperor accorded with the ordained succession;[2]
The regime is prosperous, the imperial way splendid.
The Nine Provinces all submit and obey,
His awesome virtue penetrates the eight remotenesses.
The Three Excellencies memorialized about the various lords:[3]
We were not to tarry long [at court].

1 For Eastern Father, see **5.27**, line 13.
2 "Ordained succession" indicates royal succession governed by the heavens.
3 The "Three Excellencies" were three of the highest ministers in the government.

蕃位任至重
8 舊章咸率由

侍臣省文奏
陛下體仁慈
沈吟有愛戀
12 不忍聽可之
迫有官典憲
不得顧恩私
諸王當就國
16 璽綬何累縗

便時舍外殿
宮省寂無人
主上增顧念
20 皇母懷苦辛
何以爲贈賜
傾府竭寶珍
文錢百億萬
24 采帛若烟雲
乘輿服禦物
錦羅與金銀
龍旂垂九旒
28 羽蓋參班輪

In the position of vassal prince, the burden is truly great:
The old regulations are all to be followed.

Attendant officials scrutinized the written memorial,
But His Majesty embodies kindness and compassion.
Mumbling to himself out of love and fondness,
He could not bear to heed and approve it.
But compelled by the officials' codes and laws,
He could not regard affection and personal feelings.
All the princes were to go to their fiefs:
Their seals and ribbons, how profuse!

We forthwith lodged in halls apart;
The palace precinct was quiet, devoid of people.
His Majesty increased his fond remembrances,
Our august mother felt anguished and distressed.[1]
What did he use as bestowals and gifts?
He upended the treasury, exhausted its precious objects:
Inscribed coins in the hundreds of millions,
Polychrome silks as plentiful as mists and clouds,
Objects of imperial use:
Brocades and gauzes, gold and silver,
Dragon flags trailing nine streamers,
Plumed canopies and painted wheels.[2]

1 I.e., Empress Dowager Bian.

2 The flag with a dragon painted on it and with nine streamers attached, as well as vermilion-painted carriage wheels, were imperial privileges.

諸王自計念
無功荷厚德
思一效筋力
糜軀以報國

鴻臚擁節衛
副使隨經營
貴戚并出送
夾道交輜軿
車服齊整設
韡曄燿天精
武騎衛前後
鼓吹簫笳聲
祖道魏東門
淚下霑冠纓
扳蓋因內顧
俯仰慕同生
行行將日暮
何時還闕庭
車輪爲徘徊
四馬躊躇鳴
路人尚酸鼻
何況骨肉情

All the princes reckoned and pondered;
Though lacking merit, we received generous favor.
Our thoughts were one: to devote strength of sinew,
And be pulverized to repay our country.

The grand herald, holding a verge, acts as escort,
Assistant envoys follow along to and fro.
Noble relatives come out together to see us off,
Lining the route curtained carts and carriages intermingle.
Vehicles and vestments are arrayed in good order,
Fulgently shining, more brilliant than the sun in the sky.
Martial cavalrymen escort us front and rear,
The flutes and pipes of musicians resound.
We sacrifice to the road at Wei's eastern gate,
Tears fall and wet our hat-strings.
I draw the canopy to turn and look back,
Instantly I long for my born brothers.
Traveling on and on, it is almost dusk;
When will I return to court?
The carriage wheels are hesitant,
My four horses falter and neigh.
Even passers-by feel the pain,
How much more those with bonds of flesh and blood!

5.43 靈芝篇

靈芝生玉池
朱草被洛濱
榮華相晃耀
4 光采曄若神
古時有虞舜
父母頑且嚚
盡孝于田壟
8 烝烝不違仁
伯瑜年七十
彩衣以娛親
慈母笞不痛
12 歔欷涕沾巾

丁蘭少失母
自傷早孤煢
刻木當嚴親
16 朝夕致三牲
暴子見凌悔
犯罪以亡形

5.43 Numinous Mushroom Song

Numinous mushrooms grow at the Jade Pond,
Vermilion plants blanket the banks of the Luo.[1]
Their luxuriant florescence mutually dazzlingly shines,
The bright colors are as brilliant as though divine.
In ancient times there was Yu Shun;[2]
His father and mother were stupid and deceitful.
He was utterly filial on the field paths,
Grandly he remained humane.
When Bo Yu was seventy,
He wore particolored clothes to delight his parents.
When his loving mother whipped him and it did not hurt,
He sobbed and tears soaked his kerchief.[3]

Ding Lan while young lost his mother,
And pitied himself early orphaned and alone.
He carved wood to represent his parents,
And morning and evening brought them the three sacrificial animals.
When they were abused and insulted by a ruffian,
Ding broke the law, with no regard for punishment.

1 Both numinous mushrooms and vermilion plants were auspicious. Gu Zhi 古直, for example, quotes the weft book to the *Classic of Filial Piety* entitled *Xiao jing wei Yuan shen qi* 孝緯援神契: "As for the ruler, when his virtue reaches plants and trees, then mushrooms and vermilion plants grow" 王者，德至於草木，則芝草朱草生.

2 This is the legendary sage emperor Shun.

3 According to *Shuo yuan*, Bo Yu 伯俞（伯瑜）was whipped by his mother and cried. Because he had never cried before when she whipped him, she asked why he was crying this time. He replied that before it had always hurt but now she was too feeble to make it hurt, so he cried. Most famously, the one who wore particolored clothes for the amusement of his senile parents was not Bo Yu but Laolaizi 老萊子, a model of filial piety.

丈人為泣血
20 免戾全其名

董永遭家貧
父老財無遺
舉假以供養
24 傭作致甘肥
責家填門至
不知何用歸
天靈感至德
28 神女為秉機

歲月不安居
嗚呼我皇考
生我既已晚
32 棄我何其早
蓼莪誰所興
念之令人老

1 Lines 13–20 tell of Ding Lan of the Later Han. He was orphaned while young, and, having no parents to serve in their old age, carved them out of wood. He served these wooden effigies as if they were alive. One day a neighbor's wife wanted to borrow something from Ding's wife. Ding's wife asked the wooden parents, and when they did not appear pleased, she denied the request. The neighbor himself was drunk and hurried over to curse the wooden parents. He even hit them over the head with a stick. When Ding got home, he killed his

The old ones wept blood for him,
And he was exonerated and preserved his reputation.[1]

Dong Yong encountered family poverty;
His father was elderly and no property remained.
He borrowed to provide support,
He worked for pay to bring him savory foods.
Creditors came filling his door,
And he did not know how to pay them back.
Heavenly spirits were moved by his perfect virtue,
And a goddess employed a loom for him.[2]

The years and months do not remain at rest;
O woe, my illustrious deceased father.[3]
Since when I was born it was already late;
Why abandon me so soon?
Who was it who composed “Tall Tansy Mustard”?
Thinking of it makes a man old.[4]

---

neighbor. Ding was arrested, and as he took leave of the wooden parents, they shed tears. Ding was let off due to his exemplary filial behavior. The “three sacrificial animals” are the ox, sheep, and pig.

2 Dong Yong was a man of the Former Han, who lost his mother while he was young. When his father died, he did not have the means to bury him, so he borrowed, pledging himself into slavery should he fail to repay the loan. After he had buried his father, Dong was on his way to take his place as a slave when he met a woman on the road. She wanted to become his wife. He hesitated because of his penury, but she insisted that that didn’t matter. Together they went to his master’s house. The master asked the woman what abilities she had, and she replied that she could weave. The master told her that when she had woven him a thousand bolts of silk, they would be freed. Within ten days the work was completed. The master was amazed and set them free. It turned out that the wife was the star Weaver Woman (Vega). Heaven had been moved to send her to help Dong because of his filial piety. She flew off after telling him this.

3 Refers to Cao Cao.

4 “Tall Tansy Mustard" is a poem in the *Classic of Poetry* (*Mao shi* 202). It is a complaint about the passing of the speaker’s parents, his missing them and his inability to depend on them and to fulfill his filial duties towards them.

退詠南風詩
36 灑淚滿禕抱

亂曰
聖皇君四海
德教朝夕宣
萬國咸禮讓
40 百姓家肅虔
庠序不失儀
孝悌處中田
戶有曾閔子
44 比屋皆仁賢
髫　無夭齒
黃發盡其年
陛下三萬歲
48 慈母亦復然

Retreating I will chant that south wind poem,
And the tears I shed fill up my embroidered robe.[1]

Envoi:
The sage emperor rules the four seas,
His virtuous influence spreads day and night.
Myriad states all are courteous and defential,
Common people of every family are reverent and respectful.
District and hamlet schools do not omit proper conduct,
The filial and dutiful to elder brothers keep to the fields.
Households have sons like Zeng and Min,[2]
Every home is humane and worthy.
Young children have no early death,
The hoary-headed fulfill their years.
Three cheers "Long Life!" for Your Majesty,
And likewise for our loving mother.[3]

1 "South wind poem" refers to the poem "Triumphal Wind" 凱風 from the *Classic of Poetry* (*Mao shi* 32). It is a poem of filial piety that deals with the inability of seven sons to comfort their mother.

2 This refers to Confucius' disciples Zengzi 曾子 and Min Ziqian 閔子騫. Both had reputations for filial piety.

3 Empress Dowager Bian.

5.44 大魏篇

大魏應靈符
天祿方甫始
聖德致泰和
神明為驅使
左右為供養
中殿宜皇子
陛下長壽考
群臣拜賀咸悦喜

積善有餘慶
寵祿固天常
眾喜填門至
臣子蒙福祥
無患及陽遂
輔翼我聖皇
眾吉咸集會
凶邪奸惡並滅亡

黄鵠游殿前
神鼎周四阿
玉馬充乘輿
芝蓋樹九華

5.44 Great Wei Song

The great Wei responded to numinous signs,
Its heaven-sent blessings were then just beginning.
The emperor's sage virtue brings great peace,
Deities serve at his beck and call.
Those about him provide sustenance,
The inner palace is proper for imperial sons.
May Your Majesty enjoy a ripe old age;
The gathered officials offer congratulations and all are happy and joyful.

Amassing good deeds brings a surfeit of blessings;
Favor and good fortune are certainly Heaven's normal way.
Manifold happiness comes filling the gates,
The officials receive good luck:
That no trouble reaches even a *yangsui*,[1]
They aid and assist our sage emperor.
Manifold auspiciousnesses all assemble and gather,
Evil and treachery are both destroyed.

A yellow swan swam in front of the palace,
Divine tripods are all around the courtyards.[2]
Jade horses fill the imperial equipage,
The mushroom canopy puts up nine blossoms.[3]

---

1 *Yangsui* is a type of carriage. I am following here Gu Zhi's interpretation of this problematic line. See *Additional Notes*.

2 The yellow swan and divine tripods are good omens. See *Additional Notes*.

3 References to jade horses and numinous mushrooms also imply the presence of a good and successful ruler. The nine blossoms echo the "nine-petal mushroom canopy" 芝蓋九葩 in Ban Gu's "Western Capital Rhapsody. See also *Additional Notes*.

白虎戲西除
舍利從闢邪
騏驥躡足舞
鳳皇拊翼歌

豐年大置酒
玉樽列廣庭
樂飲過三爵
朱顏暴已形
式宴不違禮
君臣歌鹿鳴
樂人舞鼙鼓
百官雷拚贊若驚

儲禮如江海
積善若陵山
皇嗣繁且熾
孫子列曾玄
群臣咸稱萬歲
陛下長壽樂年

御酒停未飲
貴戚跪東廂

A white tiger plays on the western steps,
A *sheli* follows a *bixie*.[1]
A unicorn dances with tapping feet,
A phoenix sings with beating wings.

In a year of plenty a great feast is made,
Jade goblets are arrayed in the broad courtyard.
Happily drinking, we exceed three cups;[2]
Our flushed faces show and give us away.
Our feasting does not violate etiquette,
And ruler and officials sing "Deer Cry."[3]
The musicians dance to the beating of the horseback war-drum,
A hundredfold officers thunderously clap and cheer as though amazed.

Your stored-up courtesy is like a river or sea;
Your accumulated good deeds are like a hill or mountain.
Your imperial sons are abundant and splendid,
Your grandsons will add great- and great-great-grandsons to the list.
The gathered officials all proclaim "Long life!
May Your Majesty live long and take pleasure in the years!"

The imperial wine pauses, not yet consumed;
Noble kin kneel in the eastern wing.

---

1 The white tiger is the guardian directional spirit of the west. The *sheli*, sometimes called *hanli* 含利, is a beast that appeared in Han period processions. See *Additional Notes*. As its name implies, the *bixie* (expels evil) is a mythical animal of apotropaic significance.

2 See **5.1**, line 9.

3 The *Classic of Poetry* poem "Deer Cry" 鹿鳴 is *Mao shi* 161, a poem about a ruler holding a feast for his ministers and presenting them with gifts.

侍人承顏色
奉進金玉觴
此酒亦真酒
福祿當聖皇
陛下臨軒笑
左右咸歡康
杯來一何遲
群僚以次行
賞賜累千億
百官並富昌

5.45 精微篇

精微爛金石
至心動神明
杞妻哭死夫
梁山為之傾
子丹西質秦
烏白馬角生
鄒衍囚燕市
繁霜為夏零

1 Qi Liang of Qi was killed in battle in 550 BCE. The story on which these lines are based says that his wife cried so hard that the city wall collapsed in response. It is unclear why the poem mentions a Liang mountain. See *Additional Notes*.

The attendants comply with the emperor's expression,
Respectfully present chalices of gold and jade.
This wine is indeed the True Wine,
A blessing fit for our sage emperor.
His majesty smiles down from the railed landing,
Those in attendance are all joyful and at ease.
How slowly the cups come!
The host of officials are served in proper order.
Gifts worth billions are bestowed,
The hundred officers are altogether rich and prosperous.

5.45 Essential Subtlety Song

Essential subtlety can break metal and stone;
The sincerest heart can move the gods.
Qi's wife cried for her dead husband,
And the Liang mountain toppled because of it.[1]
Prince Dan went west as a hostage in Qin,
And crows turned white and horses grew horns.[2]
Zou Yan was imprisoned in a town in Yan,
And profuse frost fell in summer for him.[3]

---

2 Prince Dan of Yan was a hostage in the state of Qin. He wanted to go home, and in a popular version of the events, the king of Qin listed a number of impossible conditions to be met before he could leave, among them being crows heads turning white and horses growing horns. When heaven and earth responded to Prince Dan's plight by making these things happen, he was allowed to leave.

3 Zou Yan was totally loyal to King Hui of Yan, but the king believed slander about Zou Yan and had him arrested. Zou cried to Heaven, and Heaven sent down frost in summer in response.

關東有賢女
自字蘇來卿
壯年報父仇
身沒垂功名
女休逢赦書
白刃幾在頸
俱上列仙籍
去死獨就生

太倉令有罪
遠徵當就拘
自悲居無男
禍至無與俱
緹縈痛父言
荷擔西上書
盤桓北闕下
泣淚何漣如
乞得並姊弟
沒身贖父軀
漢文感其義
肉刑法用除
其父得以免
辯義在列圖

East of the pass there was a worthy daughter,
She styled herself Su Laiqing.
In her prime she took revenge on her father's enemy,
And when she died, she left behind merit and reputation.
Maid Xiu received a pardon letter,
With the naked blade nearly on her neck.
Both were on the "roster of ranked immortals;"[1]
Staving off death, only one got to live.

The Prefect of the Great Granary committed a crime;
He had been summoned from afar and was about to go to be arrested.
He lamented that his home had no sons,
And once calamity came, there was no one to accompany him.
Tiying was pained by her father's words
And undertook to present a memorial in the west.
She circled around beneath the northern gate-tower,
The tears she wept – how they streamed down!
She begged to combine in herself her older and younger sisters
And relinquish herself to redeem her father's person.
Emperor Wen of Han was moved by her dutifulness,
And mutilating punishments were hence abolished by law.
Her father was able thereby to be exonerated,
And her eloquence and dutifulness are in the *Exemplary Illustrations*.[2]

---

1 Huang Jie explains this as a euphemism for a roll of the dead. In addition to this piece, the story of Maid Xiu, or Daughter Xiu, is told in more detail in other poems also from the third century. See *Additional Notes*.

2 This must be a reference to an illustrated version of the *Lie nü zhuan* (Traditions of Exemplary Women) or to paintings depicting women from the book.

多男亦何為
一女足成居

簡子南渡河
津吏廢舟船
執法將加刑
女娟擁棹前
妾父聞君來
將涉不測淵
畏懼風波起
禱祝祭名川
備禮饗神祇
為君求福先
不勝釂祀誠
致令犯罰艱
君必欲加誅
乞使知罪諐
妾願以身代
至誠感蒼天
國君高其義
其父用赦原

1 In 167 BCE, it was ordered that judicial officers arrest Chunyu Yi 淳于意, who was Prefect of the Grand Granary of Qi, and transport him to be imprisoned in the capital at Chang'an. He had five daughters and no sons. When he was about

Why in that case have many sons?
One daughter is enough to keep a family together.[1]

When Jianzi was crossing the Yellow River heading south,
The functionary at the ford caused the boats to be delayed.[2]
The law enforcement officers were about to apply the punishment,
When his daughter Juan stepped forward holding an oar:
"Since my father heard you were coming,
And were going to cross the unfathomable depths,
He has dreaded that wind and waves would arise,
And, praying and supplicating, he has made sacrifices to the famous river,
And prepared gifts to offer to the gods
To seek good blessings for you in advance,
But he was unequal to his sincerity in draining the libations,
To the point it has caused the adversity of crime and punishment.
If you are definitely going to impose death,
I beseech you, let him be conscious of his offense.
I am willing to substitute my body for his,
May my absolute sincerity move azure Heaven.
The prince held her dutifulness in high regard,
And so her father was pardoned and absolved.

---

to be taken, he cursed his daughters for being of no use in such a situation. His daughter Tiying was very hurt and followed him to Chang'an, where she presented a communication that said, "When my father was an official, everyone in Qi praised his honesty and fairness, but now he has broken the law and been sentenced to punishment. I lament that those who have died cannot live again and that those who have suffered the mutilating punishments cannot again be made whole. Even though they once more wished to correct their errors and start over, there is no way to do so. I wish to be confiscated as an official slave to redeem my father's punishment and crime so that he can start over." The communication moved Emperor Wen to show leniency and to abolish mutilating punishments.

2 The story of Daughter Juan and Zhao Jianzi 趙簡子 (Zhao Yang 趙鞅), a powerful figure of the state of Jin during the fifth century BCE, is told in *Traditions of Exemplary Women*. Zhao Jianzi was going south to attack Chu and had set a time for the officer in charge of a ford to take him across the river. When he arrived, the officer was dead drunk, and Jianzi wanted to kill him. But the officer's daughter Juan interceded and saved her father. The narrative in the poem follows the account in *Traditions of Exemplary Women* quite closely.

河激奏中流
筒子知其賢
歸聘為夫人
榮寵超後先
辯女解父命
何況健少年

黃初發和氣
明堂德教施
治道致太平
禮樂風俗移
刑措民無枉
怨女複何為
聖皇長壽考
景福常來儀

5.46 孟冬篇

孟冬十月
陰氣厲清
武官誡田
講旅統兵
元龜襲吉

"The River Roils" was performed mid-stream,[1]
And Jianzi grasped her worthiness.
On returning he took her to be his wife,
And his glorious favor surpassed any before or since.
If eloquent daughters may save fathers' lives,
How much more then might robust lads!

The Huangchu period has produced a harmonious *qi*,
From the Bright Hall virtuous teachings spread.[2]
The way of good governing has brought the Great Peace,
And with rites and music, customs and usages alter.
Punishments are disused, yet the people are not crooked,
What would an aggrieved daughter do anymore?
May our sage emperor enjoy high old age,
And great good blessings always come and make an appearance.

5.46 First Month of Winter Song

In the first month of winter, the tenth month,
The *yin* force is keen and crisp.
Military officials ordered the hunt,
To exercise the army and train the troops.
The great turtle repeated auspicious results,

1 This song is in *Traditions of Exemplary Women.*

2 A Bright Hall was a building for ceremonial functions that was constructed according to cosmological beliefs, being round above and square below.

元光著明
蚩尤蹕路
8 風弭雨停

乘輿啟行
鸞鳴幽軋
虎賁採騎
12 飛象珥鶡
鐘鼓鏗鏘
簫管嘈喝
萬騎齊鑣
16 千乘等蓋

夷山填谷
平林滌藪
張羅萬里
20 盡其飛走

趯趯狡兔
揚白跳翰
獵以青骹
24 掩以修竿

A great light brought forth its brightness.[1]
Chiyu cleared the road,[2]
Winds abated, rain ceased.

The imperial carriage begins to move,
Simurgh-bells sounding, clank clash.
The Rapid-as-Tigers riding horseback are colorfully clad,[3]
The fast ivory carriage is ornamented with pheasant plumes.
Bells and drums clang and crash,
Pipes and flutes bellow and bawl.
Ten thousand riders keep their bits in line,
A thousand carriages keep their canopies even.

They flatten mountains and fill valleys,
Level forests and sweep away marshes,
Spread nets for myriad *li*,
Take all that walks or flies.

Leaping and hopping the wily rabbit,
Flashing its white fur, bobbling its long fur.
They hunt it with the blue-legged goshawk,
Ambush it with long bamboo poles.

---

1 "Great turtle" is a reference to divination by reading cracks produced by heat on turtle shells, or plastromancy. A "great light" means here a comet, as a good omen ushering out the old and bringing in the new.

2 There are multiple traditions regarding the warrior figure Chiyou. Relevant to his appearance here, he appears in *Han Feizi* as a member of the vanguard that leads the Yellow Emperor up Mount Tai. He also figures in the hunt that takes place in the first month of winter in Zhang Heng's "Western Metropolis Rhapsody." David R. Knechtges suggests that Chiyou there is "a person in the procession who impersonates Chiyou." In connection with the previous line of the present poem, note that the comet that appeared in 135 BCE was called the Banner of Chiyou 蚩尤旗.

3 The Gentlemen Rapid-as-Tigers were an imperial guard.

韓盧宋鵲
呈才騁足
噬不盡緤
牽麋掎鹿

魏氏發機
養基撫弦
都盧尋高
搜索猴猨
慶忌孟賁
蹈穀超巒
張目決眥
發怒穿冠

頓熊扼虎
蹴豹搏貙
氣有餘勢
負象而趨

獲車既盈
日側樂終
罷役解徒
大饗離宮

Hanlu and Songque[1]
Show their skill, sprint fleet of foot,
Bite before their leads run out,
Drag down elàphure, pull down sika deer.

Mr. Wei pulls the crossbow trigger,
Yang Ji plucks the bowstring.[2]
A Dulu climbs up high
Hunting for macaques and gibbons.[3]
Qing Jis and Meng Bens
Tread valleys and cross ridges;[4]
They open their eyes wide, split their sockets,
Their hair standing on end in anger pokes through their caps.

They knock down bears, seize tigers,
Trample leopards, wrestle leopard-cats,
And their energy having strength to spare,
They hurry along bearing an elephant.

The game carts now filled,
The sun slants and the festivities come to an end.
They dismiss the conscripts and release the troops,
And hold a great banquet in a detached palace.

---

1 Hanlu and Songque are the names of archetypal hunting hounds.

2 Mr. Wei is the same as Da Wei 大魏, who is mentioned in *Wu Yue Chunqiu* and elsewhere as an early figure in the use of the crossbow. Yang Ji is Yang Youji 養由基, a skilled archer of the sixth century BCE.

3 Dulu was the name of an old Burmese country. Its acrobats were good at climbing poles.

4 Qing Ji was a man of Wu during the Spring and Autumn period. He supposedly could chase down fleeing animals and catch flying birds with his bare hands. Meng Ben was a brave man of Qi during the Warring States period. It was said of him that in the water he wasn't afraid of lamia or dragons and that on land, he did not fear rhinoceroses or tigers.

亂曰
聖皇臨飛軒
論功校獵徒
死禽積如京
流血成溝渠
明詔大勞賜
大官供有無
走馬行酒醴
驅車布肉魚
鳴鼓舉觴爵
擊鐘釂無餘
絕網縱麟麑
弛罩出鳳雛
收功在羽校
威靈振鬼區
陛下長歡樂
永世合天符

Envoi:
The sage emperor looks down from a high landing,
Appraises merit, evaluates the hunters.
Dead game is piled like hills,
The streaming blood forms races and rivulets.
The emperor brilliantly orders a grand gift of rewards,
And the Grand Provisioner furnishes everything.
Racing horses move wine and ale,
Speeding carts distribute meat and fish.
With the sounding drums they raise chalice and beaker,
With the striking bells they drain the last drop.
Loose the net, free the unicorn fawns;
Remove the lid, let out the phoenix chicks.
Achieving success rests in the plumed battalion,
Their formidable power jolts the farthest lands.
May Your Majesty always be happy and joyful
And forever accord with Heaven's token of approbation.

5.47 棄婦篇

石榴植前庭
綠葉搖縹青
丹華灼烈烈
璀采有光榮
光榮曄流離
可以處淑靈
翠鳥飛來集
撫翼以悲鳴
悲鳴夫何爲
丹華實不成
撫心長歎息
無子當歸寧
有子月經天
無子若流星
天月相終始
流星沒無精
棲遲失所宜
下與瓦石并
憂懷從中來
歎息通雞鳴
反側不能寐

5.47 The Rejected Wife

A pomegranate grows in the forecourt;
Its green leaves shimmer pale green.
The cinnabar blossoms blaze brilliantly,
Their gem-like colors have a glossy luster –
A glossy luster as resplendent as lapis lazuli,
And thus fit to lodge a supernal creature.
A kingfisher comes flying to roost;
Beating its wings it sadly cries –
Sadly cries, but over what?
The cinnabar blossoms do not form fruit.
I beat my breast and heave a long sigh;
Not having a son, I must go back to my parents:
Having a son, you're the moon plying the sky;
Without a son, you're like a falling star.
The moon in the sky waxes and wanes,
But a falling star dies without a glimmer.
Dallying and dawdling, it loses its appointed place
And descends to join with rubble and stones.
Anxious cares come from within,
And I sigh all the way till cockcrow.
I toss and turn and cannot sleep,

逍遙於前庭
踟躕還入房
24 肅肅帷幕聲
搴帷更攝帶
撫弦調鳴箏
慷慨有餘音
28 要妙悲且清
收淚長歎息
何以負神靈
招搖帶霜露
32 何必春夏成
晚穫爲良實
願君且安寧

5.48 長歌行

墨出青松煙
筆出狡兔翰
古人感鳥跡
4 文字有改判

Wander in the forecourt.
Pacing to and fro, I return to my room;
The curtains make a swishing sound.
Drawing the curtains, I tie the cords;
Strumming its strings, I tune the singing zither:
Where impassioned, it has a sound that lingers;
Where subtle, it is both sad and clear.
Holding back tears, I heave a long sigh;
Why blame this miraculous bird?
Sweet olive needs a frosty dew;
What need to ripen in spring or summer?[1]
Late harvest makes good fruit;
I wish my lord to be calm and serene.

5.48 Long Song Ballad (fragment)

Ink comes from the soot of green pines,
Brushes come from the long fur of wily rabbits.
Ancient people were influenced by bird tracks,
But for writing there were changes and differentiations.[2]

1 Sweet olive is an evergreen that often flowers in autumn and winter, so the speaker is here and in the following line telling the husband not to be so impatient for the birth of a child.

2 One tradition says that Chinese script originated from humans observing bird tracks. The postface to *Shuo wen jie zi* 說文解字 says in part: "Huang ti's scribe Ts'ang Chieh saw the traces of the footprints of birds and beasts. He recognized that these partiform structures could be distinguished and differentiated one from another. Thus he first created writing" 黃帝之史倉頡見鳥獸蹏迒之迹。知分理之可相別異也初造書契 (tr. William Boltz).

List of Abbreviations

AM	*Asia Major*
BMFEA	*Bulletin of the Museum of Far Eastern Antiquities*
BSOAS	*Bulletin of the School of Oriental and African Studies*
Cao Haidong	Cao Haidong 曹海東, trans. *Xin yi Cao Zijian ji* 新譯曹子建集. Taipei: Sanmin shuju, 2003.
Ccbz	Hong Xingzu 洪興祖 (1090–1155), ed. *Chu ci buzhu* 楚辭補注. Beijing: Zhonghua shuju, 1983.
Cheng	Ming dynasty Wanli 萬曆 period (1573–1620) edition by Cheng shi 程氏 that served as Ding Yan's base text.
Cjky	*Cao ji kaoyi* 曹集考異. Edited by Zhu Xuzeng 朱緒曾 (fl. 1837). In *Jinling congshu* 金陵叢書, 3rd series.
CLEAR	*Chinese Literature: Essays, Articles, Reviews*
Concordance	Jean-Pierre Diény, comp. *Concordance des oeuvres completes de Cao Zhi*. Paris: Institut des Hautes Études Chinoises, Collège de France, 1977.
Cxj	Xu Jian 徐堅 (659–729) et al., comps. *Chu xue ji* 初學記. Beijing: Zhonghua shuju, 1962.
Ding	Ding Yan 丁晏 (1794–1875), ed. *Cao ji quanping* 曹集銓評. Edited by Ye Jusheng 葉菊生. Beijing: Wenxue guji kanxingshe, 1957.
EMC	*Early Medieval China*
Fu Yashu	Fu Yashu 傅亞庶, ed. *San Cao shi wen quanji yizhu* 三曹詩文全集譯注. Changchun: Jilin wenshi chubanshe, 1997.
HHs	Fan Ye 范曄 (398–445). *Hou Han shu* 後漢書. Beijing: Zhonghua shuju, 1963.
HJAS	*Harvard Journal of Asiatic Studies*
Hnz	He Ning 何寧, ed. *Huainanzi jishi* 淮南子集釋. Beijing: Zhonghua shuju, 1998.
Hs	Ban Gu 班固 (32–92). *Han shu* 漢書. Beijing: Zhonghua shuju, 1962.

https://doi.org/10.1515/9781501507038-004

Huang Jie	Huang Jie 黃節 (1873–1935), ed. *Cao Zijian shi zhu* 曹子建詩注. Rev. ed. Beijing: Renmin chubanshe, 1957.
Hydcd	*Hanyu dacidian* 漢語大辭典.
JAOS	*Journal of the American Oriental Society*
Li ji	*Li ji zheng yi* 禮記正義, in *Shisan.*
Lu	Lu Qinli 逯欽立, ed. *Xian Qin Han Wei Jin Nanbeichao shi* 先秦漢魏晉南北朝詩. Beijing: Zhonghua shuju, 1983.
MS	*Monumenta Serica*
Mszy	*Mao shi zhengyi* 毛詩正義, in *Shisan.*
QHHw	Yan Kejun 嚴可均 (1762–1843), comp., *Quan Hou Han wen* 全後漢文, in Yan Kejun, comp. *Quan shanggu sandai Qin Han Sanguo Liuchao wen* 全上古三代秦漢三國六朝文. (Beijing: Zhonghua shuju, 1991.
QSgw	Yan Kejun 嚴可均 (1762–1843), comp., *Quan Sanguo wen* 全三國文, in *Quan shanggu sandai Qin Han Sanguo Liuchao wen.*
QWJ	Han Geping 韓格平 et al., eds. *Quan Wei Jin fu jiaozhu* 全魏晉賦校注. Jilin: Jilin wenshi chubanshe, 2008.
Sbby	*Sibu beiyao* 四部備要.
Sbck	*Sibu congkan* 四部叢刊.
Sgz	Chen Shou 陳壽 (233–297). *San guo zhi* 三國志. Beijing: Zhonghua shuju, 1959.
Shisan	*Shisan jing zhushu* 十三經注疏. Beijing: Beijing daxue chubanshe, 2000.
Shj	Yuan Ke 袁珂, ed. *Shanhai jing jiaozhu* 山海經校注. Shanghai: Shanghai guji chubanshe, 1980.
Shuchao	Kong Guangtao 孔廣陶 (1832–1890), ed. *Beitang shuchao* 北堂書鈔. Nanhai: Kong shi, 1888.
Sj	Sima Qian 司馬遷 (145–86? BCE). *Shi ji* 史記. Beijing: Zhonghua shuju, 1959.
Ss	Shen Yue 沈約 (441–513), *Song shu* 宋書. Beijing: Zhonghua shuju, 1974.
Sszy	*Shang shu zhengyi* 尚書正義, in *Shisan.*
TP	*T'oung Pao*

Tpyl — Li Fang 李昉 (925–996) et al., comps. *Taiping yulan* 太平御覽. Beijing: Zhonghua shuju, 1995.

Wenji — *Songben Cao Zijian wenji* 宋本曹子建文集. Facsimile of a Song edition in the collection of Qu shi [Qu Yong 瞿鏞] of Changshu 常熟瞿氏藏本影印. In *Xu Gu yi congshu* 續古逸叢書. Shanghai: Shangwu yinshuguan, 1922.

Wx — Xiao Tong 蕭統 (501–531), ed. *Wen xuan* 文選. Shanghai: Shanghai guji chubanshe, 1986.

Xj — *Xiao jing*孝經, in *Shisan*.

Xu — Xu Gongchi 徐公持. *Cao Zhi nianpu kaozheng* 曹植年譜考證. Beijing: Shehui kexue wenxian chubanshe, 2016.

Yfsj — Guo Maoqian 郭茂倩 (twelfth century), ed. *Yuefu shi ji* 樂府詩集. Beijing: Zhonghua shuju, 1979.

Ytxy — Wu Zhaoyi 吳兆宜(fl. 1672), annot. *Yutai xinyong jianzhu*玉臺新詠箋注. Beijing: Zhonghua shuju, 1999.

Ywlj — Ouyang Xun 歐陽詢 (557–641) et al., comps. *Yiwen leiju* 藝文類聚. 1965. Revised edition Shanghai: Shanghai guji chubanshe, 1999.

Zhang Pu — Zhang Pu 張溥 (1602–1641), ed. *Chen Siwang ji* 陳思王集, in volume 2 of Zhang Pu, ed. *Han Wei Liuchao baisan mingjia ji* 漢魏六朝百三名家集. 6 vols. Taipei: Wenjin chubanshe, 1979.

Zhao — Zhao Youwen 趙幼文, ed. *Cao Zhi ji jiaozhu* 曹植集校注. Beijing: Renmin wenxue chubanshe, 1984.

Zz — *Zuo zhuan* 左傳.

Additional Notes

These notes are arranged in the order in which the pieces appear in this book. The numbers in the left margin are line numbers.

1.1
東征賦 ***Fu* on the Eastern Campaign**
Ding 1; Zhao 63–65
Additional notes
Pref. Reading 宮 for 官 with Zhang Pu 1.1b. See Zhao 64. This preface is also translated in David R. Knechtges, "Group Literary Composition at the Court of Ye in the Late Eastern Han," unpub. paper, 22, and Shih, "Jian'an Literature Revisited," 165.
9 The extra length of this line in Chinese indicates there is a problem here. Perhaps, as Zhao 64n suggests, text is missing.
13–16 Ding 1 states that these lines were not in his base text. He added them from *Tpyl* 336.8a, where they appear in isolation. The *Tpyl* text, however, does not have the two 兮 graphs in lines 13 and 15, so Ding adds them based on Zhang Pu 1.2a. I understand 戈櫓 in line 13 as 戈船 (*Hydcd*, s. v. 戈櫓); cf. Zhao 65n. On "halberd ships," see Joseph Needham, *Science and Civilisation in China*, vol. 4, *Physics and Physical Technology*, part 3, *Civil Engineering and Nautics* (Cambridge: Cambridge Univ. Press, 1971), 440, 680–81.

1.2
遊觀賦 ***Fu* on Visiting a Lookout (fragment)**
Ding 1–2; Zhao 66–67
Additional notes
Some scholars – Zhao 67, for example – think this piece may date to the same period as **1.1**.

1.3
懷親賦 ***Fu* on Longing for a Loved One (fragment)**
Ding 2; Zhao 407–9
Additional notes
5 Reading 存 for 在, with *Ywlj* 20.372, *Wenji* 1.2a. See Zhao 408.

https://doi.org/10.1515/9781501507038-005

1.4

玄暢賦 *Fu* on Communicating with the Mysterious (fragment)

Ding 2–3; Zhao 241–43

Additional notes

Xu 222 rather speculatively place this *fu* in Jian'an 22 (217).

Pref. Reading 旨 for 情, with *Cxj* 17.422. See Zhao 242.

6 Reading 之 for 以, with *Ywlj* 26.470.

7–8 Line 8, which is found as an isolate in Li Shan's commentary in *Wx* 27.1275, is appended to the *fu* in Ding 3. It is inserted here following *QSgw* 13.5a. See also *QWJ* 30, Fu Yashu 777–78, Zhao 243. The blank line 7 is assumed for prosodic reasons.

10 See Richard John Lynn, *The* Classic of Changes*: A New Translation of the* I Ching *as Interpreted by Wang Bi* (New York: Columbia Univ. Press, 1994), 133–34.

12 On Yi Yin and Lü Shang, see *Sj* 3.94, 32.1477–78.

15 On the connection between yellow bell and dynastic succession, see Martin Kern, rev. of *Writing and Authority in Early China*, by Mark Edward Lewis, *China Review International* 7.2 (Fall 2000), 363–64.

19 Reading 傅 for 摶, with *Wenji* 1.3a; Zhao 244.

21 Reading 舍余駟 for 企駟躍, with *Ywlj* 26.470; Zhao 244.

23 Reading 軌 for 軏, with *Ywlj* 26.470; Zhao 244.

1.5

幽思賦 *Fu* on Hidden Thoughts

Ding 3–4; Zhao does not have this *fu*

1.6

節遊賦 *Fu* on Curtailing Excursions

Ding 4–5; Zhao 183–86

Additional notes

Xu 171–72 dates this to Jian'an 19 (214) or a bit later.

9 The term 西嶽 here must not literally refer to the Western Sacred Peak Mount Hua 華山, which is far away from Ye. Fu Yashu 772 suggests that Cao is using Mount Hua as a metaphor for the imposing height of the Three Terraces, as Zuo Si later does in his "Wei Capital Rhapsody" 魏都賦: "The three Terraces, standing in a row, rise rugged and tall. / With high platforms rearing up from shadowy bases, / They resemble the sheered slopes of Mt. Hua" 三臺列峙以崢嶸亢陽臺於陰基擬華山之削成; Knechtges, *Wen xuan*, 1: 445. See *Wx* 6.273.

11 This line is almost exactly the same as a line from "Rhapsody on the Tall Gate Palace" 長門賦, attributed to Sima Xiangru; see *Wx* 16.714.

14 This line is almost exactly the same as a line from Ban Gu's 班固 (32–92) "Western Capital Rhapsody" 西都賦; see *Wx* 1.18.

26 Wang Tianhai 王天海, trans., *Mu Tianzi zhuan quan yi*; *Yan Danzi quan yi* 穆天子傳全譯; 燕丹子全譯 (Guiyang: Guizhou renmin chubanshe, 1997), 25.

35 Reading 沈浮 for 浮沈, with *Ywlj* 28.507 and *Wenji* 1.4b.

1.7

感節賦 *Fu* on Responding to the Season

Ding 5–6; Zhao 502–4

Additional notes

It is possible that this was written in his ancestral home of Qiao in Jian'an 14 (209); see Xu 105.

16 Reading 末 for 未, with Zhao 503.

17–18 See Xu Weiyu 許維遹, ed., *Han Shi waizhuan jishi* 韓詩外傳集釋 (Beijing: Zhonghua shuju, 1980), 10.350–51; James R. Hightower, *Han Shih Wai Chuan: Han Ying's Illustrations of the Didactic Applications of the Classic of Songs* (Cambridge, Mass.: Harvard Univ. Press, 1952), 333; Wu Zeyu 吳則虞, ed., *Yanzi chunqiu ji shi* 晏子春秋集釋, 2 vols. (Beijing: Zhonghua shuju, 1962), 1: 63.

1.8

離思賦 *Fu* on Thoughts on Parting

Ding 6; Zhao 40–41

Additional notes

Pref. On the campaign, see *Sgz* 1.34–36. The preface to Cao Pi's rhapsody "Moved by Parting" 感離賦 says, "In Jian' an 16, His Highness went on a military expedition west. I stayed to guard. My elderly mother and all my younger brothers went along ..." 建安十六年，上西征，余居守。老母諸弟皆從……; Yi Jianxian 易健賢, trans., *Wei Wendi ji quanyi* 魏文帝集全譯 (Guiyang: Guizhou renmin chubanshe, 2009), 20. Both of these prefaces postdate the *fu* to which they are attached, and while it is conceivable that they are not authentic, I have seen no evidence that is the case. Cao Zhi's use of "heir-designate" in his preface is anachronistic, for Cao Pi was not made heir-designate until Jian'an 22. Zhao 41 seems to think 太子 is simply an error for 世子 ("eldest son of the principal wife"). Another possibility is that Cao Pi's title in the preface was changed sometime later to reflect his new status. On the dating of the piece, see also Xu 123–24.

1.9

釋思賦 *Fu* on Relieving Troubled Thoughts

Ding 6–7; Zhao 51–52

Additional notes

Pref. On Cao Zheng and Cao Shao, see *Sgz* 20.579, 588; Rafe de Crespigny, *A Biographical Dictionary of Later Han to the Three Kingdoms (23–220 AD)* (Leiden: Brill, 2007), 47, 50. Xu 94 estimates that this *fu* dates from about Jian'an 13 (208).

2 Zhao 52 and Fu Yashu 726 think the contents of *Mao shi* 186 and the Mao interpretation of the poem do not match well with this *fu*. They believe Cao Zhi had another version in mind, with Zhao suggesting the Han version of the *Classic of Poetry*.

1.10

臨觀賦 *Fu* on Looking Out from a Lookout

Ding 7; Zhao 505–6

1.11

潛志賦 *Fu* on Focusing the Will

Ding 7; Zhao does not have this *fu*

Additional notes

4 Reading 呈藝 for 藝窟, with *Wenji* 2.1a, Zhang Pu 1.2b, and the Ming movable-type edition, 2.1a (*Sbck*).

12 Reading 天路 for 徇天 and 焉 for 為, with *Ywlj* 36.645.

1.12

閒居賦 *Fu* on Living in Idleness (fragment)

Ding 7–8; Zhao 130–32

Additional notes

8 Reading 而 for 之, with *Ywlj* 64.1144.

15 Reading 廓 for 廊, with *Ywlj* 64.1144.

16 Reading 廣 for 高, with *Ywlj* 64.1144.

1.13

慰子賦 *Fu* on Condolence for a Departed Child

Ding 8–9; Zhao does not have this *fu*

Additional notes

Cao Zhi had two daughters who died as infants and for whom he wrote laments 哀辭. Given the use of the term 中殤 in this *fu*, since they died so young, the piece would not appear to be about them.

1.14

敍愁賦 *Fu* on Expressing Sorrow (fragment)

Ding 9; Zhao 61–63

Additional notes

There were actually three Cao daughters given to Liu Xie 劉協 (181–234), who was still emperor in Jian'an 18 (213), when this event took place. The youngest was Cao Hua 曹華, who remained home because of her age. The two who did move to the emperor's household were Cao Xian 曹憲 and Cao Jie 曹節; see *Sgz* 1.42, and *HHs* 10B.455.

3 Partly quoted from *Mao shi* 32.

8 The explanation for 六列 given in the note to this line derives from a comment by Sun Xingyan 孫星衍 (1753–1818) in *Xu Guwen yuan* 續古文苑 (Changsha: Shangwu yinshuguan, 1940), 2.105. Zhao 62 offers a somewhat different explanation, opining that 六 is an error for 女 and that it should come after 列, instead of before, rendering 列女.

1.15

秋思賦 *Fu* on Autumn Thoughts

Ding 9; Zhao 471–73

Additional notes

Following line 6, some texts of the *fu* have two lines that are not included in Ding or translated here. They are translated in Kroll, "Seven Rhapsodies of Ts'ao Chih," *JAOS* 120 (2000): 4. See Kroll's n. 14 for the texts that contain those lines.

4 Reading 衣 for 璣, with *Shuchao* 154.8a, *Wenji* 2.3b, and others (see Fu Yashu 801).

1.16

九愁賦 *Fu* on Nine Sorrows

Ding 10–11; Zhao 252–57

Additional notes

This *fu* adopts the persona of Qu Yuan and speaks of having been slandered and exiled. But at the same time it is also surely a comment by Cao Zhi on his own experiences under Cao Pi's reign. See Xu 323–24. Some commentators tie parts of the *fu* to specific events in his life. See Cao Haidong 37–43; Fu Yashu 780–85.

6 Reading 顧 for 顧, with *Ywlj* 35.621.

26 Reading 惆悵 for 悵望, with *Ywlj* 35.621.

33 See Zhang Heng's "Rhapsody on Pondering the Mystery" 思玄賦; David R. Knechtges, *Wen xuan: Selections of refined Literature*, vol. 3, *Rhapsodies on Natural Phenomena, Birds and Animals, Aspirations and Feelings, Sorrowful Laments, Literature, Music, and Passions* (Princeton: Princeton Univ. Press, 1996), 3: 123. See *Wx* 15.665.

48 Reading 悗 for 挽, as suggested by *Cjky* 2.4b.

50 Reading 乎 for 兮, with *Ywlj* 35.621.

61 Reading 收 for 長, with *Ywlj* 35.621.

67 Reading 軌 for 軏, with *Ywlj* 35.621.

69 Reading 而 for 以, with *Ywlj* 35.621.

77 Reading 徑 for 隧, with *Ywlj* 35.621.

82 Reading 若 for 苦 and 刃 for 忍, with *Ywlj* 35.621.

1.17

娛賓賦 *Fu* on Entertaining Guests

Ding 11–12; Zhao 47–48

Additional notes

Xu 130–31 dates this to Jian'an 16 (211) or after.

1–2 These two opening lines do not appear in Ding, but they are in *Cxj* 10.240 by themselves and identified as part of this *fu*. Zhao follows *QSgw* 13.9b in adding them here.

13–14 *Sj* 33.1518 has the Duke of Zhou saying, "Even so, whenever I wash my hair, I must squeeze it out thrice, and when I eat, I have to spit out three mouthfuls to rise and welcome someone, for still I fear losing a worthy man of the empire" 然我一沐三捉髮，一飯三吐哺，起以待士，猶恐失天下之賢人. This information also appears in *Han shi waizhuan*; see Xu, *Han shi waizhuan jishi*, 3.117, and Hightower, *Han Shih Wai Chuan*, 114. *Kongzi jiayu* 孔子家語 3.15b (*Sbck* ed.) talks about him going to humble homes in search of men.

16 Reading 乾 for 甘, with *Wenji* 2.6b. As Zhao 48n points out, 甘 does not fit the rhyme scheme. For the allusion in this line, see *Li ji* 63.1946.

1.18

愍志賦 *Fu* on Compassionate Thoughts (fragment)

Ding 12; Zhao 32–33

Additional notes

For the bracketed addendum, see *Shuchao* 84.7b (the text in this edition of *Beitang shuchao* differs slightly from Ding).

1.19

歸思賦 *Fu* on Homeward Thoughts (fragment)

Ding 12–13; Zhao 32–33

Additional notes

2 Reading 北 for 他, with *Ywlj* 30.529.

1.20

靜思賦 *Fu* on Stilling Desire (fragment)

Ding 13; Zhao 37

Additional notes

James Robert Hightower, "The *Fu* of T'ao Ch'ien," *HJAS* 17 (1954): 180n, erroneously gives the title as "Jing qing fu" 靜情賦, citing *QSgw* 13.4a. However, in *QSgw* the title is "Jing si fu" 靜思賦, as it is here. See also *Ywlj* 18.333. In any case, it is obvious that much – perhaps most – of this *fu* is missing.

1 The first lines of the several *fu* on the stilling the passions theme studied by Hightower all follow a stock pattern; see Hightower, "The *Fu* of T'ao Ch'ien," 170n. Note the similarity between the first line of this *fu* and the first line of **5.15**.

2.1

感婚賦 *Fu* on Fretting about Marriage (fragment)

Ding 15; Zhao 30–32

Additional notes

Xu 144, on weak grounds, dates this to Jian'an 17 (212). Fu Yashu 712–13 understands this *fu* to be spoken by the woman.

6 Cf. *Mao shi* 42/1: "I scratch my head and vacillate" 搔首踟躕.

2.2

出婦賦 *Fu* on the Spurned Wife

Ding 15–16; Zhao 35–36

Additional notes

Xu 185 puts this *fu* in Jian'an 20 (215), but that is because he puts the two poems entitled "Miscellaneous Poem on Behalf of Madam Wang, Wife of Liu Xun" 代劉勳妻王氏雜詩 in that year. But those poems are elsewhere attributed to Cao Pi and are not in Ding. See *Ytxy* 2.58–59; Lu 1: 403, 455.

1–2 These two opening lines do not appear in Ding's base text; he added them from *Beitang shuchao* 84.

3 Reading 而 for 之, with Ding 15 from *Beitang shuchao* 84, and 質陋 for 陋質, with *Ywlj* 30.528 and *Shuchao* 84.8a. See also Zhao 36n. But note that the three editions of *Beitang shuchao* I have checked write 之.

12 Reading 忉怛 for 忉忉, with *Ywlj* 30.528 and *Wenji* 3.1b.

2.3

洛神賦 *Fu* on the Goddess of the Luo River

Ding 16–19; Zhao 282–93; *Wx* 19.895–901.

Additional notes

Title This *fu* is often read as an allegorical piece about a worthy subject's quest for an understanding ruler. But another, much more dubious interpretation has existed side-by-side with that one. That interpretation says that the original title was "Gan Zhen fu" 感甄賦 (*Fu* on Being Moved by Zhen) and understands the *fu* as dealing with a romantic relationship between Cao Zhi and his sister-in-law Empress Zhen, Cao Pi's wife. It is not clear when such a story originated, but it is found in an anonymous "*Ji*" 記 ("record" or "note") that is included in Li Shan's seventh-century commentary (*Wx* 19.895) just before the *fu*'s preface. The notion of a love affair between Cao Zhi and Empress Zhen is almost universally rejected by scholars. Furthermore, as Hu Kejia 胡克家 (1757–1816) points out in his *Wen xuan kaoyi* 文選考異 (*Wx* 19.901), this "*Ji*" appears to be an interpolation by You Mao 尤袤 (1127–1194) in his 1181 edition of *Wen xuan*, not part of Li Shan's original commentary. See Cutter, "The Death of Empress Zhen: Fiction and Historiography in Early Medieval China," *JAOS* 112 (1992): 577–83. The information in that article also appears in a revised form in Robert Joe Cutter and William Gordon Crowell, *Empresses and Con-*

sorts: Selections from Chen Shou's Records of the Three States *with Pei Songzhi's Commentary* (Honolulu: Univ. of Hawai'i Press, 1999), 72–79.

Pref. Li Shan (*Wx* 19.896) already noted a potential problem with the date. See also K. P. K. Whitaker, "Tsaur Jyr's 'Luohshern fuh,'" *AM* 2nd ser., 4 (1954): 48–49; Ruan Tingzhuo 阮廷卓, "'Luo shen fu' cheng yu Huangchu sinian kao" 洛神賦成於黃初四年考, *Dalu zazhi* 大陸雜誌 16 (1958): 23, 29; Jiang Zhuxu 江竹虛, *Cao Zhi nianpu* 曹植年譜, coll. Jiang Hong 江宏 (Taipei: Shangwu yinshuguan, 2013), 237–8; Zhang Keli, *San Cao nianpu*, 193; Knechtges, *Wen xuan*, 3: 412. But cf. Gu Nong 顧農, "Cao Zhi shengping zhong de san'ge wenti" 曹植生平中的三個問題, *Yangzhou shiyuan xuebao* 揚州師院學報 (*shehui kexue ban* 社會科學版), 1993.1: 3–4. The more speculative parts of Gu's theory need not invalidate his idea about the date in the preface being correct. The preface mentions Song Yu, who is sometimes referred to as the pseudo-Song Yu, reflecting how little is known about this figure and the doubtful authenticity of the works attributed to him. On the Song Yu corpus, see Gao Qiufeng 高秋鳳, *Song Yu zuopin zhenwei kao* 宋玉作品真偽考 (Taipei: Wenjin chubanshe, 1999) and Wu Guangping 吳廣平, *Song Yu yanjiu* 宋玉研究 (Changsha: Yuelu shushe, 2004), 86–103. For translations of these two *fu* attributed to Song Yu, see Knechtges, *Wen xuan*, 3: 325–49; Eduard Erkes, "Shen nü fu: The Song of the Goddess," *TP* 25 (1928): 387–402; Lois Fusek, "The Kao-t'ang fu," *MS* 30 (1972–73): 392–425. *Mao shi* 9/1 has the line "The Han River has a roaming nymph" 漢有遊女. Although the line there seems to have no supernatural meaning, its appearance in the Han 韓 version of the *Shi jing* is explained by Xue Han 薛漢 (fl. 25–60 CE) as follows: "'Roaming nymph' refers to the goddess of the Han [River]" 游女漢神也; *Xue jun Han shi zhangju* 薛君韓詩章句, A.2a, in *Yuhan shanfang ji yishu* 玉函山房輯佚書, comp. Ma Guohan 馬國翰 (1794–1857). He Zhuo 何焯 (1661–1722), *Yimen dushu ji* 義門讀書記 (Beijing: Zhonghua shuju, 1987), 45.883 sees this as the basis for the idea of a goddess of the Luo River. It can also be seen as an instance of what some see as Cao Zhi's tendency to draw on the Han version of the *Shi*; see Xing Peishun 邢培順, "Cao Zhi yu *Han Shi*" 曹植與韓詩, *Chaohu xueyuan xuebao* 巢湖學院學報 13.5 (2011): 30.

3–6 On these places, see also Knechtges, *Wen xuan*, 2: 354.

10 See Li Shan's commentary in *Wx* 19.896; *Wei Jin Nanbei chao wenxueshi cankao ziliao* 魏晉南北朝文學史參考資料 (Beijing: Zhonghua shu-

ju, 1962), 1: 96; Whitaker, "Tsaur Jyr's 'Luohshern Fuh,'" 53; Fu Lipu 傅隸僕, *Fu xuanzhu* 賦選注 (Taipei: Zhengzhong shuju, 1977), 118.
11 Li Shan notes the variant 楊林 (poplar grove) for "sunny grove," but "sunny grove" seems better attested. See *Wx* 19.896.
12 Reading 眄 for 盼, with *Wx* 19.896 and *Ywlj* 8.162. See Zhao 286.
75 For the parable involving Zheng Jiaofu, see Wang Shumin 王叔岷 (1914–2008), ed., *Liexian zhuan jiaojian* 列仙傳校箋 (Beijing: Zhonghua shuju, 2007), A.52–57.
97–98 On these lines, see *Wx* 19.899; Knechtges, *Wen xuan*, 3: 362; Kroll, "Seven Rhapsodies of Ts'ao Chih," 11. The similar lines in Ruan Yu's "Zhi yu fu" 止欲賦 are quoted by Li Shan in *Wx* and are also found in *Ywlj* 18.332.
116–17 On the identification of these deities, see also Knechtges, *Wen xuan*, 3: 362 and Kroll, "Seven Rhapsodies of Ts'ao Chih," 11.
128 Reading 陽 for 揚, with *Wx* 19.900, Zhang Pu 1.6a, and *Wenji* 3.5a. See Zhao 291.

2.4
愁霖賦 *Fu* on Distress at the Downpour (fragment)

Ding 19; Zhao 52–54

Additional notes

This piece possibly dates from after the fourth month of Jian'an 18 (8 May–6 June 213). Cao Pi also has a *fu* by this title in which he says he was on his way back to Ye. If that date is correct, this would have been following an expedition Cao Cao led to the south against Sun Quan; see Zhao 53–54. There were heavy rains and flooding that year from the fifth through the eighth month; see *HHs* 9.387, *zhi* 15.3312. Ding 19 includes a second fragment by this title, but based on Li Shan's commentary to *Wx*, which quotes similar lines and attributes them to a "*Fu* on a Downpour" 霖賦 or 霖雨賦 by Cai Yong 蔡邕 (132–192), *QSgw* omits this second *fu* fragment. See *QSgw* 13.1a–b; Zhao 53n, 531. See also *Wx* 27.1288, 29.1379. This dubious second fragment is also omitted here. Xu 220 disagrees with the dating above and puts it in Jian'an 22 (217) or a bit earlier.
7–8 On this myth, see ch. 2, "Sons of Suns," in Sarah Allan, *The Shape of the Turtle: Myth, Art, and Cosmos in Early China* (Albany: State Univ. of New York Press, 1991), 19–56.

2.5

喜霽賦 *Fu* on Joy at the Clearing Sky (fragment)

Ding 19; Zhao 211–12

Additional notes

This piece could have been written in 213, sometime after the preceding piece. But another possible date is the first year of the Yankang reign period (21 April–11 December 220). The *Wei lüe* 魏略 says that it rained for over fifty days in a row and that the weather cleared with the founding of Wei; *Cxj* 2.41. Zhao 212 suggests that the references to Yu and Tang, the founding emperors of the Xia and Shang, respectively, would have been especially appropriate at a time when Cao Pi was preparing to accept the abdication of the last Han emperor. Xu 220 disagrees and puts it in or near Jian'an 22 (217), like the preceding piece. He thinks it has to date from before Cao Pi was designated heir.

1 Reading 盱 for 旰, with Zhao 211n. This line appears to draw on *Hnz* 19.1317.

2 See *Sszy* 6.204.

3–4 See Zhao 79n; Allan, *The Shape of the Turtle*, 41–46.

2.6

登臺賦 *Fu* on Ascending the Terrace

Ding 20; Zhao 44–47

Additional notes

This *fu* dates from Jian'an 17 (212); see Xu 141–42.

1 Reading 而 for 之, with *Sgz* 19.558, comm. quoting the *Wei ji* 魏紀 of Yin Dan 陰澹.

2 Reading 登層 for 聊登, with *Sgz* 19.558, comm. quoting the *Wei ji* of Yin Dan.

3 Reading 太 for 天, with *Sgz* 19.558, comm. quoting the *Wei ji* of Yin Dan.

5 Reading 門 for 殿, with *Sgz* 19.558, comm. quoting the *Wei ji* of Yin Dan. The *Ye zhong ji* 鄴中記 of Lu Hui 陸翽 (ca. fourth century CE) says, "The southern face of the Ye palace compound had three gates. The one on the west was Fengyang Gate. It was twenty-five *zhang* [just under 200 ft.] tall, with six floors on top and upturned eaves facing the sun. Beneath opened two portals. Seven or eight *li* [about 2 miles] before reaching Ye, one could spy this gate in the distance. Furthermore, they secured a large bronze phoenix at its apex, its head rising one

zhang 6 *chi* [almost 13 ft.]." 鄴宮南面三門西鳳陽門高二十五丈上六層反宇向陽下開二門未到鄴臺七八里遙望此門又安大銅鳳于其巔舉頭一丈六尺; Lu Hui, *Ye zhong ji*, 1a, in *Wuyingdian juzhenban shu* 武英殿聚珍版書 (Beijing, 1776).
10 Reading 園 for 眾, with *Sgz* 19.558, comm. quoting the *Wei ji* of Yin Dan.

2.7

九華扇賦 *Fu* on the Many-Splendored Fan

Ding 20–21; Zhao 38–40
Additional notes
This *fu* may be incomplete.
3 Reading 淥 for 綠, with *Ywlj* 69.1212.
7 Reading 析 for 華, with Zhao 39. Note that Zhao is following Ding in saying this 析 comes from *Tpyl*. However, *Tpyl* 702.6a has 折, as does *Ywlj* 69.1212.
12 Reading 絢 for the missing graph marked by □ in Ding, with *Shuchao* 134.5a. See also Han Geping 韓格平 et al., eds., *Quan Wei Jin fu jiaozhu* 全魏晉賦校注 (Changchun: Jilin wen shi chubanshe, 2008), 47.
15 Reading 以 for the missing graph marked by □ in Ding, with *Shuchao* 134.4b.

2.8

寶刀賦 *Fu* on Precious Sabers (fragment)

Ding 21–22; Zhao 159–63
Additional notes
Title *Shuchao* 123.3a gives the title as "Precious Sabers and Swords *Fu*" 寶刀劍賦.
Pref. *Wenji* 3.8a does not have 家父, "paterfamilias," nor did Ding's base text. He added it from *Tpyl* 346.5a. On Cao Lin, see *Sgz* 20.582; see also Cutter and Crowell, *Empresses and Consorts*, 145. Cf. Cao Haidong 73n, where the marquis is inexplicably identified as Cao Bao 曹豹. On Cao Cao becoming king, see *Sgz* 1.47.
3 This line can be understood in the context of Cao Cao's attempts to recruit talented men for office. Three edicts by Cao Cao, the most famous of which is often called "Edict Seeking Worthies" ("Qiu xian ling" 求賢令), are indicative of his emphasis on achievement and talent over affiliation. The other two edicts are "Edict Ordering Officials Not

to Spurn Those with Partial Failings in Selecting Officials" ("Chi yousi qu shi wufei pianduan ling" 敕有司取士毋廢偏短令) and "Edict on Not Being a Stickler for Status in Recommending Worthies" ("Ju xian wuju pinxing ling" 舉賢勿拘品行令); see *Cao Cao ji* 曹操集 (Beijing: Zhonghua shuju, 1973), 2.40–41, 46, 48–9. The edicts are translated in Paul W. Kroll, "Portraits of Ts'ao Ts'ao: Literary Studies on the Man and the Myth" (Ph.D. diss., Univ. of Michigan, 1976), 17–19; Rafe de Crespigny, *Imperial Warlord: A Biography of Cao Cao, 155–220 AD* (Leiden: Brill, 2010), 367–69.

7–8 On Wu Huo, see, for example, *Mengzi*, 6B.2. See also Herrlee G. Creel, *Shen Pu-hai: A Chinese Political Philosopher of the Fourth Century BC* (Chicago: Univ. of Chicago Press, 1974), 317–20. The ancient southern kingdoms of Wu and Yue are known to have been skilled in the production of iron and steel and the manufacture of high-quality swords. The *Yue jue shu* 越絕書 has a famous account concerning five precious swords owned by King Goujian 勾踐 (r. 496–465 BCE) of Yue that mentions Ouye. See Le Zumou 樂祖謀, ed., *Yue jue shu* (Shanghai: Shanghai guji chubanshe, 1985), 11.79–80. For translations of this passage, see Cutter, "'Well, how'd you become king, then?' Swords in Early Medieval China" *JAOS* 132 (2012): 527–28; Donald Wagner, *Iron & Steel in Ancient China* (Leiden: Brill, 1996), 111–12; Olivia Milburn, "The Weapons of Kings: A New Perspective on Southern Sword Legends in Early China," *JAOS* 128 (2008): 426–27. The authorship and date of the *Yue jue shu* are uncertain, although the text was probably compiled in the first century CE.

10 For the identification of Celestial Court 天庭 with Grand Tenuity 太微, see, for example, Kong Yingda's 孔穎達 (574–648) commentary to *Li ji* 14.540. On Grand Tenuity, see Edward H. Schafer, *Pacing the Void: T'ang Approaches to the Stars* (Berkeley: Univ. of California Press, 1977), 52, 208; Gustav Schlegel, *Uranographie chinoise*, 2 vols. (Leiden: Brill, 1875; reprt. Taipei: Ch'eng-wen Publishing Co., 1967), 1: 534–36; Joseph Needham and Lu Gwei-djen, *Science and Civilisation in China*, vol. 5: *Chemistry and Chemical Technology*, Part 2: *Spagyrical Discovery and Invention: Magisteries of Gold and Immortality* (Cambridge: Cambridge Univ. Press, 74), 101n.

14 Reading 鑿 for 鑿, with *Tpyl* 346.5b. Scholars have understood 中黃 here as either the name of an ancient unidentifiable kingdom (Fu Yashu, 767, for example) or as the equivalent of 中央, "the center" (*Hydcd*

s. v. 中黄). I followed the former explanation in "Well, how'd you become king, then?" 534. However, another meaning for 中黄 that was well established long before Cao Zhi's day – it appears in Zhang Heng's 張衡 (78–139) "Nan du fu" 南都賦 – is as an abbreviation for 石中黄子 (brown hematite), which was used as a longevity medicament; see Knechtges, trans., *Wen xuan, or Selections of Refined Literature*, vol. 1: *Rhapsodies on Metropolises and Capitals* (Princeton: Princeton Univ. Press, 1982), 312n. When present in soil, hematite gives it a reddish hue. One use of hematite, beyond iron and steel manufacture (and the quest for longevity), is as jewelers rouge, a reddish paste used for polishing gems and metals.

16 Reading 功 for 思, with *Ywlj* 60.1084.

19 Ding 22 says that the three extrametrical words 故其利 have been inserted from *Beitang shuchao* 123, but they are not in the *Siku quanshu* edition of that work. The words 故其 do appear without 利 in *Shuchao* 123.3b.

23–24 See *Yue jue shu*, 11.79–80; Wagner, *Iron & Steel*, 111–13.

26 The last line appears to draw from lines in two canonical texts. *Mao shi* 303/5 has "That Yin received the appointment was entirely right, / A hundred blessings they bore" 殷受命咸宜，百祿是何; Bernhard Karlgren, *The Book of Odes* (Stockholm: Museum of Far Eastern Antiquities, 1974), 263. The "Da Yu mo" 大禹謨 section of the *Shang shu* has "If within the four seas there are hardship and poverty, Heaven's blessings will end forever" 四海困窮，天祿永終; *Sszy*, 112, in *Shisan*.

2.9

車渠椀賦 *Fu* on a *Musāragalva* Bowl

Ding 22–23; Zhao 137–39

Additional notes

Title The preface to Cao Pi's "*Fu* on a *Musāragalva* Bowl" says, "*Musāragalva* is a kind of jade. It has many fine veins and elaborate patterns. It is produced in the western lands whose people treasure it. Small ones are tied to the neck, and large ones are used to make vessels" 車渠玉屬也多纖理縟文生於西國其俗寶之小以繫頸大以為器; trans. David R. Knechtges, "Group Literary Composition at the Court of Ye in the Later Eastern Han," unpub. paper, 19. See *Ywlj* 84.1443. *Juqu* is also identified as mother-of-pearl or giant clam; Paul W. Kroll, *A Student's Dictionary of Classical and Medieval Chinese*, rev. ed. (Leiden: Brill,

2017), 44. As Hsiang-Lin Shih writes, "We do not know whether Cao Pi saw a precious stone that was translated into Chinese as *juqu*, or a seashell that was somehow identified as a type of jade from the Western Regions;" Shih, "Jian'an Literature Revisited," 133n. Xu 199–200 dates this to Jian'an 16 (221)

2 Reading 峻 for 浚, with *Ywlj* 73.1262.

3 Reading 以 for 之, with *Ywlj* 73.1262.

17 On Gongshu Ban, see Knechtges, *Wen xuan*, 1: 192n; Nicholas Morrow Williams, "The Brocade of Words: Imitation Poetry and Poetics in the Six Dynasties" (Ph.D. diss., Univ. of Washington, 2010), 153n.

2.10

迷迭香賦 *Fu* on *Midie*

Ding 23; Zhao 139–40

Additional notes

Xu 200–1 dates this to Jian'an 21 (216), essentially because Wang Can, who also wrote on the topic, died in 217.

Title "*Midie*" is the Chinese word for the herb rosemary, and that is what the topic of this *fu* has been understood to be in modern times. Perhaps that is how it should be understood here, but it is difficult to know whether rosemary was the plant that Cao Zhi and others in his day were writing about. It is identified by them as an import from the west, but there does not seem to be a very robust textual tradition regarding this herb after that. Even Li Shizhen 李時珍 (1518–1593), in his *Compendium of Materia Medica*, essentially relies on third-century *fu* for his information; see Chen Guiting 陳貴廷, ed., *Bencao gangmu tong shi* 本草綱目通釋, 2 vols. (Beijing: Xueyuan chubanshe, 1992), 1: 697–98.

2 Reading 發 for 凝, with *Ywlj* 81.1395.

2.11

大暑賦 *Fu* on a Heat Wave (fragment)

Ding 23–24; Zhao 148–51

Additional notes

This *fu* may date from the summer of Jian'an 21 (216). See Zhang Keli 張可禮, *San Cao nianpu* 三曹年譜 (Ji'nan: Qi Lu shushe, 1983), 144–45; Xu 198–99. Note that the bracketed lines at the end are appended by Ding Yan from *Tpyl* 1.6a. In addition to Cao Zhi's piece, fragments of *fu* with the same title by Chen Lin, Liu Zhen, Po Qin, and Wang Can are in *Cxj* 3.50 and *Ywlj* 5.89–90. See also Shih, "Jian'an Literature Revisited," 255–63.

5–6 Ding 23 states that these lines were not in his base text. He added them from *Beitang shuchao* 156 (see *Shuchao* 156.7a).

7–8 Ding 23 states that these lines were not in his base text. He added them from *Tpyl* 34.3b (where 玄 is written 元).

17 Reading 遠 for 近 with *Tpyl* 34.3b.

26 Reading 綏 for 緩 with *QSgw* 13.1b.

33 See *Tpyl* 591.9a; Zhang Hua 張華 (232–300), *Bowu zhi* 博物志 (Changsha: Shangwu yinshuguan, 1939), 72. On Plain Girl, see R. H. Van Gulik, *Sexual Life in Ancient China* (1961; rpt. Leiden: Brill, 1974), 74–75.

3.1

神龜賦 *Fu* on the Divine Turtle

Ding 26; Zhao 96–100

Additional notes

Dated to Jian'an 22 (217) by Zhao 99 and Xu 221.

20 See Fabrizio Pregadio, ed., *The Encyclopedia of Taoism*, 2 vols. (London: Routledge, 2008), 2: 1193.

21–26 *Wenji* 4.1b has 白靈 (white numen) for 白龍 (white dragon). Zhao 98 thinks 白靈 is the correct reading and that white numen refers to a white turtle 白龜. But Cao Zhi's use of 翔翥, "soaring and ascending," seems to fit a dragon better. It is almost as though Cao Zhi is conflating the parable in *Zhuangzi*, in which Yu Ju catches a large white turtle, which is killed and whose shell is used for prognostication, with the one in *Shuo yuan*, in which a white dragon changes into a fish and has its eye shot out by Yu Ju. The lodging of a complaint with the High God in lines 25–26 seems to reflect the version in *Shuo yuan*. See Wang Shumin 王叔岷, ed., *Zhuangzi jiaoquan* 莊子校詮, 3 vols. (Taipei: Zhongyang yanjiuyuan Lishi yuyan yanjiusuo, 1988), 3: 1066; Xiang Zonglu 向宗魯, ed., *Shuo yuan jiaozheng* 說苑校證 (Beijing: Zhonghua shuju, 1987), 9.237.

31–32 Wang, *Zhuangzi jiaoquan*, 2: 631.

44 Zhang Zongxiang 張宗祥, ed., *Lun heng jiaozhu* 論衡校注 (Shanghai: Shanghai guji chubanshe, 2010), 7.144; Alfred Forke, *Lun-Hêng*,

Part 1: *Philosophical Essays of Wang Ch'ung* (Leipzig, 1907), 333. For Chisongzi, see Pregadio, *Encyclopedia of Taoism*, 1: 271–72; for Wangzi Qiao, see Pregadio, *Encyclopedia of Taoism*, 2: 1028–29.

3.2
白鶴賦 *Fu* on a White Crane

Ding 25–26; Zhao 238–40

Additional notes

5 Reading 挾 for 狹 with Zhao 239.
7 Shj 2.47. See also Knechtges, *Wen xuan*, 2: 92.
12 Reading 而 for 之 with *Ywlj* 90.1567.
23 See David R. Knechtges, "Ssu-ma Hsiang-ju's 'Tall Gate Palace Rhapsody,'" *HJAS* 41 (1982): 57, n. 45.
24 Reading 託 for 記 with Zhao 240.

3.3
蟬賦 *Fu* on the Cicada

Ding 27–28; Zhao 92–95

Additional notes

7 For 皦皦, *Cxj* 30.749 and *Wenji* 4.3a have 噭噭. Poem **4.8** also has 噭噭. But the connotation of sadness in 噭噭 does not fit the context here.
27 See *Mengzi* 4A.1. Li Zhu appears several times in *Zhuangzi* as the name of a man with keen eyesight.
39 Reading 膳 for 庖 with *Ywlj* 97.1679 and *Wenji* 4.4a.
40 Reading 歸 for 熾 with *Ywlj* 97.1679 and *Wenji* 4.4a.
48 Cf. *Mao shi* 197/4: "The singing cicadas go chirr chirr" 鳴蜩嘒嘒.
52 See *Sj* 61.2122–5.
53–54 Sima Biao's 司馬彪 (240–306) "Treatise on Carriages and Robes, II" 輿服下 states: "As for the military hat, also called the military cap great hat, all of the military officers wear it. Palace attendants and Regular Palace Attendants add yellow gold cap ornaments and attach cicadas as embellishments" 武冠，一曰武弁大冠，諸武官冠之。侍中、中常侍加黃金璫，附蟬為文; *HHs, zhi* 30.3668. On this passage see the discussion in B. J. Mansvelt Beck, *The Treatises of Later Han: Their Author, Sources, Contents and Place in Chinese Historiography* (Leiden: Brill, 1990), 248–50. See also the additional note to line 19 of **3.5**.

3.4

鸚鵡賦 *Fu* on the Parrot

Ding 28; Zhao 57–59

Additional notes

2 Reading 而 for 之, with *Cxj* 30.738.

6 Reading 而 for 之, with *Cxj* 30.738 and *Ywlj* 91.1576.

9–10 Cf. Mi Heng's "Yingwu fu": "It is not that he cares about his remaining years, / But he grieves for the innocent fledglings;" Knechtges, *Wen xuan,* 3: 55. See *Wx* 13.614.

19 Reading 以 for 其, with *Ywlj* 91.1576 and *Wenji* 4.5a.

3.5

鶡賦 *Fu* on the Brown Eared Pheasant

Ding 28–29; Zhao 151–53

Additional notes

Xu reasonably dates this to Jian'an 21 (216).

Pref. The following words are attributed to a "Heji fu xu" 鶡雞賦序 (Preface to the Brown Eared Pheasant *Fu*) by Cao Cao: "Brown Eared Pheasants have fierce temperaments, and when they fight there is after all no losing – they pin their expectations on fighting to the death. When people today use brown eared pheasant [feathers] for their hats, it symbolizes this" 鶡雞猛氣其鬬終無負期於必死今人以鶡為冠像此也; *Cao Cao ji*, 13. This preface is preserved in *QSgw* 1.1b, whose source was *Daguan bencao* 大觀本草 (full title *Jingshi zhenglei beiji Daguan bencao* 經史證類備急大觀本草) by Tang Shenwei 唐慎微 (ca. 1056–1093). Almost no trace remains of *fu* attributed Cao Cao – just this and two other minuscule fragments – so it simply seems more likely that this is a version of the preface attributed to Cao Zhi.

9 Reading 擅 for 檀, with *Wenji* 4.5b.

19 Sima Biao's "Treatise on Carriages and Robes, II" states: "With regard to the military hat, one commonly refers to it as the grand hat. ... They attach a pair of brown eared pheasant tail [feathers], setting them erect on the left and right, so it is said to be a brown eared pheasant cap. The Gentlemen of the Household for All Purposes, the Left and Right Rapid as Tigers, the Feathered Forest, the General of the Gentlemen of the Household for All Purposes, and the Inspectors of the Left and Right of the Feathered Forest all were capped with brown eared pheasant caps ... The Cavalry Rapid as Tigers all wore brown eared pheasant caps and tiger-striped unlined garments. It is said that Xiangyi annually presented woven tiger-striped [fabric]. Brown eared pheasants are valiant pheasants. When they fight, they only stop when one is dead. 武冠，俗謂之大冠……加雙鶡尾，豎左右，為鶡冠云。五官、左右虎賁、羽林、五中郎將、羽林左右監皆冠鶡冠……虎賁武騎皆鶡冠，虎文單衣。襄邑歲獻織成虎文云。鶡者，勇雉也，其鬬對一死乃止; *HHs zhi* 30.3670. See also Shen Congwen 沈從文 (1902–1988), *Zhongguo gudai fushi yanjiu* 中國古代服飾研究 (Beijing: Shangwu yinshuguan, 2011), 199, 202 and the additional note to lines 53–54 of **3.3**.

3.6

離繳雁賦 *Fu* on a Wild Goose Who Encountered an Arrow Cord

Ding 29–30; Zhao 100–2

Additional notes

6 What is translated as "season" here and in line 11 is 節, which refers to the twenty-four solar nodes into which the year was divided. But since the reference here is to four nodes, it means the four seasons as marked by the primary nodes – the solstices and equinoxes. On the nodes see, for example, Derk Bodde, *Festivals in Classical China: New Year and Other Annual Observances during the Han Dynasty (206 BC–AD 220)* (Princeton: Princeton Univ. Press, 1975), 28–9.

13 As Paul Kroll notes, the 南北 in this line is a "biased compound" 偏義複詞, in which one element, in this case 南, is the "active" word; Kroll, "Seven Rhapsodies of Ts'ao Chih," 8n. For other examples of directions used in this way, see [Yu Guanying 余冠英 (1906–1995)], *Han Wei Liuchao shi luncong* 漢魏六朝詩論叢 (Taipei: He Luo tushu chubanshe, n. d.), 40, 45.

19 Reading 逝 for 遠, with *Cxj* 30.735 and *Ywlj* 91.1580.

23 Cf. *Mao shi* 202.

3.7

鷂雀賦 *Fu* on the Sparrow Hawk and Sparrow

Ding 30–31; Zhao 302–5

Additional notes

This piece is discussed in the Introduction. The text of this *fu* is probably incomplete. Ding 31 is able to append a stray line from *Tpyl* 841.7a at the end of the piece (not translated here), and when Yan Zhitui's 顏之推 (531–591) *Yanshi jiaxun* quotes two lines from it, they are not in the same order as in the transmitted text; see Zhou, *Yanshi jiaxun huizhu*, 106. One scholar does seem to think it is complete; see Hou Libing 侯立兵, *Han Wei Liuchao fu duowei yanjiu* 漢魏六朝賦多維研究 (Beijing: Renmin chubanshe, 2007), 335. Xu 290 dates it to Huangchu 2 (221).

27 *Yanshi jiaxun* identifies the term *ke suan* 果 (=顆) 蒜 in line 20 as an "everyday usage among the common people" 俗間常語; Zhou, *Yanshi jiaxun hui zhu*, 106.

51–55 There are significant differences in the explications or translations of these lines by modern scholars; see Zhao 304; Cao Haidong, 103–4; Fu Yashu, 797–98; Wei Gengyuan 魏耕原, ed., *Lidai xiaofu guanzhi* 歷代小賦觀止 (Xi'an: Shaanxi renmin jiaoyu chubanshe, 1998), 172.

3.8

蝙蝠賦 *Fu* on the Bat

Ding 31; Zhao 301–2

Additional notes

Xu 290 dates it to Huangchu 2 (221).

13 Ding 31 thought that 空 might be a mistake for 穴, but Zhao 302 shows that 空 did have the meaning of a cave or den.

3.9

芙蓉賦 *Fu* on the Lotus

Ding 31–32; Zhao 179–81

Additional notes

At the end of this piece, Ding appends two additional lines quoted from Li Shan's commentary to *Wx* 31.1445. It is not apparent where they would fit in the *fu* as we have it, and they are not translated here.

7–8 Reading 木 for 桑, with *Tpyl* 999.4a. On the mythology underlying these lines, see Sarah Allan, "Sons of Suns: Myth and Totemism in Early China," *BSOAS* 44.2 (1981): 293–301. This is also included in a slightly different form in her book *The Shape of the Turtle*, 27–36.

14 On the candle dragon, see Paul W. Kroll, "Li Po's *Rhapsody on the Great P'eng Bird*," *Journal of Chinese Religions* 12 (1984): 9; Xiaofei

Tian, "Illusion and Illumination: A New Poetics of Seeing in Liang Dynasty Court Literature," *HJAS* 65 (2005): 14n.
21 Reading 擢 for 耀, with *Wenji* 4.8a and other texts (see *Concordance* 3.32).

3.10

酒賦 *Fu* on Wine

Ding 32–33; Zhao 124–28

Additional notes

Although most of this piece is the same from edition to edition, there are serious textual problems, including lacunae and variant readings that are not simply matters of orthography. Xu 202–3 dates it to Jian'an 21 (216), largely because Wan Can, who also wrote on the topic, died in 217.

3 On Wine Pennant, see Ho Peng Yoke, *The Astronomical Chapters of the* Chin shu (Paris: Mouton, 1966), 93.
5 See *Hs* 36.1923.
6 See *Sj* 77.2378–81.
7–8 *Kongcongzi*, 13.79a (*Sbck*). See also Yoav Ariel, *K'ung-ts'ung-tzu: The K'ung Family Masters' Anthology* (Princeton: Princeton Univ. Press, 1989), 136.
12 The lines quoted in the note are from Zhang Hua's "Qing bo pian" 輕薄篇. See Wang Ping, "Southern Girls or Tibetan Knights: A Liang (502–557) Court Performance," *JAOS* 128 (2008): 78n; Lu 1: 611.
16 Cf. Zhang Heng, "Nan du fu": "With 'floating ants' like duckweed" 浮蟻若萍; Knechtges, *Wen xuan*, 1: 325. See *Wx* 4.156.
19 Reading 歡 for 芬, with *Ywlj* 72.1249.
20 Reading 之 for 於, with *Ywlj* 72.1249.
21 This line is a quote from *Shi jing*; see *Mao shi* 209/3. But also cf. Zhang Heng, "Nan du fu": "Pledges and toasts are exchanged" 獻酬既交; Knechtges, *Wen xuan*, 1: 325. See *Wx* 4.157.
29 Wen Ying's 文穎 (fl. 196–220) commentary in *Han shu* contains line said to be from this poem; see *Hs* 88.3611.
30 Karlgren, *The Book of Odes*, 118.
36 Following Zhao 128 in understanding 作者 as probably equivalent to 賢者, based on *Lun yu* 14.37. Fu Yashu 750n also thinks it refers to 賢者, but apparently not because of the *Lun yu* passage. Cao Haidong

112n, on the other hand, thinks it refers back to the inventors of winemaking.

A This comes from *Shuchao* 148.1a.

B This is from *Shuchao* 148.11a. On the incidents involving Duke Mu and Liu Bang, see *Sj* 5.189, 8.347. See also William H. Nienhauser, Jr., ed., *The Grand Scribe's Records*, vol. 1: *The Basic Annals of Pre-Han China* (Bloomington: Indiana Univ. Press, 1994), 97; William H. Nienhauser, Jr., ed., *The Grand Scribe's Records*, vol. 2: *The Basic Annals of Han China* (Bloomington: Indiana Univ. Press, 2002), 14–15.

C This is from *Shuchao* 148.8a.

E From Wu Yu 吳棫 (d. 1155), *Yun bu* 韻補, 4.135 (*Congshu jicheng* 叢書集成 ed.). For the "Proclamation on Alcohol," see Bernard Karlgren, *The Book of Documents* (Stockholm: Museum of Far Eastern Antiquities, 1950), 41, 43–46; See *Sszy* 14.440–52. See also Roel Sterckx, "Food and Philosophy in Early China," in *Of Tripod and Palate: Food, Politics, and Religion in Traditional China*, ed. Sterckx (New York: Palgrave Macmillan, 2005), 53–54. Cao Cao is also known for having restricted the use of wine in 196, which drew the criticism of Kong Rong, who adduced the example of Liu Bang having killed the white snake while drunk, as well as other allusions also found in Cao Zhi's *fu*. See Xu 34–35. For Kong Rong's letters, see Wu Yun 吴云, ed., *Jian'an qizi ji jiaozhu* 建安七子集校注 (Tianjin: Tianjin guji chubanshe, 2005), 89–94.

3.11
槐賦 *Fu* on the Pagoda-tree

Ding 33; Zhao 146–48

Additional notes

In *Cxj* 28.689 the title is given as 槐樹賦. Xu 201–2 dates it to Jian'an 21 (216).

5 Reading 榱 for 欀 and 以 for 之, with *Ywlj* 88.1518.

3.12
橘賦 *Fu* on the Sourpeel Tangerine

Ding 33; Zhao 146–48

Additional notes

Xu 145 dates this to Jian'an 17 (212) but admits there is no real proof. He also says it could be sometime between 212 and 220, favoring a date earlier in that span.

2 See *Zz*, Xi 5; Stephen Durrant, Wai-yee Li, and David Schaberg, *Zuo Tradition/Zuo zhuan* (Seattle: Univ. of Washington Press, 2016), 1: 278–79. See also Shih, "Jian'an Literature Revisited," 77–78; Cao Haidong 116n. Cf. Fu Yashu 731n, where an alternative reading is suggested.
9 Reading 江洲 for 山川, with *Cxj* 28.681 and Li Shan's commentary to *Wx* 43.1941. See also Zhao 60n.
25 On understanding 激 as synonymous with 明, see Ding 34; Zhao 61n; Liao, *Wei Jin yongwu fu yanjiu*, 436.

3.13
述行賦 *Fu* Recounting a Journey
Ding 34; Zhao 132–33
Additional notes
This *fu* may well have been written at or about the same time as **4.26** (see the *Additional Notes* to that poem). Ding 34 supplied the bracketed line at the end here from Li Shan's commentary to Pan Yue's 潘岳 (247–300) "*Fu* on a Westward Journey" 西征賦 in *Wx* 10.442. There it is called "述征賦." Despite the difference in title, these are likely to be the same piece; Xu 127.
3 See *Sj* 6.239.
5 Reading 神 for 秦, with *Cxj* 7.146. See Zhao 133n. An extant fragment of Zhang Heng's "*Fu* on the Hot Springs" 溫泉賦 includes what seems to be a preface. It says, in part, "Next I went to Mount Li to view the hot springs and bathed in the divine well ..." 余適驪山，觀溫泉，浴神井……; Zhang Zhenze 張震澤, ed., *Zhang Heng shiwen ji jiaozhu* 張衡詩文集校注 (Shanghai: Shanghai guji chubanshe, 2009), 15; *Cxj* 7.146. See also Edward H. Schafer, "The Development of Bathing Customs in Ancient and Medieval China and the History of the Floriate Clear Palace," *JAOS* 76 (1956): 73.

4.1
公宴 Lord's Feast
Ding 35; Zhao 48–50
Additional notes
Xu 143–44 dates this to Jian'an 17 (212). In any case, it seems likely to pre-date 217, the year others – including Wang Can, Ruan Yu, Liu Zhen who wrote seemingly related poems died in the epidemic.

3 See Cutter, "Cao Zhi's (192–232) Symposium Poems," *CLEAR* 6 (1984): 9n; Tsao, *The City of Ye in the Chinese Literary Landscape*, 23. Cf. Huang Shoucheng 黄守誠, *Cao Zijian xintan* 曹子建新探 (Taipei: Yunlong chubanshe, 1998), 187.

4.2

侍太子作 Seated in Attendance on the Heir Designate

Ding 35; Zhao 178–79

Additional notes

Titles of works in this period are often problematic. That seems to be the case here, since the title does not comport with the 公子 in line 9; see Xu 130. Xu dates it to Jian'an 16 (211), not very confidently; at any rate, before Jian'an 22, when Cao Pi became heir designate.

1 *Wenji* 5.1b has 春 ("spring") for 天 ("sky"). Huang Jie 1.2, follows this reading, pointing out that the opening verse of "Da zhao" 大招 is 青春受謝白日昭只 "Green spring takes its turn, and the white sun shines." See *Ccbz* 10.1b. Huang says that although the poem is set in summer, when the sun emerges following a rain, it is as pleasant as spring. He also thinks that 青春 is a metonym for the heir designate, since the heir designate can be referred to metonymically as 春宮 ("spring palace") and 青宮 ("verdant palace").

4.3

元會 New Year's Audience

Ding 35–36; Zhao 491–94

Additional notes

8 On the zigzag and meander motifs, see Knechtges, *Wen xuan*, 1: 86n; Wang Guanshi 王關仕, *Yili fushi kaobian* 儀禮服飾考辨 (Taipei: Wenshizhe chubanshe, 1979 rpt.), 114–19, 122–23, 127, 132–35, and 248 (plate).

19 Cf. Zhao 493n, which argues that 喜 should be replaced with the variant 善, which appears in some texts.

4.4

送應氏（其一） Seeing off Mr. Ying, No. 1

Ding 36; Zhao 3

Additional notes

It is not clear whether the title refers to one Mr. Ying or two. In fact, there is no explicit reference to any individual. But the poems already bear this title in *Wx* 20.974, and Huang Jie 1.8 has proposed that Cao Zhi composed this poem for Ying Yang and Ying Qu 應璩 (190–252) in Jian'an 16 (211) when he passed Luoyang while accompanying Cao Cao on an expedition against Ma Chao 馬超 (176–222). He is followed by Cao Haidong 128 and Fu Yashu 555n. Huang's dating is open to challenge; see David R. Knechtges, "Ruin and Remembrance in Classical Chinese Literature: The 'Fu on the Ruined City' by Bao Zhao," in *Reading Medieval Chinese Poetry: Text, Context, and Culture*, ed. Paul W. Kroll (Leiden: Brill, 2015), 62–63. Xu 124–25 also dates the poem to 211, based on what he sees as a poetic dialogue between these poems and two "Parting Poems" 別詩 by Ying Yang.

4.5

送應氏（其二） Seeing off Mr. Ying, No. 2

Ding 36–37; Zhao 4–6

Additional notes

1 "Da Su Wu shu" 答蘇武書, a piece of doubtful authenticity attributed to Li Ling 李陵 (d. 74 BCE), says, "You have assiduously made known your fine virtue, and inscribed your name on bamboo strips in an idyllic time" 勤宣令德，策名清時; *Wx* 41.1847.

2 The second of the "Yu Su Wu san shou" 與蘇武三首 in *Wx* 29.1353, also dubiously attributed to Li Ling, has the line "A happy gathering is hard to happen upon again" 嘉會難再遇.

4 *Hs* 54.2464 has Li Ling saying to Su Wu (ca. 143–60 BCE), "Human life is like the morning dew" 人生如朝露. If Cao Zhi, as seems likely, did have Li Ling in mind, he changed 露 to 霜 for the sake of the rhyme.

5 The binomial 嬿婉, which is translated here as "comfort and joy," appears in *Wx* 29.1355 in the third of the four poems supposedly written by Su Wu: "Our pleasure is just for this evening now, / joy must be had while the time is here" 歡娛在今夕，嬿婉及良時; Stephen Owen, *An Anthology of Chinese Literature: Beginnings to 1911* (New York: Norton, 1996), 251.

4.6

雜詩 Unclassified Poem, No. 1

Ding 37; Zhao 393–94

Additional Notes
Xu 166–70 dates it to Jian'an 19 (214).

4.7
雜詩（其二） Unclassified Poem, No. 2
Ding 37; Zhao 393–94
Additional Notes
Xu 406–7 dates it to the Taihe reign period but also gives the opinions of other scholars..

4.8
雜詩（其三） Unclassified Poem, No. 3
Ding 37–38; this poem is missing in Zhao's edition

4.9
雜詩（其四） Unclassified Poem, No. 4
Ding 38; Zhao 387
Additional Notes
3 Reading 江北 for 北海, with *Wenji* 5.4b.

4.10
雜詩（其五） Unclassified Poem, No. 5
Ding 38; Zhao 379–80

4.11
雜詩（其六） Unclassified Poem, No. 6
Ding 38; Zhao 65–66
Additional Notes
10 On Emperor Wu's sacrifices, see *Hs* 25B.1243. Michael Loewe translates an inscription from a TLV mirror of Late Han date: "If you climb Mount T'ai, you may see the immortal beings. They feed on the purest jade, they drink from the springs of manna. They yoke the scaly dragons to their carriage, they mount the floating clouds. The white tiger leads them ... they ascend straight to heaven. May you receive a never-ending span, long life that lasts for ten thousand years, with a fit place in office and safety for your children and grandchildren;" see Loewe, *Ways to Paradise: The Chinese Quest for Immortality* (London: George Allen & Unwin, 1979), 97, 200.

4.12

喜雨 Welcome Rain

Ding 39; Zhao 366–67

Additional notes

Ding appends what he suspects is a preface to this poem from *Shuchao* (see *Shuchao* 156.10b): "In the second year of the Taihe reign period [228 CE], a great drought. The three grains were not harvested, and the people were dispersed by famine" 太和二年大旱、三麥不收、百姓分於饑餓. There indeed was a drought in the second year of Taihe (see *Sgz* 3.94), but the *Shuchao* text quoted by Ding – who is followed by Huang Jie 1.16 and Zhao 367 – has "third year of the Taihe period." As Xu Gongchi notes, there is really no proof that this so-called preface has anything to do with the poem. He dates the poem to 229; see Xu, 372–73.

4.13

離友 Parting from a Friend, No. 1

Ding 39; Zhao 54–55

Additional notes

Pref. Xiahou Wei, who eventually held office as inspector of Jingzhou 荊州 and of Yanzhou 兗州, was a son of Xiahou Yuan 夏侯淵 (d. 219). He is said to have had a chivalrous spirit; *Sgz* 9.272 and Pei's commentary (9.273) quoting *Shiyu* 世語. Some scholars believe this poem dates from the autumn of Jian'an 18 (213), that Cao Zhi and Cao Pi accompanied the army to Qiao in the spring and returned to Ye in the summer, and Xiahou Wei returned to Qiao in the autumn. See *Cjky* 5.10a; Jiang, *Cao Zhi nianpu*, 169–72. Zhang Keli, *San Cao nianpu*, 127–28. However, Xu Gongchi rather convincingly argues for a date in the autumn of Jian'an 15 (210); Xu, 116–17.

4.14

離友 Parting from a Friend, No. 2

Ding 39; Zhao 54–55

Additional notes

This second poem is not in some editions of Cao's works. The bracketed lines at the end are appended by Ding Yan from *Cxj* 18.448. As Zhang Pu 2.15a notes, these seem to be from a different poem. Ding also includes another line – in tetrasyllabic meter – from Li Shan's

commentary in *Wx* 21.999, 27.1275, where it is said to be from a poem entitled "Parting from a Friend," by Cao Zhi.
2 Reading 絛 for 柔, with *Ywlj* 29.515.

4.15

應詔 Responding to an Edict
Ding 40–41; Zhao 276–78
Additional notes
This poem and the poem "Blaming Myself" (**4.27**) were submitted, together with the confessional "Memorial Presenting the Poems 'Blaming Myself' and 'Response to an Edict,'" to Cao Pi in Huangchu 4 (223), before the fifth month. The impetus for the poems and memorial came from the fact that Cao Zhi had just survived the threat of death by execution. A combination of relief, awareness of his precarious position, and the deferential style appropriate to addressing an emperor color these works.
3 Cf. *Mao shi* 50/3: "While it was still starry he harnessed up early" 星言夙駕.
13–14 Cf. *Mao shi* 4/1, 2, 3: "In the South there are trees with down-curving branches;" Karlgren, *The Book of Odes*, 4. *Mao shi* 9/1 has "In the South are tall trees, / But you may not stop and rest" 南有喬木不可休息.
21 Following roughly for 藹藹 the *Guang ya* 廣雅 gloss 盛 (see Li Shan's commentary, *Wx* 20.934), instead of the gloss 整齊貌 in Zhao 277n.
27 Cf. *Mao shi* 71/1: "On the river's edge" 在河之滸.
32 Cf. *Mao shi* 189/6: "He sleeps and rises" 乃寢乃興.
42 Zhao 278n thinks that "western rampart" may refer to the area in Luoyang called Metal Rampart 金墉城. However, Metal Rampart seems to have been built by Cao Pi's son and successor Cao Rui (Emperor Ming). See Nancy Shatzman Steinhardt, *Chinese Architecture in an Age of Turmoil, 200–600* (Honolulu: Univ. of Hawai'i Press, 2014), 9–11. Cf. Wang Zhongshu, *Han Civilization*, trans. K. C. Chang et al. (New Haven: Yale Univ. Press, 1982), 35–36.
48 See the identical line in *Mao shi* 191/6.

4.16

贈徐幹 Presented to Xu Gan
Ding 41; Zhao 42–44

Additional notes
Xu 219–20 dates this to Jian'an 22 (217).
19–20 See Chen Qiyou 陳奇猷, ed., *Han Feizi xin jiaozhu* 韓非子新校注 (Shanghai: Shanghai guji chubanshe, 2000), 13.271.

4.17
贈丁儀 Presented to Ding Yí
Ding 41; Zhao 129–30
Additional notes
Title Li Shan's note to the title (*Wx* 24.1119) indicates that in the edition of Cao's works he had, the title was "Yu Duting hou Ding Yì" 與都亭侯丁翼 (For the Duting Marquis Ding Yì). He adds that for the title to say Ding Yí 丁儀 is an error (誤也), but he also goes on to quote the *Wei lüe* on who Ding Yí was. Note, too, that in *Wen xuan ji zhu* Li Shan's note is slightly less definite, saying "perhaps it is an error" (恐誤也); *Tangchao Wen xuan jizhu huicun* 唐鈔文選集註彙存 (Shanghai: Shanghai guji chubanshe, 2000), 1: 232. In any case, if they are written for either Ding brother, **4.17**, **4.19**, and **4.21** must date from 220 or earlier, since Cao Pi had both brothers killed in 220; *Sgz* 19.561–62.
12 Cao Zhi seems to draw on a story from the *Yanzi chunqiu*: In the time of Duke Jing, it rained and snowed for three days without clearing. The duke, wearing a fur garment made from the white fur from under the legs of foxes, sat on the steps beside the hall. Yanzi entered for an audience and immediately got some time. The duke said, "Strange! It has rained and snowed for three days but the weather isn't cold." Yanzi replied, "The weather isn't cold?" The duke laughed. Yanzi said, "I have heard that the worthy rulers of old were full but knew of the people's hunger, were warm but knew of their people's cold, were leisured but knew of their people's toil. Now you do not know these things" 景公之時，雨雪三日而不霽。公被狐白之裘，坐堂側陛。晏子入見，立有間，公曰：「怪哉！雨雪三日而天不寒。」晏子對曰：「天不寒乎？」公笑。晏子曰：「嬰聞古之賢君飽爾知人之飢，溫而知人之寒，逸而知人之勞。今君不知也; Wu, *Yanzi chunqiu ji shi*, 1:74.
13–14 See *Sj* 31.1459. See also Shi Guangying 石光瑛, ed., *Xin xu jiaoshi* 新序校釋 (Beijing: Zhonghua shuju, 2001), 867–69.

4.18
贈王粲 Presented to Wang Can
Ding 42; Zhao 29–30

Additional notes
The date of this poem is disputed. Xu 152 argues for Jian'an 18 (213).
16 Reading 自 for 遂 with *Wx* 24.1121.

4.19
贈丁儀王粲 Presented to Ding Yí and Wang Can
Ding 42; Zhao 133–35; *Wx* 24.1121–22
Additional notes
This poem probably dates to Jian'an 20 (215). See Xu 182.
Title In *Wen xuan* (24.1121), the title is "Also Presented to Ding Yí and Wang Can" 又贈丁儀王粲. Li Shan's note to the title indicates that in the edition of Cao's works he had the title was "Da Ding Jingli Wang Zhongxuan" 答丁敬禮王仲宣 ("In Response to Ding Jingli and Wang Zhongxuan"). Jingli was the *zi* of Ding Yí's brother Ding Yì 丁翼, so Li Shan thought that the title given in *Wx* was an error. This has been disputed by Huang Jie and others.
7–8 See *Wx* 2.57, 2.60; Knechtges, *Wen xuan*, 1: 196–7, 200–1; David R. Knechtges, "Interpreting the Former Han Imperial Court in the Later Han: The Western Capital *Fu* of Ban Gu and Zhang Heng," unpub. paper, 25, 28; He Qinggu 何清谷, ed., *Sanfu huangtu jiaoshi* 三輔黃圖校釋 (Beijing: Zhonghua shuju, 2005), 2.127, 3.180–81. On Grand Clarity, see, for example, Paul W. Kroll, "Lexical Landscapes and Textual Mountains in the High T'ang," *TP* 84 (1998): 79.
12 This is an allusion to the "Mou gong" 謀攻 ("Planning Attacks") chapter of *Sunzi*: "Sunzi said, 'In general, with regard to the method of engaging in warfare, preserving the [enemy] state intact is best, destroying it is inferior to this'" 孫子曰：凡用兵之法，全國為上，破國次之; see Cao Cao, *Sunzi zhu* 孫子注, in *Cao Cao ji* 曹操集 (Beijing: Zhonghua shuju, 1973), 83.

4.20
贈白馬王彪 Presented to Biao, Prince of Baima
Ding 42–45; Zhao 294–301; *Wx* 24.1122–26
Additional notes
Title Li Shan (*Wx* 24.1122) indicates that in the edition of Cao's works he had the title was "Yu Juancheng zuo" 於圈城作. Lu 1: 453 and Xu 316 agree that this was the original title and that it was changed by *Wx*. See also *Wei Jin Nanbeichao wenxueshi cankao ziliao*, 72n.

Pref. The preface is not included in *Sgz* 19.564–65, where Pei's commentary quotes the poem from the *Wei shi chunqiu* 魏氏春秋 of Sun Sheng 孫盛. Sun does provide a context similar to that of the preface, however. The preface does appear, somewhat ambiguously placed, in Li Shan's *Wx* commentary (24.1122–23), but it is also missing from some editions of Cao Zhi's collected works, including *Wenji*. We cannot be certain it is by Cao Zhi. Cao Biao was Prince of Wu in Huangchu 4. He seems not to have become Prince of Baima until three years later, so if the preface is authentic, Cao Biao's title was updated at some point. See Xu 316–17. A minority view holds that he may have been twice appointed to Baima. See *Cjky* 5.17b and Huang 36–37. As noted, Autumn's Beginning (立秋) was the twenty-fourth day of the sixth month (August 8, 223). But the ceremony was scheduled for eighteen days before that. Thus, Cao Zhi and the others left for Luoyang during the fifth month. See *HHs*, *zhi* 5.3123, 8.3182; Bodde, *Festivals in Classical China*, 192–95; *Wei Jin Nanbeichao wenxueshi cankao ziliao*, 73n.
18 *Mao shi* 3/3. See *Mszy*, 47.
25 Reading 軶 (栀) for 軏, with Pei's commentary (*Sgz* 19.565); *Wenji* 5.9b.
27 Cf. *Mao shi* 3/3.

4.21

贈丁廙 Presented to Ding Yì

Ding 45; Zhao 294–301; *Wx* 24.1126–27

Additional notes

Title *Wx* 24.1126 writes Ding Yì's name as 丁翼.
15 This is allusion to the "Wen yan" commentary to the hexagram *kun* 坤: "A family that accumulates good deeds will surely have a surplus of blessings" 積善之家必有餘慶.
20 Zhang, *Lun heng jiaozhu*, 28.556; Alfred Forke, *Lun-Hêng*, Part 2, 231–32. See also Wiebke Denecke, *The Dynamics of Masters Literature: Early Chinese Thought from Confucius to Han Feizi* (Cambridge, Mass.: Harvard Univ. Asia Center, 2010), 82–83.

4.22

朔風 Boreal Wind

Ding 45–46; Zhao 173–75; *Wx* 29.1361–63

Additional notes

This poem seems to be informed by the poet's separation from his brothers Cao Biao and, especially, Cao Zhang, who died in Huangchu 4. But it is difficult to date (see Xu 321–23) and seems to include a pledge of fealty to the ruler, either Cao Pi or Cao Rui.

3 & 7 Cf. lines 7–8 of the first of the Nineteen Old Poems: "A Hu horse leans into the northerly wind, / a Yue bird nests on a southern branch" 胡馬依北風 / 越鳥巢南枝; *Wx* 29.1343.

23 "Close companions" is 同袍, which I am taking to be a reference to Cao Zhang and Cao Biao, as do others. The source is, of course *Shi jing* (*Mao shi* 133), which "is about comradeship between fellow coldiers;" Xiaofei Tian, "Woman in the Tower: 'Nineteen Old Poems' and the Poetics of Un/concealment," *EMC* 15 (2009): 14.

38 Reading 憐 for 隣, with *Wenji* 5.12a.

4.23

矯志 Resolve

Ding 46–47; Zhao 317–19

Additional notes

Ywlj 23.416 has this as two poems, the first ending at line 8, the second beginning at line 9.

1 Reading 桂 for 樹, with *Wenji* 5.12b.

17–20 Cf. Liu Xiang's 劉向 (77–6 BCE) "Zhang ming" 杖銘: "Sugar cane may be sweet, but it hardly can make a staff; flatterers may please, but they cannot serve as chancellors" 都蔗雖甘，殆不可杖，佞人悅己，亦不可相; *Ywlj* 69.1210.

24 This line is identical to one in *Mao shi* 235.

25 See *Mengzi* 4B.24.

29–30 See Xu, *Han shi waizhuan jishi*, 8.303–4; Hightower, *Han Shih Wai Chuan*, 288; *Hnz* 18.1299–1300.

31–32 See Chen Qiyou, ed., *Han Feizi xin jiaozhu*, 9.598.

35–36 Huang Jie 1.50 suggests inserting these lines from Li Shan's *Wx* commentary (36.1636) at this point: "Kindly tigers hide their claws; / Divine dragons conceal their scales" 仁虎匿爪 / 神龍隱鱗. See also Zhao 318.

37 See *Li ji* 53.1704; Andrew Plaks, Ta Hsüeh *and* Chung Yung (The Highest Order of Cultivation *and* On the Practice of the Mean) (London: Penguin, 2003), 51. Zhao 317 writes the variant 燾.

43 Reading 闔 for 關, with Zhang Pu 2.10b.

4.24

閨情 Boudoir Feelings, No. 1

Ding 47; Zhao 317–19

Additional notes

Title The title of this poem is sometimes simply given as "Za shi," after *Ytxy* (2.61). Zhu Xuzeng suggests that the title "Gui qing" may be from Song times and derive from the poem's placement in the "Gui qing" category in *Ywlj* (32.563); see *Cjky* 5.23b. Although the poem is, in fact, a kind of boudoir lament, "Gui qing" may not have been the original title.

19 Reading 儻願終顧盼 for 儻終顧盼恩, with *Ytxy* 2.61.

4.25

閨情（其二） Boudoir Feelings, No. 2

Ding 47–48; Zhao 516

4.26

三良 Three Good Men

Ding 48; Zhao 135–36

Additional notes

On this and related poems, see also K. P. K. Whitaker, "Some Notes on the Background and Date of Tsaur Jyr's Poem on the Three Good Courtiers," *BSOAS* 18.2 (1956): 303–11; Cutter, "On Reading Cao Zhi's 'Three Good Men': *Yong shi shi* or *deng lin shi*?" *CLEAR* 11 (1989): 1–11; Tian, *The Halberd at Red Cliff*, 140–48. "Three Good Men" dates from Jian'an 16, possibly the twelfth month (January 21–February 19, 212). See Xu 126; Jiang, *Cao Zhi nianpu*, 164–5. Zhang, *San Cao nianpu*, 118–19, puts the date a couple of months earlier. Cao Zhi was with Cao Cao's army at that time and was in Yongzhou 雍州, the site of the tumulus of Duke Mu and the Three Good Men. Ruan Yu, who also wrote a poem on this topic – his is entitled "Poem on History" 詠史詩 – was along on this expedition; Cutter, "On Reading Cao Zhi's 'Three Good Men,'" 8. Xu accidentally writes Ying Yang for Ruan Yu.

5–6 For Sima Qian's account of the sacrifice of the three brothers known as the Three Good Men, see *Sj* 5.194. The commentary of Ying Shao 應劭 (140–206) in *Hs* 81.3336 says: "Duke Mu of Qin was drinking with a gathering of officials. When drunk he said, 'In life we share this joy, in death let us share the sorrow.' Thereupon, [Ziju] Yanxi, [Ziju] Zhonghang, and [Ziju] Qianhu assented. When the duke died, they followed him into death. This is why the 'Yellow Birds' poem was composed." 秦穆公與羣臣飲酒，酒酣，公曰：『生共此樂，死共此哀。』於是奄息、仲行、鍼虎許諾。及公薨，皆從死。黃鳥詩所為作也。

4.27

責躬 Blaming Myself (with memorial)

Ding 48–50; Zhao 268–75

Additional notes to the memorial

Some editions of Cao's works do not have the memorial, and in some it appears in the memorial section (as in the *Sbby* edition), not with the poem. Zhang Pu places it among Cao's memorials (1.19a), with the title "Memorial Presenting the Poem 'Blaming Myself'" 上責躬詩表. But he also places it at the head of the two poems (2.9a–b), with the title "Presenting the Poems 'Blaming Myself' and 'Responding to an Edict'" 上責躬應詔詩. There are small differences in the two texts. In *Wx* 20.927–29 it is with the two poems and bears the title "Memorial Presenting the Poems 'Blaming Myself' and 'Responding to an Edict'" 上責躬應詔詩表.

For "reform in the evening," see Huang Huaixin 黃懷信, with Kong Deli 孔德立 and Zhou Haisheng 周海生, eds., *Da Dai Li ji huijiao jizhu* 大戴禮記彙校集注 (Xi'an: San Qin chubanshe, 2004), 49.465.

Zhao 271n says that "the poet" here means the poet who composed *Mao shi* 198 "Qiao yan" 巧言, the fifth "stanza" of which says: "The glib words are like a reed-pipe, / It's just the thickness of their faces" 巧言如簧顏之厚矣. See also Zhu Jian 朱珔 (1759–1850), *Wen xuan jishi* 文選集釋, preface dated 1836 (Taipei: Guangwen shuju, 1966), 16.4a.

Li Shan (*Wx* 20.928) relates the phrase 胡顏 back to the meaning of *Mao shi* 52/3 seen here in the previous note ("Why doesn't he hurry up and die?"). Li Shan goes on to say, "*Mao shi* says 'With what face does he not quickly die'" 何顏而不速死也. The fact that these words do not appear in the *Mao shi* as we have it has attracted the attention of scholars, and attempts have been made to explain why; see Zhao 271n and Zhu Jian, *Wen xuan jishi*, 16.4a. It does not seem to appear among the preserved passages of the other three schools of *Shi jing* interpretation either, so one wonders whether it is possible that Li Shan did not intend to quote the Mao version but was instead offering a paraphrase.

Mao shi 152/1: 鳲鳩在桑，其子七兮. The Mao commentary says, "As for the way the cuckoo feeds its chicks, at dawn it is from high to low, and at dusk it is from low to high. Its fairness to all of them is as though they are one" 鳲鳩之養其子，朝從上下，莫從下上，平均如一; *Mszy* 7.557. Li Shan's quotation of this line also differs slightly. On the identification of 鳲鳩 as the cuckoo, see C. M. Lai, "Avian Identification of *jiu* 鳩 in the *Shijing*," *JAOS* 117 (1997): 350–52, and her "Messenger of Spring and Morality: Cuckoo Lore in Chinese Sources," *JAOS* 118 (1998): 530–42.

Additional notes to "Blaming Myself"

8 The language in this line seems to draw on *Shang shu*. "Yu gong" 禹貢 says: "Five hundred *li* [beyond the restricted zone 要服] is the wild zone" 五百里荒服, and "Da Yu mo" 大禹謨 says: "Be not indolent, be not neglectful, and the four Yi will come to pay allegiance" 無怠無荒，四夷來王; *Sszy* 4.105, 6.202.

9 Reading 超商 for 越商; see Diény et al., *Concordance des œuvres completes de Cao Zhi*, 4.49.

12 The phrase 時雍, here translated as "harmonious and concordant," appears in the "Yao dian" 堯典 (Canon of Yao) of the *Shang shu*; see *Sszy* 2.31. There 時 is explained by the pseudo-Kong Anguo commentary as 是, apparently in the sense of "therefore." Fan Wang's 范望 (fl. 265 CE) commentary to *Tai xuan jing* 太玄經 glosses 時雍 by stating that 時 means 調 ("harmonious") and 雍 means 和 ("concordant"); *Tai xuan jing*, 1.4a (*Sbck*). See also Zhao 272n.

22 See *Sgz* 19.557. It usually been thought that Cao Zhi did not go to Linzi until after Cao Pi became emperor, but Gu Nong, based largely on a poem by Handan Chun, thinks that he went there as early as 217; see Gu, "Cao Zhi shengping zhong de sange wenti," 1–2.

24 For an informative discussion of the Duke of Zhou, see Edward L. Shaughnessy, "The Duke of Zhou's Retirement in the East and the Beginnings of the Ministerial-Monarch Debate in Chinese Political Philosophy," *Early China* 18 (1993): 41–72.

29–32 In line 29, reading 予 for 爾, with *Sgz* 19.563. On the incident involving the Major's Gate, see *Sgz* 19.558; Cutter, "The Incident at the Gate," 228–62.

29–56 On these lines, see "Introduction," pp. xxiv–xxv. They have to do with Cao's first offense, in 221, involving Guan Jun. But there was a second offense not in his biography that is referred to in his "Order of Huangchu 6" 黃初六年令, which states: "Formerly, because I was of a trusting nature, I harbored no suspicions of those about me and, so, was seriously and unjustly slandered by Grand Administrator of Dong commandery Wang Ji, Guardian Assistant Cang Ji, and others, and offended the imperial court. My body was lighter than down, and the calumny was weightier than Mount Tai. I depended on receiving the emperor's sweeping benevolence, and in the face of the legal opinions of the mass of officials, he pardoned this most serious among the three thousand felonies. I returned to my old residence, donned my original attire. This gift of clouds and rain, how can it be measured? Upon returning to my fief, I shut my door and retired to household duties. My body and shadow kept company with each other for two years. Ji and the others searched for the tiniest flaw by every possible means, but in the end there was nothing they could say. When I got to Yong, I was again informed on by the regent-receptionist, and because of this, too, things have been complicated for another three years up to now. However, they have not been able to find fault with me." 吾昔以信人之心無忌於左右，深爲東郡太守王機、防輔吏倉輯等枉所誣白，獲罪聖朝。身輕於鴻毛，而謗重於太山，賴蒙帝王天地之仁，違百師之典議，舍三千之首戾，反我舊居，襲我初服，雲雨之施，焉有量哉！反旋在國，揵門退掃，形景相守，出入二載。機等吹毛求瑕，千端萬緒，然終無可言者。及到雍，又爲監官所舉，亦以紛若，於今復三年矣。然.不能有病於孤者。

The surviving source of Cao's "Order of Huangchu 6" is *Wenguan cilin*; see Luo Guowei 羅國威, ed., *Ri cang Hongren ben* Wenguan cilin *jiaozheng* 日藏弘仁本文館詞林校證 (Beijing: Zhonghua shuju, 2001), 695.443. Li Shan does quote from the order, simply calling it a *ling*, or command, in his commentary to Yan Yanzhi's 顏延之 (384–456) "Zhe bai ma fu" 赭白馬賦; *Wx* 14.629. Huang Jie 1.25n called attention to the incident involving Wang Ji and Cang Ji in his influential collection of Cao's poems, and Xu Gongchi, taking issue with part of Huang's theory, provides a logical reconstruction of the events in Xu 295–301, 310–11. The enigmatic lines 53–56, especially lines 53–54, have attracted a good deal of attention for a long time. Xu explains them well, but the most audacious interpretation of what Cao Zhi is talking about is that of Gu, "Cao Zhi shengping zhongde san'ge wenti," 2–5. Whereas

Huang and Xu both say Cao Zhi went to Ye (here signified by the name Ji) to be punished, Gu argues that the lines only say the coachman went to Ye. He quotes two items. The first is from a memorial attributed to Cao Zhi that is in *Tpyl* 820.7b. Just this single sentence is preserved there: "I intended to send someone to Ye to buy fifty bolts of Shangdang cloth to make little curtains for carriages, but the regent-receptionist would not permit it" 欲遣人到鄴市上黨布五十疋作車上小帳帷謁者不聽. Gu also quotes a fragment that he believes is from the same memorial: "Your servant has heard that those who are cold do not crave a foot of jade but rather yearn for a short rough tunic, and those who are hungry do not wish for a thousand in gold but rather relish a single meal. Now the reason the great wealth of a thousand in gold or a foot of jade is not as good as a single meal or a short rough tunic is due to the urgent necessity of the thing" 寒者不貪尺玉而思短褐，飢者不願千金而美一餐。夫千金尺玉至貴而不若一餐短褐者，物有所急也; see *Ywlj* 5.92. This fragment is also in Ding 7.123–24 and Zhao 3.406–7, both of which give the title as "Hoping for a Kindness" 望恩表. Gu's argument is that for Cao Zhi the purchase of cloth was a pressing necessity. When he was not only not allowed to do so but also accused of a serious offense, he had no choice but to write this memorial (of which we only have a couple of fragments) to clear himself. A clue to the general nature of his offense is in "Order of Huangchu 6," which says, "this most serious among the three thousand felonies." Gu quotes this statement: "The categories under the five punishments number three thousand, and no crime is greater than being unfilial" 五刑之屬三千; 罪莫大於不孝. Despite the fact that he misattributes it to *Shang shu* (it is actually from *Xj* 6.47; cf. *Sszy* 19.64), it is quite possible that the offense was some act that qualified as unfilial (or unfilial and unfraternal). Texts from *Li ji* to *Xiao jing* do conflate filiality and service to the ruler, and the Han emphasized this principle; see Michael Nylan, "Confucian Piety and Individualism in Han China," *JAOS* 116 (1996): 1–27. Gu's theory about the specific nature of the false accusation against Cao Zhi is highly speculative and need not detain us here.

4.28
情詩 Love Poem
Ding 50–51

Additional notes
Ytxy 2.61 makes this the second of five "Za shi" it attributes to Cao Zhi.
9–10 *Mao shi* 65 and 36, respectively.

4.29
妬 Jealousy
Ding 51; Zhao 539

4.30
芙蓉池 Lotus Pond (fragment)
Ding 51; Zhao 539

4.31
雜詩 Unclassified Poem
Ding 51; Zhao 512
Additional notes
Cao Haidong 183 thinks that because this is not in Huang Jie or collected by Ding Fubao, "a lot of people" 很多人 do not think it is by Cao Zhi. But at the same time, he acknowledges that his collected works, as well as *Ywlj*, do have it.

4.32
雜詩 Unclassified Poem
Ding 51; Zhao 512–3
Additional notes
Ding appends an additional line found in Li Shan's *Wx* commentary but essentially says that he just placed it with **4.31** and **4.32** because he didn't know what else to do with it. I have not included it.
2 In "Letter to Yang Dezu," this name appears in Ding 146 as 龍泉, but he notes the variant 龍淵 in Pei's commentary to *Sgz*. See *Sgz* 19.559. On the efficacy of the waters of Dragon Pool for tempering swords, see Pei Yin's 裴駰 (fl. 438 CE) commentary to *Sj* (69.2252), citing *Taikang di ji* 太康地記. *Taikang di ji*, which is known by other titles, may date to the third year of the Taikang reign period (280–289); see *Shi ji suoyin yinshu kaoshi* 史記索隱引書考實, 2 vols. (Beijing: Zhonghua shuju, 1998), 2: 596–98.

5–6 The bracketed Chinese text of line 5 reflects the reading suggested by Kong Guangtao in *Shuchao* 122.1a. For line 6, Kong suggested that there was a character missing after the word 刀 (not before it as shown in Ding). I have taken the liberty of inserting the word 劍, in keeping with the topic of this fascicle. This is pretty audacious, especially since 劍 already appears in the poem. But Cao Zhi does repeat words in his poems from time to time. Note that Fu Yashu 577 has made □刀 into 刀刃, implying that Kong Guangtao suggests this, which he does not, insofar as I can see.

4.33
言志 Stating My Aims (fragment)
Ding 52; Zhao 539

4.34
七步詩 Poem in Seven Paces
Ding 52; Zhao 278–79
Additional notes
For the anecdote in n. 1, see Yu Jiaxi 余嘉錫, ed., *Shishuo xinyu jianshu* 世說新語箋疏 (Shanghai: Shanghai guji chubanshe, 1993), 4.244. There is another translation of it in Richard B. Mather, trans., *Shih-shuo Hsin-yü: A New Account of Tales of the World*, 2nd ed. (Ann Arbor: Univ. of Michigan Center for Chinese Studies, 2002), 133–34. On the background of this poem, see Cutter, "On the Authenticity of the 'Poem in Seven Paces,'" In *Studies in Early Medieval Chinese Literature and Cultural History, Dedicated to Donald Holzman and Richard B. Mather*, ed. Paul W. Kroll and David R. Knechtges, 1–26 (Boulder: T'ang Studies Society, 2003).

4.35
離別詩 Parting (fragment)
Ding 52; Zhao 540

4.36
失題 Title Lost
Ding 52; Zhao 569

5.1

箜篌引 Harp Lay

Ding 55–56; Zhao 459–62

Additional notes

7 See *Hs* 97B.3988; Li Shan's commentary in *Wx* 27.1286. Yang'e is also mentioned in *Huainanzi*, where the commentary of Gao You 高誘 (fl. ca. 212 CE) explains that it was the name of a famous performer. *Hnz* 2.150–51.

9 See, for instance, *Zz*, Xuan 2: "When a subject attends his lord's feast, to exceed three goblets is a violation of etiquette" 臣侍君宴過三爵非禮也. See also the commentary in Yang Bojun 楊伯峻, ed., *Chunqiu Zuozhuan zhu* 春秋左傳注, 2nd ed. (Beijing: Zhonghua shuju, 1995), 2: 659.

11 The biography of Lu Zhonglian 魯仲連 (third century BCE) says: "Thereupon, the Lord of Pingyuan wanted to enfeoff Lu [Zhong]lian, but Lu thrice turned away envoys and was in the end unwilling to accept. The Lord of Pingyuan then held a feast and, when he was tipsy, rose and went forward, giving Lu a present of a thousand in gold." 於是平原君欲封魯連，魯連辭讓者三，終不肯受。平原君乃置酒，酒酣起前，以千金為魯連壽; *Sj* 83.2465.

13 Cf. *Lun yu*, 14.12.

15 Cf. *Zhou yi*, hexagram 15, 6/1.

24 The "Xici zhuan" 繫辭傳 of the *Zhou yi* says, "He rejoices in Heaven and his knowledge of fate, therefore he is free of care" 樂天知命故不憂; Richard Wilhelm, *The I Ching or Book of Changes*, trans. Cary F. Baynes, 3rd ed. (Princeton: Princeton Univ. Press, 1967), 295.

5.2

野田黃雀行 Ballad of the Sparrow in the Field

Ding 56; Zhao 206–7

5.3

七哀 Seven Sorrows

Ding 56–57; Zhao 313–14

Additional notes

Ding includes two versions of this poem. He points out that *Yfsj* 41.611 also has two. As it often does in such cases, *Yfsj* indicates the second is the one performed by Jin dynasty musicians and that the one translated here is the original. The two are almost the same. In *Yfsj*, the title is "怨詩行," and it is referred to elsewhere by that title, as well.

5.4
鬭雞 Cockfight

Ding 58; Zhao 1–2

Additional notes

Liu Zhen and Ying Yang both have poems to this title and both died in 217. Ying Yang's poem has the lines, "The elder and younger brother roamed to the gaming ground, / And ordered carriages to pick up their crowd of guests" 兄弟遊戲場命駕迎衆賓; Lu 1: 384. The elder and younger brother here are widely understood to be Cao Pi and Cao Zhi, and the "gaming ground" or "field of sport" refers to a cockpit. Xu 128 dates it to Jian'an 16 (211), but in any case it is pre-217.

9 Reading 激流 for 邀清, with *Ywlj* 91.1585 and *Cxj* 30.730.

15 On raccoon-dog grease, see Cutter, *Chinese Culture and the Cockfght* (Hong Kong: Chinese Univ. Press, 1989), 19.

5.5
升天行 Ascending to Heaven, No. 1

Additional notes

Title On questions about the title of this work and its attribution to Cao Zhi, see Lu 1: 423. Li Shan quotes the first and second couplets of the poem – in Cao Zhi's name but in a tetrasyllabic form – under the title "Ku han xing" 苦寒行. The first occurrence is in his commentary to the "Hai fu" 海賦 and the second is in his commentary to the last of Guo Pu's 郭璞 (276–324) "You xian shi" 遊仙詩. The latter is at *Wx* 21.1024, but the former is missing from this edition of *Wx*. It is, however, in the "standard edition" of 1809; see *Wen xuan* 文選 (1809; Beijing: Zhonghua shuju, 1977), 12.7b. *Wenyuan yinghua* 文苑英華 attributes both of the "Sheng tian xing" poems to Liu Xiaowei 劉孝威 (496–549); Li Fang 李昉 (925–996) et al., eds., *Wenyuan yinghua* (Beijing: Zhonghua shuju, 1966), 193.2a–b.

1 On "sandal-borne" 乘蹻, see Stephen Shih-tsung Wang, "Tsaur Jyr's Poems of Mythical Excursion" (M.A. thesis, Univ. of California, Berkeley, 1963), 47–48. See also James R. Ware, trans., *Alchemy, Medicine, Religion in the China of AD 320: The Nei P'ien of Ko Hung (Pao-p'u tzu)* (Cambridge, Mass.: Mass. Institute of Technology Press, 1966),

258–59; Joseph Needham, with Wang Ling, *Science and Civilisation in China*, vol. 4: *Physics and Physical Technology*, Part 2, *Mechanical Engineering* (Cambridge: Cambridge Univ. Press, 1965), 582–83.

5.6

升天行 Ascending to Heaven, No. 2

Additional notes

2 See *Shj* 9.256.

5.7

仙人篇 Transcendents

Ding 59; Zhao 263–65

Additional notes

1–2 See Yang Lien-sheng, "A Note on the So-called TLV Mirrors and the Game *Liu-po*," *HJAS* (1947): 202–6; and "An Additional Note on the Ancient Game *Liu-po*," *HJAS* 15 (1952): 124–39; Loewe, *Ways to Paradise*, 60–85; Y. Edmund Lien, "Wei Yao's Disquisition on *boyi*," *JAOS* 126 (2006): 567–71.

3–4 *Sj* 6.248 says: "Traveling in a southwesterly direction he crossed over the R. Huaí and came at length to Heng-shan. At Nan-chün he took boat and was sailíng down the river to the Hsiang-shan shríne when a great wind arose and nearly prevented hís gettíng to land. The emperor inquíred of his wise men who Hsíang-chün was. They replied, "Accordíng to our ínformation, Hsíang-chün are the daughters of Yao and the wíves of Shun who are buríed in thís place;" David Hawkes, "The Quest of the Goddess," in *Studies in Chinese Literary Genres*, ed. Cyril Birch (Berkeley: Univ. of California Press, 1974), 56. See also Liang Duan 梁端 (d. 1825), ed., *Lie nü zhuan jiaozhu* 列女傳校注, 1.1a–2a (*Sbby* ed.); Albert Richard O'Hara, *The Position of Women in Early China* (Taipei: Mei Ya Publications, 1978), 13–17; Anne Behnke Kinney, *Exemplary Women of Early China: The Lienü zhuan of Liu Xiang* (New York: Columbia Univ. Press, 2014), 1–3; Bernhard Karlgren, "Legends and Cults in Ancient China," *Bulletin of the Museum of Far Eastern Antiquities* 18 (1946): 296. For the story of the Daughter of Qin and Xiao Shi, see Wang Shumin 王叔岷, ed., *Liexian zhuan jiaojian* 列仙傳校箋 (Beijing: Zhonghua shuju, 2007), 80–84.

9 On Han Zhong's being sent on this quest, see *Sj* 6.252; Needham, *Science and Civilisation in China*, 5.3, 18.

15–16 Purple Tenuity is Edward Schafer's translation of Ziwei 紫微; see Schafer, *Pacing the Void*, 47. On the stars of the two walls, eastern and western, of this constellation, see Schlegel, *Uranographie chinoise*, 1: 507–10; see also Joseph Needham and Wang Ling, *Science and Civilisation in China,* vol. 3: *Mathematics and the Sciences of the Heavens and the Earth* (Cambridge: Cambridge Univ. Press, 1959), 259–61.
27–28 *Sj* 28.1394.

5.8
妾薄命 I Am Ill-Fated, No. 1
Ding 59; Zhao 480–81
Additional notes
This poem and the following one are usually treated as two distinct works; however, *Ywlj* 41.742 treats them as a single poem, and *Cjky* 6.3b-4b gives them as three poems.
3–4 In line 4, reading 靈 for 觀, with *Ywlj* 41.742. On the places mentioned here see Niu, *Gudu Yecheng yanjiu*, 14, 75–76; Tsao, *The City of Ye in the Chinese Literary Landscape*, 17, 58.

5.9
妾薄命（其二） I Am Ill-Fated, No. 2
Ding 59–60; Zhao 480–84
Additional notes
1 Reading 日既逝矣 for 日月既逝, with *Ywlj* 41.742 and the textual note in *Wenji* 6.3a.
14 Two texts may be relevant to Cao Zhi's reference to "broken cap strings." *Sj* 126.3198 has Chunyu Kun 淳于髡 laugh so hard at being offered a paltry sum by King Wei of Qi 齊威王 that he broke his cap strings. Broken cap strings also figure in an anecdote that involves ribaldry at a drinking party and that appears in different versions in *Shuo yuan* and *Han shi wai zhuan*. See Xiang Zonglu, *Shuo yuan jiao zheng*, 6.125–26; Xu, *Han shi waizhuan jishi*, 7.256; Hightower, *Han Shih Wai Chuan*, 238.
24 Cf. *Mao shi* 138/2.
28–29 Cf. *Mao shi* 298/2 and, especially, 174/1.

5.10
白馬篇 White Horse
Ding 60–61; Zhao 411–13

Additional notes
10–12 On the Yuezhi and horse-hoof targets, see Knechtges, *Wen xuan,* 3: 70; Shih, "Jian'an Literature Revisited," 167.
17 See *Hs* 1B.69, Yan Shigu's 顏師古 (581–645) commentary.

5.11
名都篇 Famous Cities
Ding 61–62; Zhao 484–87
Additional notes
Xu 128–29 thinks this dates from Jian'an 16 (211), but this does not seem based on anything very concrete.
1–2 Zhang Xian 張銑 (fl. ca. early eighth century) notes: "'Famous cities' means those like Handan and Linze" 名都邯鄲臨淄之類也; *Liuchen zhu Wen xuan* 六臣注文選 (Beijing: Zhonghua shuju, 1987), 27.27b. Another opinion is that "famous city" is singular and refers to Luoyang, capital of both Later Han and Wei; Zhao 3.485. Wu Chaoyi 吳朝義 argues that the setting of the poem is meant to be Chang'an 長安, the old Han dynasty capital, and understands *jing* Luo to mean the two capitals Chang'an and Luoyang, with *ming du* referring to the large cities of the empire, in effect making *ming du* and *jing* Luo synonyms for grand places; Wu Chaoyi, "Cao Zhi 'Ming du pian' xinzheng" 曹植名都篇新証, *Xi'nan minzu xueyuan xuebao* (*zhexue shehui kexue ban*) 西南民族學院學報（哲學社會科學版） 1988.4:76.
17 There was a structure by this name in the imperial hunting park, the Shanglin yuan 上林苑, that is mentioned in Ban Gu's "Western Capital Rhapsody," as well as in *Hs* 6.198. It was a site for competitive games. See *Wx* 2.75; Knechtges, *Wen xuan,* 1: 226–27; Homer H. Dubs, *History of the Former Han Dynasty,* vol. 2 (Baltimore: Waverly Press, 1944), 98. See also Wu, "Cao Zhi 'Ming du pian' xinzheng," 75. *Sanfu huangtu* 三輔黃圖, a work perhaps initially compiled at the end of the Han or beginning of the Wei, says that Emperor Wu of Han 漢武帝 (r. 140–87 BCE) had the Feilian Lodge 飛廉觀 constructed in the Shanglin Park in 109 BCE. In the Later Han, in 62 CE, Emperor Ming 明帝 (r. 58–75) took the bronze statues from there and had them installed outside the western gate of Luoyang, where he erected the Pingle Lodge; *Sanfu huangtu jiaoshi*, 5.328. Li Shan's commentary to Zhang Heng's "Eastern Metropolis Rhapsody" ("Dong jing fu" 東京賦) has the same information; *Wx*, 3.105. But indications are that Pingle

in Luoyang was not a place for pleasure, and, in any case, it must have been destroyed when Dong Zhuo 董卓 (d. 192) razed Luoyang in 190. Faced with a shortage of cash, he had its bronze statues melted down to mint coins. See Wu, "Cao Zhi 'Ming du pian' xinzheng," 75; Rafe de Crespigny, *Fire over Luoyang: A History of the Later Han Dynasty, 23–220 AD* (Leiden: Brill, 2016), 51–52, 435, 463; Ying Shao's commentary in *Hs* 6.193.

18 A fragment from Cao Pi's *Dian lun* 典論 says, "At the end of [the reign] of [Emperor] Ling the Filial [r. 168–189], the court administration was in shambles, and commandery officials and the various government functionaries were all drinking heavily – the imperial relatives were even worse. A ladle of wine was worth a thousand coins" 孝靈之末朝政墮廢郡官百司并湎於酒貴戚尤甚斗酒至千錢; *Shuchao* 148.8a–b. See also Fu Yashu 505.

20 *Wx* 27.1290 has the variant 寒 for 炮. Two texts are especially relevant. *Mao shi* 177 has the line "Soft-shelled turtle roasted in clay, minced carp" 炰[=炮]鱉[=鼈]膾鯉, while Cao Zhi's own "Seven Enlightenments" ("Qi qi" 七啟) has 寒芳蓮之巢龜, which can be rendered "Chowdered turtle that nests in fragrant lotus" (cf. *Sj* 128.3227). The meaning of 寒 in this line from "Seven Enlightenments" has engendered much discussion. Just what this method of food preparation was remains problematic. Some, but not all, of the relevant sources are mentioned in Wang Liqi's 王利器 critical edition of *Yantie lun* 鹽鐵論. See Wang Liqi, ed., *Yantie lun jiaozhu* 鹽鐵論校注 (Beijing: Zhonghua shuju, 1992), 386. A kind of stewing or chowdering seems quite likely. Note that the *wuchen* 五臣 text of *Wen xuan* has 炮, not 寒, and 炮 is the reading followed here. Yang Shen 楊慎 (1488–1559), however, condemns this reading. He first takes the position that the old text (*jiu ben* 舊本) – by which he means the pre-*wu chen Wen xuan* – had the word 寒. He then writes: "The *wu chen* [text] cavalierly changed it to *bao bie*. Now *bao bie kuai li* is an old line from the *Mao shi*, so who among those of shallow learning would not consider *han* an error and follow the reading *bao*? They do not stop to think that the forms of the graphs *han* and *bao* are far apart and that the pronunciations, too, are different. How could one make such an error?" 五臣妄改作「炰鼈」。蓋「炰鼈膾鯉」，《毛詩》舊句，淺識孰不以為「寒」字誤而從「炰」字耶？不思「寒」與「炰」字形相遠，音呼又別，何得誤至于此; Yang

Shen, *Sheng'an shihua xin jianzheng* 升菴詩話新箋證, ed. Wang Dahou 王大厚 (Beijing: Zhonghua shuju, 2008), 1: 261.
See also Yang Shen, *Danqian zonglu jianzheng* 丹鉛總錄箋證, ed. Wang Dachun 王大淳, 3 vols. (Hangzhou: Zhejiang guji chubanshe, 2013), 2: 515.
23 On *ju*, see Knechtges, *Wen xuan,* 2:294; Zhonghua renmin gongheguo tiyu yundong weiyuanhui Yundong jishu weiyuanhui 中華人民共和國體育運動委員會運動技術委員會, ed., *Zhongguo tiyushi cankao ziliao* 中國體育史參考資料, vol. 1 (Beijing: Renmin tiyu chubanshe, 1957), 33–90; Yu, *Shishuo xinyu jianshu*, 21.711; Mather, *Shih-shuo Hsin-yü*, 390. On "pegs," see the excerpt from Handan Chun, *Yi jing* 藝經, quoted in *Tpyl* 755.4b.

5.12

薤露行 Dew on the Shallots
Ding 62; Zhao 433–34
Additional notes
Title "Dew on the Shallots" is an old *yuefu* title for a pallbearers' song (挽歌) that Cao Zhi has adopted to write a poem unrelated to that original context.
11 Reading 猶 for 豈, with Zhang Pu 2.1a.

5.13

豫章行 Yuzhang Ballad, No. 1
Ding 62; Zhao 414–15
Additional notes
7–8 See *Sj* 47.1930–32.

5.14

豫章行 (其二) Yuzhang Ballad, No. 2
Ding 62–63; Zhao 415–16
Additional notes
5–6 See Edward L. Shaughnessy, "Western Zhou History," in *The Cambridge History of Ancient China: From the Origins of Civilization to 221 B.C.*, ed. Michael Loewe and Edward L. Shaughnessy (Cambridge: Cambridge Univ. Press, 1999), 310–11.
7–8 See *Zz*, Cheng 15, Xiang 14; Durrant et al., *Zuo Tradition/Zuozhuan*, 2: 819, 1011.

Additional notes
The poem is also known as "Taishan Liangfu xing" 泰山梁甫行 (Mount Tai and Liangfu Ballad) and "Taishan Liangfu yin" 泰山梁甫吟 (Mount Tai and Liangfu Chant). Liangfu, near Mount Tai, was a hill where the Shan ceremony of the Feng-Shan 封禪 ceremonial complex might be held, while the major Feng ceremony had to be on Mount Tai itself. Liangfu is sometimes written 梁父. Cao Zhi is here borrowing an existing title to compose a new poem that appears to have no connection with that title. See *Ywlj* 41.740–41; *Wx* 18.845; *Yfsj* 41.608.
4 Zhang Pu 2.3a and *Wenji* 6.7b both have 野 for 墅, and Zhao 409 thinks that is the correct reading. But either word fits the rhyme, so I retained 墅.

5.20
丹霞蔽日行 Vermilion Clouds Hide the Sun
Ding 65; Zhao 416–17
Additional notes
7 Reading 祖 for 祚, with *Ywlj* 41.742 and *Wenji* 6.8a.

5.21
怨歌行 Song of Resentment
Ding 65; Zhao 362–64
Additional notes
Although this poem is always found in editions of Cao Zhi's collected works, its attribution to him has long been open to question. See Lu 1: 426–27. Lu includes it among Cao Zhi's works due to the attribution to Cao Zhi in various sources, including *Ywlj*, *Yfsj*, and *Wenzhang zhengzong* 文章正宗. It has also been called an anonymous "old words" 古辭 poem, while other texts, quoting some of its lines, make it by Cao Pi or Cao Rui. *Js* 81.2119 has Huan Yi 桓伊 (d. ca. 392) performing this poem under the title "Poem of Resentment" 怨詩. The key source for the events recounted in the poem is, of course, the "Jin teng" 金縢 chapter of the *Shang shu*.
1–2 Cf. *Lun yu* 13.15: "To be a ruler is hard; to be a subject is not easy" 為君難為臣不易.
5 Reading 周旦 for 周公 and 文武 for 成王, with *Ywlj* 41.746 and *Wenji* 6.8b.

7 Reading 政 for 室, with *Ywlj* 41.746, *Wenji* 6.8b, and *Js* 81.2119.
10 Reading 泣 for 泫, with *Ywlj* 41.746 and *Wenji* 6.8b.

5.22

善哉行 Grand!

Ding 65–66; Zhao 532–33

Additional notes

There is a good deal of uncertainty as to whether this poem is by Cao Zhi. Zhang Pu omits it, and Ding Yan (65) says that his base text erroneously includes it. *Yfsj* 36.535 gives it as anonymous "old words," and *Tpyl* 410.1891 simply refers to it as the 古善哉行. The *Siku* editors state outright that it is not by Cao Zhi; Ji Yun 紀昀 (1724–1805) et al., eds., *Qinding Siku quanshu zongmu* 欽定四庫全是總目 (Beijing: Zhonghua shuju, 1997), 148.1984. *Ywlj* 41.747 does attribute it to Cao Zhi.
1 The 來日 in this line is usually translated as "in days to come," but here I have opted to translate it in accordance with *Hydcd*, s. v. 來日, where this poem is cited as an example. That entry also cites Li Bai's 李白 (701–762) "Lairi da nan" 來日大難 and Wang Qi's 王琦 (1696–1774) commentary to it, which says 來日，為已來之日，猶往日也. See also Wang Qi, ed., *Li Taibo quanji* 李太白全集 (Beijing: Zhonghua shuju, 1977), 5.290. In a different context, Qian *Guanzhui bian*, 1180.
11–12 See *Zz*, Xuan 2; Durrant et al., *Zuo Tradition*, 1: 595.
21–22 See John S. Major et al., *The Huainanzi: A Guide to the Theory and Practice of Government in Early Han China* (New York: Columbia Univ. Press, 2010), 8, 13.

5.23

當來日大難 Great Hardship in Days Past, A Variation

Ding 66; Zhao 467

Additional notes

Title See the *Additional Note* to line 1 of 5.22 above.
9 See Yu Guanying, *Cao Cao Cao Pi Cao Zhi shixuan* 曹操曹丕曹植詩選 (Hong Kong: Daguang chubanshe, 1976), 84.

5.24

君子行 Gentlemen

Ding 66–67; Zhao 534–35

Additional notes
The authenticity of this poem is not certain, but like Ding's base text, *Wenji* 6.9a–b includes it, and *Ywlj* 41.747 has it and says it is by Cao Zhi. Neither *Wenji* nor *Ywlj* has lines 5–8. Zhang Pu's edition of Cao's works does not contain the poem at all. The Hu Kejia edition of *Wx* does not have this poem but does quote the first two lines in a note to another poem by this title, identifying the lines as from a "古君子行," thus marking it as an "old words" poem; *Wx* 28.1294. The Liuchen version of *Wx* does have it (with variants), including it in a group of four *yuefu* specifically designated "old words;" *Liuchen zhu Wen xuan*, 27.511–12. *Yfsj* 32.467, quoting *Yuefu jieti* 樂府解題, also considers it an "old words" poem. *Yfsj* does have lines 5–8. The twelve-line versions of the piece in *Liuchen* and *Yfsj* are very similar but not exactly the same, and they are both very like but not exactly the same as this one from Ding. Due to the allusions in the poem, it seems pretty clear that it is not from a purely folk tradition; see Cao Daoheng 曹道衡 (1928–2005), "Cong yuefushi de xuanlu kan *Wen xuan*" 從樂府詩的選錄看文選, *Wenxue yichan* 文學遺產, 1994.4: 22.
7–8 As they appear in this version of the poem, these lines seem to conflate the language of two allusions, one to *Laozi* and one to the "Xici zhuan." The *Laozi* line (from chapter 4 of the transmitted version) says that the vessel of the Dao "merges with the brilliant, and becomes one with the very dust" 和其光，同其塵; see Richard John Lynn, *The Classic of the Way and Virtue: A New Translation of the* Tao-te ching *of Laozi as Interpreted by Wang Bi* (New York: Columbia Univ. Press, 1999), 57. The "Xici zhuan" says, "Modesty [Qian, Hexagram 15] is the handle of virtue" 謙，德之柄也. Note that the corresponding lines in *Yfsj* and *Liuchen* read, "Diligently modest, obtain its handle, / Merging with the brilliant is especially hard" 勞謙得其柄，和光甚獨難.

5.25
平陵東 East of Pingling
Ding 67; Zhao 400
Additional notes
6 On Penglai, see *Sj* 28.1369–70. See also the entry "Penglai" by Thomas E. Smith in Pregadio, *Encyclopedia of Taoism*, 2: 788–90; Wang, "Tsaur Jyr's Poems of Mythical Excursion," 118–20.

5.26

苦思行 Painful Thoughts

Ding 67; Zhao 316

Additional notes

8 Reading 青蔥 for 青青 with *Ywlj* 41.748 and *Wenji* 6.10a.

5.27

遠遊篇 Far Roaming

Ding 67–68; Zhao 402–3

Additional notes

5 On Fangzhang, see Pregadio, *Encyclopedia of Taoism*, 2: 788–90; Wang, "Tsaur Jyr's Poems of Mythical Excursion," 118–20.

8 On Jade Maidens, see the entry "*yunü*" by Caroline Gyss in Pregadio, *Encyclopedia of Taoism*, 2: 1206–7. *Baopuzi* notes that by taking certain minerals, one can summon or associate with these supernal beings. See Wang Ming 王明, ed., *Baopuzi neipian jiao shi* 抱朴子內篇校釋 (Beijing: Zhonghua shuju, 1986), 11.203, 208, 210; see also Conley, "Divine Medicine," 60, 74, 78.

9 Emperor Wu's eating pulverized carnelian stamens in his quest to prolong life is mentioned in Zhang Heng's "Xi jing fu" 西京賦; *Wx* 2.60; Knechtges, *Wen xuan*, 1: 201.

10 The "Far Roaming" poem of *Chu ci* has the lines 餐六氣而飲沆瀣兮漱正陽而含朝霞, translated by Paul W. Kroll as "Sup on the Six Pneumas and quaff the damps of coldest midnights – / Rinse my mouth with truest sunlight and imbibe the aurora of dawn;" Kroll, "On 'Far Roaming,'" 661. See *Ccbz* 5.166.

11 For an introduction to the lore on Kunlun, see the entry "Kunlun" by Thomas E. Smith in Pregadio, *Encyclopedia of Taoism*, 1: 602–4; John Major, *Heaven and Earth in Early Han Thought: Chapters Three, Four, and Five of the* Huainanzi (Albany: State Univ. of New York Press, 1993), 150–61.

13 He is also known by such titles as 東王, 東父王, 東王公, and 東王父. On this figure, see Loewe, *Ways to Paradise*, 121–26; Yang Lien-sheng, "A Note on the So-called TLV Mirrors and the Game *Liu-po* 六博," *HJAS* 9 (February 1947): 206 and plate 1; Yang, "An Additional Note on the Ancient Game *Liu-po*," *HJAS* 15 (June 1952):138–39; Wang, "Tsaur Jyr's Poems of Mythical Excursion," 108–9.

14 *Shj* 16.407: "South of the Western Sea, adjacent to Flowing Sands, behind the Red River, and in front of the Black River there is a great mountain. Its name is the Prominence of Kunlun" 西海之南，流沙之濱，赤水之後，黑水之前，有大山，名曰昆侖之丘. Flowing Sands is ubiquitous in poems and narratives of the Western Regions.

5.28

吁嗟篇 Alas!

Ding 68; Zhao 382–84

Additional notes

17 See *Hnz* 4.330–33; Major et al., *The Huainanzi*, 157–58. See also Zhao 383n.

5.29

鰕䱇篇 Shrimps and Eels

Ding 68–69; Zhao 381–82

Additional notes

Title The word 鰕 may refer to the pufferfish (Japanese *fugu* 河豚), but the habitat doesn't fit.

11 Reading 高念翼皇家 for 雝高念皇家, with Huang Jie 2.91 and Zhao 382n. *Yfsj* 30.446 also has this reading, but this modern edition seems to be following Huang Jie, who says it is from a Song edition of Cao's works. However, cf. *Wenji* 6.11b. Furthermore, the *Siku quanshu* text of Cao's works, which is indirectly a Song version, has 雝高念皇家.

5.30

種葛篇 Plant the Kudzu

Ding 69; Zhao 314–16

Additional notes

7–8 Cf. *Mao shi* 164/ 6, 7.

20 Reading 代 for 對, with *Wenji* 6.12a and *Yfsj* 64.929.

5.31

浮萍篇 Duckweed

Ding 69–70; Zhao 311–12

Additional notes

Title *Ywlj* 41.742 gives the title as "Cattails Grow Ballad" 蒲生行, and *Yfsj* 35.524 has "Cattails Grow Ballad Duckweed Song" 蒲生行浮萍篇.

8 Cf. *Mao shi* 164/ 6, 7.

5.32

惟漢行 Han Ballad

Ding 70; Zhao 364–65

5.33

門有萬里客 At the Gate There Is a Traveler of a Thousand *li*

Ding 70; Zhao 504–5

5.34

桂之樹行 Cinnamon Tree Ballad

Ding 70–71; Zhao 399–400

Additional notes

Title Huang Jie 2.100, calls attention to the *Chu ci* poem "Summoning a Recluse" 招隱士, which begins, "Cinnamon trees grow thickly / In the depths of the mountains;" *Ccbz* 12.232. Wang Yi's 王逸 (d. 158 CE) commentary takes the use of the fragrant cinnamon to be representative of Qu Yuan's loyalty and the mountain depths to refer to his hiding away far from court. Huang thinks Cao Zhi's *yuefu*, apparently a title he created, derives from this. The cinnamon is important not only for its fragrance as a symbol of moral integrity; in the *Chu ci* poem "Far Roaming," it is mentioned for its power to bloom in winter; *Ccbz* 5:168. See also Kroll, "On 'Far Roaming,'" 661. The implication is one of a strong life force. Not surprisingly, then, cinnamon is also mentioned in the "Elixirs of the Transcendents" 仙藥 chapter of *Baopuzi*; see *Baopuzi neipian jiaoshi*, 11.205.

10 See Kroll, "On 'Far Roaming,'" 661.

5.35

當牆欲高行 Walls Need Be High, A Variation

Ding 71; Zhao 365–66

Additional notes

5 See *Zhanguo ce* 戰國策 (Shanghai: Shanghai guji chubanshe, 1985), 4.150.

5.36

當欲遊南山行 About to Roam the Southern Mountains, A Variation

Ding 71; Zhao 424–25

5.37

當事君行 Serving the Ruler, A Variation

Ding 72; Zhao 425–26

Additional notes

7 See *Kongcongzi*, 18.28a. See also Wu, *Yanzi chunqiu jiaoshi*, 2: 589.

5.38

當車以駕行 The Carriages Are Already Harnessed, A Variation

Ding 72; Zhao 462

5.39

飛龍篇 Flying Dragon

Ding 72; Zhao 397–98

Additional notes

The bracketed lines at the end are appended by Ding Yan from Li Shan's commentary (*Wx* 28.1314) and *Beitang shuchao* 158, respectively (see *Shuchao* 158.24a). Although they are attributed to Cao Zhi, it is not known whether they are from a different version of this poem or another with the same title. It should also be noted that the text of the poem in *Ywlj* 42.755 does not have lines 7–8 and 13–14 of the version here; Owen, *The Making of Early Chinese Classical Poetry*, 143.

14 See Douglas Wile, *Art of the Bedchamber: The Chinese Sexology Classics* (Albany: State Univ. of New York Press, 1991), 36–43, 56–69.

5.40

盤石篇 Boulder

Ding 73; Zhao 260–62

Additional notes

1 Reading 盤盤 for 盤石, with *Cjky* 6.19b.

3–4 Zhao 261n thinks Cao Zhi is the speaker in this poem and calls attention to Cao's connections with the Shandong region. He also sees "east of the Huai" as indicating Yongqiu, where Cao Zhi was enfeoffed as Prince of Yongqiu from 223 or 224 until 229 or 230.

17 On doubleboats, see Guo Pu's 郭璞 (276–324) commentary in *Er ya zhushu* 爾雅注疏, 3.78, in *Shisan*. See also Joseph Needham et al., *Science and Civilisation in China*, vol. 4: *Physics and Physical Technology*, Part 3: *Civil Engineering and Nautics* (Cambridge: Cambridge Univ. Press, 1971), 392.

26 On the source of the name Nine Rivers, see *Hs* 28A.1568–69; Knechtges, *Wen xuan*, 2: 320–21n.
28 Following the reading 歸 for 師 in Chen Zuoming 陳祚明 (1623–1674), *Caishutang gushi xuan* 采菽堂古詩選, ed. Li Jinsong 李金松 (Shanghai: Shanghai guji chubanshe, 2008), 6.170.
31–32 See *Lun yu* 5.7.

5.41

驅車篇 Driving the Carriage

Ding 73–74; Zhao 404–6

Additional notes

2 Fenggao was the seat of Taishan commandery. Emperor Wu of Han had stopped here on his way to performing the *feng* and *shan* scrifices (*Hs* 25A.1234–6). The entry for Taishan commandery in the geographical treatise of the *Han shu* (*Hs* 28A.1581) says: "Fenggao has a Hall of Brightness located four *li* southwest of the town and built in Yuanfeng 2 [109 BCE] during the reign of Emperor Wu." Fenggao was 17 *li* east of the town of Tai'an, which was near the foot of Mount Tai. It was made the seat of Taishan commandery in the reign of Emperor Wu; see Edouard Chavannes, *Le T'ai Chan: Essai de monographie d'un culture chinois* (1910; rpt. Taipei: Ch'eng Wen, 1970), 165n.
11–12 Ma Dibo's 馬弟伯 (fl. 56 CE) *Fengshan yiji* 封禪儀記 mentions two Mount Tai vistas that are relevant to these lines: Wu Vista 吳觀 and Sunrise Vista 日觀; *QHHw* 29.4a. For translations of *Fengshan yiji*, see Stephen Bokenkamp, "Record of the Feng and Shan Sacrifices," in *Religions of China in Practice*, ed. Donald S. Lopez, Jr. (Princeton: Princeton Univ. Press, 1996), 251–60; Richard Strassberg, *Inscribed Landscapes: Travel Writing from Imperial China* (Berkeley: Univ. of California Press, 1994), 57–62. There is an anecdote in *Lun heng* about a visit by Confucius to Mount Tai in which Confucius claims to be able to see a white horse at the Chang Gate of the Wu capital. See Zhang, *Lun heng jiaozhu*, 4.80–82; Forke, *Lun-Hêng*, Part 2, 242–43. See also Chavannes, *Le T'ai chan*, 47, 60; Wang, "Tsaur Jyr's Poems of Mythical Excursion," 142–43.
18 Reading 祀 for 記, with *Yfsj* 64.929.
19 When Emperor Wu of Han was on Mount Tai, he is said to have consulted a fortune stick. Ying Shao's *Fengsu tongyi* says: "It is commonly said that atop Daizong [i.e., Mount Tai] there is a golden chest with

jade fortune sticks, and one can know whether the years of a person's lifespan will be long or short. Emperor Wu took a stick and got eighteen, so he read it inverted as eighty. Later, it turned out he was long lived." 俗說：岱宗上有金篋玉策，能知人年壽修短。武帝探策得十八，因到讀曰八十，其後果用耆長; Wang, *Fengsu tongyi jiaozhu*, 2.65.
21–22 *Sj* 28 is, of course, dedicated to the *feng* and *shan* sacrifices. See Mark Edward Lewis, "The *Feng* and *Shan* Sacrifices of Emperor Wu of Han," in *State and Court Ritual in China*, ed. Joseph P. McDermott (Cambridge: Cambridge Univ. Press, 1999), 50–80.

5.42–46
鞞舞歌 Horseback War-Drum Dance Songs

5.42
聖皇 Sage Emperor

Ding 74–75; Zhao 324–26
Additional notes
Pre-imperial and early imperial China had a long tradition of hymns and dances for sacrifices and ceremonies. See, for example, Martin Kern, *Die Hymnen der chinesischen Staatsopfer* (Stuttgart: Franz Steiner, 1997). The "Horseback War-Drum Dance Songs" in Han and Wei times seem to have been used as entertainment at the banquets following the annual New Year Assembly. According to their preface, Cao Zhi's suite of five "Horseback War-Drum Ballet Hymns," each bearing its own title, was not meant for imperial use, though the poems clearly were meant for his brother Cao Pi, as emperor of the Wei. It is instructive to compare this to the poet's more famous (and more lyrical and accusatory) "For Biao, Prince of Baima" 贈白馬王彪 which was probably composed at about the same time. For a description of the steps taken in Cao Pi's reign regarding sacrificial music, songs, and dances, see Kevin A. Jensen, "Wei-Jin Sacrificial Ballets: Reform versus Conservation" (Ph.D. diss., Univ. of Washington, 2012), 101 ff. Xu Gongchi dates the poems to Huangchu 4 (223); Xu 330–31.
Title *Gu jin yue lu* 古今樂錄 compiled by Shi Zhijiang 釋之匠 (sixth century CE) and quoted in *Yfsj* 53.772, says about the "Horseback War-Drum Dance Songs" title:

> There were five Han songs: the first was called "East of the Pass There Was a Worthy Daughter;" the second was called "In the

> Second Year of Zhanghe;" the third was called "Joy Endures;" the fourth was called "Emperor of the Four Quarters;" and the fifth was called "Before the Hall Grows a Cinnamon Tree." All were made by Emperor Zhang (r. 76–88). There were five Wei songs: 1) "Brilliantly Enlightened Emperor of Wei;" 2) "The Great Harmony Has a Sage Emperor;" 3) "Wei Rule Will Endure;" 4) "Heaven Begets the People;" and 5) "To Be a Ruler Is Not Easy." All were composed by Emperor Ming to replace the Han songs. Their lyrics are all lost. King Si of Chen [Cao Zhi] also has five pieces: 1) "Sage Emperor Song," to replace "In the Second Year of Zhanghe;" 2) "Numinous Mushroom Song," to replace "Before the Hall Grows a Cinnamon Tree;" 3) "Great Wei Song," to replace "The Han Is Auspicious and Splendid;" 4) "Essential Subtlety Song," to replace "East of the Pass There Was a Worthy Daughter;" and 5) "First Month of Winter Song," to replace "Wily Rabbit." Note the Han songs do not contain "The Han Is Auspicious and Splendid" or "Wily Rabbit." I suspect they are "Joy Endures" and "Emperor of the Four Quarters."
> 漢曲五篇：一曰《關東有賢女》，二曰《章和二年中》，三曰《樂久長》，四曰《四方皇》，五曰《殿前生桂樹》，並章帝造。魏曲五篇：一《明明魏皇帝》，二《大和有聖帝》，三《魏曆長》，四《天生烝民》，五《為君既不易》，並明帝造，以代漢曲。陳思王又有五篇：一《聖皇篇》，以當《章和二年中》；二《靈芝篇》，以當《殿前生桂樹》；三《大魏篇》，以當漢吉昌；四《精微篇》，以當《關中有賢女》；五《孟冬篇》，以當狡兔。按漢曲無漢吉昌、狡兔二篇，疑《樂久長》《四方皇》，是也。

See also *Js* 23.710.

9 There is a typographical error in Zhao 324. Instead of 省, it has the graphically similar 有.

5.43

靈芝篇 Numinous Mushroom Song

Ding 75–76; Zhao 326–29

Additional notes

1–2 Reading 玉池 for 天地, with Li Shan's commentary in *Wx* 31.1474. Another possible reading is 玉地, from *Ss* 4.627. If the reference is indeed to a pond, Jade Pond may be the same as Numinous Mushroom

Pond, which was dug in Huangchu 3 (222); see *Sgz* 2.82 and Zhao 327. See also Tsao, *The City of Ye*, 57–60. For Gu Zhi's commentary, see Gu Zhi, *Cao Zijian shijian* 曹子建詩箋 (1935; Taipei: Guangwen shuju, 1976 rpt.), 4.9b. Cf. Chen Li 陳立 (1809–1869), ed., *Bohu tong shuzheng* 白虎通疏證 (Beijing: Zhonghua shuju, 1994), 6.284; Tjan Tjoe Som, *Po Hu T'ung: The Comprehensive Discussions in the White Tiger Hall*, 2 vols. (Leiden: Brill, 1949), 1: 241, 335. Note that an edict from Emperor Ming to Cao Zhi says, "Of old, during the time of the former emperor, sweet dew frequently fell before the Renshou Hall and numinous mushrooms grew in the Fanglin Park" 昔先帝時甘露屢降於仁壽殿前靈芝生芳林園中; *Cxj* 2.34. Cf. *Ywlj* 98.1699; Tsao, *The City of Ye*, 57–60. Similarly, *Tpyl* 873.7a quotes *Wei lüe* 魏略 as follows: "When Emperor Wen was about to accept the abdication, vermilion plants grew by the side of the Wenchang Hall" 文帝欲受禪朱草生於文昌殿側.

5–8 The "Canon of Yao" of the *Classic of Documents* says of Shun, "his father was stupid, his mother was deceitful ... he has been able to be concordant and to be grandly filial" 父頑母嚚……克諧以孝烝烝; Karlgren, *The Book of Documents,* 4. See *Sszy* 2.53. See also Bernhard Karlgren, "Glosses on the Book of Documents," *BMFEA* 20 (1948): 70.

18 Understanding 亡形 as 忘刑, with Huang Jie 2.114 and Zhao 328. Although Ding 75 has 形 (as do Gu, *Cao Zijian shijian* 4.10a and *Ss* 22.627), the graph is 刑 in *Cjky* 6.22b and *Yfsj* 53.773.

36 For the meaning of 褘, see Wang, *Mu Tianzi zhuan quanyi*, 15.

5.44

大魏篇 Great Wei Song

Ding 76–77; Zhao 329–31

Additional notes

13 Readers and commentators have struggled with this line, as can be seen in the vastly different interpretations offered by three respected scholars – Huang Jie, Gu Zhi, and Xiaofei Tian. For their readings of the line, see Huang Jie 117; Gu, *Cao Zijian shijian*, 4.8b; and Tian, *The Halberd at Red Cliff*, 91. I have adopted Gu Zhi's explanation but cannot claim it is definitive. On *yangsui* (陽燧 or 陽遂) as the term for a burning-mirror, see Joseph Needham and Wang Ling, *Science and Civilisation in China*, vol. 4: *Physics and Physical Technology*, Part 1: *Physics* (Cambridge: Cambridge Univ. Press, 1962), 87–89. It was also, as Gu Zhi indicates, a type of auxiliary carriage in the emperor's train. Gu Zhi sees this as a metonymical usage parallel to that of 乘輿 for the emperor. He writes, "If calamity does not reach to the *yangsui*, the safety of the *shengyu* is obvious" 禍患不及於陽遂乘輿之安可知矣.

17–18 *Hs* 7.218 records that in 86 BCE "a yellow swan came down upon the T'ai-yi Pond of Chien-chang Palace. The high ministers presented their congratulations and the Emperor granted gold in terms of cash to the vassal kings, the marquises, and the members of the imperial house, to each proportionately;" Dubs, *History of the Former Han Dynasty*, 2: 152–54. For the discovery of a tripod cauldron during the reign of Emperor Wu of Han and lore on the magical significance of earlier cauldrons, see *Sj* 28.1392–94, 12.464–68. *Bohu tong* says of the ruler that "when his virtue reaches the mountains and hills ... the wetlands produce the divine tripod;" Chen, *Bohu tong shuzheng*, 6.284. Cf. Tjan, *Po Hu T'ung*, 1: 241–42. On the divine tripod, Tjan draws on the *Ruiying tu* 瑞應圖, writing that it is "the essence of substance and form; it has knowledge of luck and disaster, of gain and loss; it can be light and it can be heavy; it rests quiet and it moves; its contents boil without being heated; it is always full without being refilled; whatever is in it will comprise the Five Tastes;" Tjan, *Po Hu T'ung*, 1: 337. See *Ruiying tu* 5b, in Ma Guohan 馬國翰 (1794–1857), comp., *Yuhan shanfang ji yishu* 玉函山房輯佚書 (Changsha: Langhuan guan, 1883), 77.

19–20 *Ruiying tu* 6b also notes that jade horses appear under a good ruler who honors worthy men. Regarding the mushroom canopy, *Hs* 6.193 quotes an edict saying that in the year 109 BCE, "In an inner chamber of Kan-ch'üan Palace, there has sprung up a fungus of immortality with nine stalks and interconnected leaves;" Dubs, *History of the Former Han Dynasty*, 2: 91. *Ruiying tu* also says, "When [true] kings respectfully serve the aged and old and do not neglect their former old [subjects], then the *chih* plant is produced"; Dubs, *History of the Former Han Dynasty*, 2: 91n. See *Hs* 6:193, Ying Shao quoting *Ruiying tu* 13a.

21–24 *Bohu tong* says of the ruler, "When his virtue reaches the birds and beasts, then the phoenix soars, the simurgh dances, the unicorn arrives, the white tiger comes, the nine-tailed fox and the white pheasant come down, the white deer appears, and the white crow descends;" Chen, *Bohu tong shuzheng*, 6.284. Cf. Tjan, *Po Hu T'ung*, 1: 241. For more detailed information on the *sheli*, see Knechtges, *Wen xuan*, 1: 232n. On the *bixie*, see Ian D. Chapman, "Carnival Canons: Calendars,

Genealogy, and the Search for Ritua Cohesion in Medieval China" (Ph.D. diss., Princeton Univ., 2007), 269n, 294–95. Note that *Xiandi zhuan* 獻帝傳, quoted in Pei Songzhi's commentary, contains a section in which Assistant Grand Astrologer Xu Zhi 許芝 records the appearance of some of the same auspicious signs that appear here in lines 17–24 and cites prognostications from the apocrypha in order to support Cao Pi's ending the Han and beginning his own dynasty. See *Sgz* 2.63–65.

5.45

精微篇 Essential Subtlety Song

Ding 77–78; Zhao 332–34

Additional notes

Title Commentators on this poem suggest that "essential subtlety" 精微 means here something like "perfect sincerity." Yu Guanying explains line 1 by saying, "*Jing* means sincerity; it says that when absolute sincerity reaches an extremely profound and subtle degree, it can break metal and stone" 精是誠的意思，言精誠到極深微的程度可以糜爛金石; Yu, *Cao Cao Cao Pi Cao Zhi shixuan*, 87. Also see, for example, Huang Jie 2.119 and Gu, *Cao Zijian shijian*, 4.11a, as well as, more recently, Fu Yashu 643 and Cao Haidong 274. Note that the stories alluded to in lines 3–8 of the poem also figure in a *Lun heng* chapter whose purpose is to refute them. See Zhang, *Lun heng jiaozhu*, 5.106–18.

3–4 The wife of Qi Liang 杞梁, or Qi Zhi 杞殖, appears in *Zz*, Xiang 27 (as well as in other early texts) as a paragon of virtue who instructs a man in proper behavior. She does not cry and nothing falls down. See Durrant et al., *Zuo Tradition*, 2: 1120–21. However, her crying does cause a city wall to collapse in the *Shuo yuan* and *Lienü zhuan* versions of the story; see Xiang Zonglu, *Shuo yuan jiao zheng*, 4.85 and Liang Duan, *Lienü zhuan jiaozhu*, 4.5a. See also O'Hara, *The Position of Women in Early China*, 113–15; Kinney, *Exemplary Women of Early China*, 75–76. We don't know why the poem refers to a mountain of Liang collapsing; this does not agree with the tradition represented by *Shuo yuan* and *Lienü zhuan*. Cao's works as we have them seem to be informed by two traditions: "Order Dated Huangchu Six" 黃初六年令 also refers to a Liang shan collapsing: "Qi's wife cried in Liang, and the mountain collapsed over it" 杞妻哭梁山為之崩 (Ding 129), whereas "Memorial Seeking to Communicate with Relatives" 求通親親表 seems to allude to the tradition represented in *Shuo yuan* and *Lienü zhuan*: "making walls collapse and frost fall, I used to believe in these things" 崩城隕霜臣初信之 (Ding 116, *Wx* 37.1688). The collapse of Mount Liang in noted in *Zz*, Cheng 5; see Durrant et al., *Zuo Tradition*, 2: 752–53. It is worth noting that *Lun heng* also contains an account of the collapse of Mount Liang; see Zhang, *Lun heng jiaozhu*, 5.117–18 and Forke, *Lun-Hêng*, 2: 187–89.

5–6 One place the story appears is *Lun heng*. Forke translates: "It has been chronicled that, when Tan, the heir-prince of Yen, paid a call at the court of Ch'in, he was not allowed to go home again. He asked of the king of Ch'in permission to return, but the king detained him and said with an oath, 'In case the sun reverts to the meridian, Heaven rains grain, crows get white heads and horses horns, and the wooden elephants on the kitchen door get legs of flesh, then you may return.' At that time Heaven and Earth conferred upon him their special favour: — the sun returned to the meridian, Heaven rained grain, the crows got white crowns and the horses horns, and the legs of the wooden elephants on the kitchen door grew fleshy. The king of Ch'in took him for a Sage and let him off;" Forke, *Lun-Hêng*, 2: 176. See Zhang, *Lun heng jiaozhu*, 5.109. On the narrative account *Prince Dan of Yan* 燕丹子, which differs somewhat from the *Lun heng* treatment, see David R. Knechtges and Taiping Chang, eds., *Ancient and Early Medieval Chinese Literature: A Reference Guide*, Part 3 (Leiden: Brill, 2014), 1767–69.

7–8 Li Shan (*Wx* 37.1688) quotes *Huainanzi*: "Zou Yan was totally loyal to King Hui of Yan, but the king believed slander about Zou Yan and arrested him. Master Zou looked to the sky and cried, and even though it was then summer, Heaven sent down frost for his sake" 鄒衍盡忠於燕惠王，惠王信譖而繫之，鄒子仰天而哭，正夏而天為之降霜也. The passage is not in the current *Huainanzi*; *Hnz* 6.444. A version does appear in *Lun heng*, where it is refuted; see Zhang, *Lun heng jiaozhu*, 5.110–11.

13–14 On poems regarding Maid Xiu and their prose sources, see Joseph Roe Allen III, "Early Chinese Narrative Poetry: The Definition of a Tradition" (Ph.D. diss., Univ. of Washington, 1982), 313–41. See also Owen, *The Making of Early Chinese Classical Poetry*, 341–45.

17–32 See *Sj* 10.427. See also the version in Liang Duan, *Lienü zhuan jiaozhu*, 6.13b–14b. Line 30 apparently refers to a *Lienü zhuan* with illustrations. The *Han shu* bibliographical treatise mentions a *Lienü*

zhuan songtu (Traditions of Exemplary Women, with Eulogies and Illustrations); *Hs* 30.1727. See also O'Hara, *The Position of Women in Early China*, 9. The bibliographical sections of the *Sui shu* and *Xin Tang shu* contain a *Lienü zhuan song* attributed to Cao Zhi.
33–56 See Liang Duan, *Lienü zhuan jiaozhu*, 4.5a;
39 Reading 畏 for 長, with *Ss* 22.628.
44 Reading 至 for 教, with *Ss* 22.628.
64 On 來儀, see Karlgren, "Glosses on the Book of Documents," 142–3.

5.46

孟冬篇 First Month of Winter Song

Ding 78–79; Zhao 334–37

Additional notes

6 On the comet as an auspicious omen, see *Sj* 12.460–61. See also Dubs, *History of the Former Han Dynasty*, 2: 121; Nienhauser, *Grand Scribe's Records*, 2: 229–30.
7 See Chen Qiyou, *Han Feizi xin jiaozhu*, 10.206; Nienhauser, *Grand Scribe's Records*, 2: 229–30, n. 77.
31 On the name and location of Dulu, see Knechtges, *Wen xuan*, 1: 196n.
33 On Qing Ji, see Zhang Jue 張覺, *Wu Yue Chunqiu quanyi* 吳越春秋全譯 (Guiyang: Guizhou renmin chubanshe, 1994), 4.113. On Meng Ben, see Paul Fischer, *Shizi: China's First Syncretist* (New York: Columbia Univ. Press, 2012), 147 and Sima Zhen's 司馬貞 (679–732) commentary in *Sj* 101.2739.
57 "Plumed battalion" translates 羽校. One wonders whether this might be understood instead as "plume hunt and barricade hunt." On Yang Xiong's use of these words to describe the same hunt, see Knechtges, *Wen xuan*, 2: 114n, 116n.
58 "Farthest lands" 鬼區 is glossed by Cai Yong 蔡邕 (132–192) as "extremely distant realm" 絕遠之區 in his commentary to Ban Gu's "Canon Adduced" 典引; *Wx* 48.2162. Li Shan says 鬼區 is the same as 鬼方, which appears in *Mao shi* 255/6 and is glossed in the Mao commentary as 遠方.

5.47

棄婦篇 The Rejected Wife

Ding 75–76; Zhao 33–35

Additional notes

Xu 185 puts this *fu* in Jian'an 20 (215), but that is because he puts the two poems entitled "Miscellaneous Poem on Behalf of Madam Wang, Wife of Liu Xun" 代劉勳妻王氏雜詩 in that year. But those poems are elsewhere attributed to Cao Pi and are not in Ding. See *Ytxy* 2.58–59; Lu 1:403, 455. Some sources give the title as "棄婦詩."

7 Reading 翠 for 有, with *Tpyl* 970.6a.

31–32 What is translated as "sweet olive" is actually the toponym 招搖. *Shj* 1.1 says that on the mountain of Zhaoyao there are many 桂 trees. This is often understood to refer to Chinese cinnamon (*Cinnamomum cassia*). See, for example, Anne Birrell, *The Classic of Mountains and Seas* (London: Penguin, 1999); H. T. Huang, *Science and Civilisation in China*, vol. 6: *Biology and Biological Technology*, Part 5: *Fermentations and Food Science* (Cambridge: Cambridge Univ. Press, 2000), 52, 91. *Lüshi chunqiu* 呂氏春秋 mentions 招搖之桂 as one of the finest seasonings, and this has been translated as "the cinnamon from Zhaoyao" in John Knoblock and Jeffrey Riegel, trans., *The Annals of Lü Buwei* (Stanford: Stanford Univ. Press, 2000), 310. But since Cao Zhi is emphasizing the autumnal (i.e., late) florescence of the 桂 tree, it is likely that he meant the *gui* in its other identity of *Osmanthus fragrans*, or sweet olive.

5.48

長歌行 Long Song Ballad

Ding 79; Zhao 540

Additional notes

This poem was not in Ding's base text. He included it from *Shuchao*, 104.7b. Zhang Pu 2.15b simply calls it "Yuefu."